IN THE ABSENCE OF GOD

IN THE ABSENCE OF GOD

The Early Years of an Indian Sect

A translation of *Smṛtisthaḷ* with an introduction

Anne Feldhaus *and* Shankar Gopal Tulpule

University of Hawaii Press / Honolulu

Printed in the United States of America
92 93 94 95 96 97 5 4 3 2 1

Library of Congress Cataloging-in-Publication Data

Smṛtisthaḷ. English
In the absence of God : the early years of an Indian sect / a translation of Smṛtisthaḷ, with an introduction, by Anne Feldhaus and Shankar Gopal Tulpule.
p. cm.
Translation of: Smṛtisthaḷ.
Includes bibliographical references and indexes.
ISBN 0-8248-1335-9 (alk. paper)
1. Mahānubhāva—History. I. Feldhaus, Anne. II. Tulpule, Shankar Gopal, 1914– . III. Title.
BL1277.83.S6713 1992
294.5'51—dc20 92-15883
CIP

University of Hawaii Press books are printed on acid-free paper and meet the guidelines for permanence and durability of the Council on Library Resources

Designed by Kenneth Miyamoto

Contents

A Note on Transliteration

MARĀṬHI WORDS have been romanized according to the standard system of transliteration from the *devanāgarī* script, with the following modifications:

Silent *a* has been omitted in most cases. In names and terms judged to be much more familiar in the Sanskrit than in the Marāṭhī form, *a*s that are silent in Marāṭhī have been retained, both within compounds and at the ends of words. Thus we have written Parameśvar, Nāgdev, and *Rukmiṇī Svayaṃvar* (instead of Parameśvara, Nāgadeva, or *Rukmiṇī Svayaṃvara*), but Śiva, *jīva,* and *Bhāgavata Purāṇa.*

The *anusvār,* usually represented by *ṃ* in romanized Sanskrit, is expressed here in one of three ways: by the nasal *(ṅ, ñ, ṇ, n, m,* or *ṃ)* corresponding to the following consonant; by a tilde (˜), indicating nasalization, over a short vowel or an *e;* or by an *ṃ* following a nasalized long vowel marked with a macron.

A diaeresis mark (¨) has been used to indicate that an *i* or a *u* following an *a* or *ā* is a separate vowel and not an element of a diphthong. A tilde over an *i* that follows an *a* or *ā* (as in Mhāĩbhaṭ) indicates diaeresis as well as nasalization.

IN THE ABSENCE OF GOD

Part One
Introduction

1. Context

THE TEXT we have translated here is a medieval Indian religious group's account of its early, formative years. The text portrays the period of leadership of a man understood to have been the appointed successor of a divine incarnation. Written by members of the group, for members of the group, sometime not long after the successor's death, the text provides an exceptionally detailed and delightfully unembarrassed portrait of the transformation of the followers of a divine incarnation into a sect.

The group that produced this text is the one now known as the Mahānubhāv sect. The Mahānubhāvs are one of several medieval Indian devotional *(bhakti)* movements that have survived to modern times, and one of two such movements stemming from thirteenth-century Maharashtra. Even more than most other *bhakti* groups, the Mahānubhāvs stress exclusive devotion to a single God. They understand this God, whom they call simply Parameśvar, "the supreme Lord," to have become embodied in a number of different incarnations (*avatārs*). One of these was Cakradhar, the Mahānubhāvs' founder and the last of a series of five human incarnations called the "Five Kṛṣṇas" *(pañcakṛṣṇa)*.

Like the other thirteenth-century Maharashtrian *bhakti* movement, the more popular, less ascetic, and less exclusivistic Vārkarīs, the Mahānubhāvs are devotees of Kṛṣṇa. But for the Mahānubhāvs, Kṛṣṇa is not, as he is for the Vārkarīs and for some other devotees of Kṛṣṇa, an incarnation of Viṣṇu. Rather, Kṛṣṇa is an incarnation of the one God, Parameśvar, and Viṣṇu is but one of numerous deities (*devatās*), beings of a sort qualitatively different from and inferior to Parameśvar.[1] For Mahānubhāvs, Cakradhar and the other four of the "Five Kṛṣṇas"—Guṇḍam Rāüḷ or Śrīprabhu, Cakradhar's guru; Cāṅgdev Rāüḷ, Guṇḍam Rāüḷ's guru; the god Dattātreya; and Kṛṣṇa himself—were the supreme God Parameśvar in human form.

The central figure in the present text is Nāgdev, a human being whom the Mahānubhāvs understand Cakradhar to have appointed as his successor. In the text, Nāgdev is most often referred to as "Bhaṭ" or "Bhaṭobās," while Cakradhar is called "the Gosāvī" and the group of his followers the "*mārg*," the "way" or "path." *Smṛtisthaḷ* shows Bhaṭobās and his fellow members of the *mārg* as they remember, interpret, and try to apply the teachings of the departed Gosāvī.

The period portrayed in the text is the late thirteenth century and the beginning of the fourteenth. It was during this period that the Mahānubhāvs became transformed from the followers of a divine incarnation into a sect, in the years from the disappearance of Cakradhar[2] and the subsequent death of Guṇḍam Rāüḷ to the death of Bhaṭobās. This is the period in which *Smṛtisthaḷ* is set. The first chapter of the text tells of the departure of Cakradhar, and the penultimate tells of the death of Bhaṭobās (chapter 260). Guṇḍam Rāüḷ's death is related in chapter 5, and—with the exception of chapters 23 and 247, which the text itself explicitly assigns to other periods—the subsequent chapters, from 5 to the end of the book, are concerned with the time from Guṇḍam Rāüḷ's death to that of Bhaṭobās.

Smṛtisthaḷ itself gives us dates for Cakradhar's departure (late in Śaka 1194—that is, early A.D. 1273: chapter 1), for the death of Guṇḍam Rāüḷ (A.D. 1286 or 1287: chapter 5), and for the death of Bhaṭobās (Śaka 1224, or A.D. 1302: chapter 260). But the text also presents other evidence that puts this last date into question, making it seem likely that Bhaṭobās died closer to A.D. 1312 than to 1302.[3] The date of Nāgdev's birth is not known, but the mention of his old age pension in chapter 107 suggests that he must have been fairly old when he died.

The locus of the text is Maharashtra, the Marāṭhī language region of western India, with its two distinct subregions of the Godāvarī Valley and Varhāḍ or Vidarbha.[4] During the period in which the text is set, this was the realm of the Yādavs, whose capital was Devgiri (modern Daulātabād, near Auraṅgābād). Political figures and events of the Yādav period made their mark on the Mahānubhāvs,[5] and on this text (see chapters 77, 83–87, 92–93, 145–146, and 148–150, in particular). But the main focus of *Smṛtisthaḷ*'s interest is not events or personages of the outside world, but rather the group of Cakradhar's followers and their relations to their God, to one another, and to the way of life that brought them together as followers of their God.

The principal concern of *Smṛtisthaḷ* is to portray the life of the group of Cakradhar's followers during the period of Nāgdev's leadership. The text was written by members of the group, for members of the group. One gets the impression that it was written primarily out of a desire to preserve the recollection of the events of those early years, because of their inherent interest and importance to the members of the group. This "inherent interest" may have been based in part on a conservative tendency that seems to be typical of religious and other movements: the tendency to idealize beginnings. In portraying to themselves the occurrences and words of the period of Nāgdev's leadership, members of the group—those who composed the text initially, those who revised it subsequently, and those who preserved it, memorized it, recited it, and copied it over the centuries—portrayed the group's ideals. And yet this text, like the other early Mahānubhāv hagiographical texts, manages to portray its ideal period with an astonishing lack of idealization, romanticization, or abstraction.

It is the concrete detail of this text, and its matter-of-fact attitude in reporting the concrete detail, that will delight the modern, non-Mahānubhāv reader. For the modern scholar of religion, the same concreteness and matter-of-fact attitude provide a rare glimpse into the process by which a sect is formed, as well as into the primary concerns of this particular sect. Not only for its intended, Mahānubhāv audience, but for anyone who has the opportunity to read it, *Smṛtisthaḷ* reveals the central aspects of the group's understanding of itself. These include, on the one hand, the substantive matters of ascetic practice and devotion to an absent God; and, on the other hand, the formal matters of the group's boundaries, its internal structure and relations, and its scriptures. All of these aspects of the group's identity are shown in *Smṛtisthaḷ* in their formative period. The text thus provides a candid picture of a fluid moment in what were later to become more rigidly solidified rules, practices, and institutions.

2. Devotion

Viraha

The first chapter of *Smṛtisthaḷ* reports a fact that is basic to the situation of Bhaṭobās and the other followers as we find them in this text: Cakradhar is gone. The second chapter reports Bhaṭobās' initial response to this fact, and thereby introduces a theme that is fundamental not only to this text but to Mahānubhāv religion generally and to the religion of several other devotional movements in medieval India. The theme is that of desolation at the absence of God.

Bhaṭobās' desolation at Cakradhar's absence is so intense that he wanders far off alone, falls unconscious, lies still for a long enough time to allow mushrooms to grow on him, and eats nothing but the drops of fruit juice squeezed into his mouth by some kindly cowherds on the hillside. Meanwhile, his cousin and fellow-disciple Māhādāïsẽ travels hundreds of miles, from Belopur, on a tributary of the Godāvarī River, to Ṛddhipur, in Varhāḍ, and from there to Bhānkheḍe (see the map), searching for him. When she finds him, she must wake him up, brush him off, wrap him up, and carry him off on her back. She feeds him by dipping a twisted end of cloth in some milk and putting it into his mouth. Telling people along the way, "God's absence has made him go crazy" (chapter 4), she finally gets him to Ṛddhipur. Here he and she and Cakradhar's other disciples settle down in the presence of Śrīprabhu (Guṇḍam Rāüḷ), who is Cakradhar's guru and another divine incarnation.

Fourteen years (and one chapter) later, Śrīprabhu dies, and the disciples are again desolate. In their grief, Bhaṭobās and a sizeable group of them go wandering off together, visiting places in the Godāvarī Valley where Cakradhar once stayed. This time Bhaṭobās remains relatively calm. It is another disciple, Bāïdevbās, who is overcome by emotion: he licks so hard at a place where Cakradhar once spat that he scrapes his tongue and must be told to stop (chapter 6). Later, Bhaṭobās changes his travel plans for fear that Bāïdevbās will die if Bhaṭobās too goes away (chapter 9).

The term for such desolation is *viraha.*[6] *Viraha* is an important theme for many of the *bhakti* movements of medieval India.[7] The theme of *viraha* is particularly characteristic of Kṛṣṇa *bhakti.* In this type of devotion, the desolation of Kṛṣṇa's milkmaid lovers (*gopīs*) when Kṛṣṇa leaves the pastoral world of Braj serves as the mythological model for human devotees' love of a god from whom they are temporally and ontologically separated.[8] Mahānubhāvs ally themselves to the great movement of Kṛṣṇa *bhakti* by including Kṛṣṇa, along with Cakradhar and Guṇḍam Rāüḷ, in their list of five principal incarnations of Parameśvar, the one God.[9]

Among the Mahānubhāvs, as in other groups practicing Kṛṣṇa *bhakti,* the story of Kṛṣṇa provides a focus for literary activity, rhetorical skill, and musical talent. *Smṛtisthaḷ* tells of two disciples composing verses specifically about the *gopīs*' pining for Kṛṣṇa (Kāḷe Kṛṣṇabhaṭ in chapter 114 and Nāïkbāï in chapter 165). The composition of other Mahānubhāv works dealing with various aspects of the life of Kṛṣṇa is also narrated in *Smṛtisthaḷ:* Narendra's *Rukmiṇī Svayaṃvar* and Haragarva's *Gadya*[*rāj*] in chapter 113; and the second half of Māhādāïsē's *Rukmiṇī Svayaṃvar* in chapter 174.

In addition, *Smṛtisthaḷ* describes with approval early Mahānubhāv litterateurs who are characterized by the kind of intense emotion that often marks the literary world of Kṛṣṇa devotion elsewhere in India. Kavīśvarbās, whom Bhaṭobās praises (in chapter 242) as "a poet of love," evokes such strong emotion through his exposition of the *Bhāgavata Purāṇa* (the principal Sanskrit compendium of Kṛṣṇa stories) that he turns Bhaṭobās' heart to nectar (chapter 120). Unable to support any further melting of his heart, Bhaṭobās has another, less-skilled reciter expound the *Bhagavadgītā* (chapter 121). Despite the fact that Bhaṭobās has forbidden Paṇḍitbās to sing (chapter 89), his grief *(dukha)* is so great that he sings a song of longing. His song is addressed to "King Govind" (this could be either Kṛṣṇa or Guṇḍam Rāüḷ) and to "the Lord of Nāgdev, Cakrapāṇī"—that is, Cakradhar. Bhaṭobās overhears Paṇḍit's song and removes the prohibition against singing (chapter 90). Another episode tells of a work in Sanskrit verse composed by a disciple who is called "Virahe Lakṣmīdharbhaṭ" because of his desolation *(viraha)* at his separation from God. Lakṣmīdharbhaṭ composes his work in a state of intense pining for God *(īśvarvirahē)* (chapter 18): "As he was writing, he would faint sometimes from grief. Then he would return to consciousness and go out to beg. Some days he would just lie there. Then the priest of the place [where he was doing his writing] would come; he would lift him up and bring him to consciousness." Bhaṭobās is delighted with the work, *Jñānbhāskar,*[10] as well as, implicitly, with the state in which its author wrote it.

Viraha, pining—primarily for Cakradhar (and Guṇḍam Rāüḷ) rather than for Kṛṣṇa—provides the motivation for other words and actions reported in *Smṛtisthaḷ* as well. Bhaṭobās avoids long stays in Paiṭhaṇ and Ṛddhipur (chapter 201), the headquarters of Cakradhar and Guṇḍam Rāüḷ, respectively, apparently because these places remind him too painfully of the loved ones who are no longer there. Āüsē, who stays on as a kind of caretaker in Ṛddhipur (chapter 11), refuses Bhaṭobās' invitation to accompany him to the Godāvarī (Gaṅgā) Valley. "Without Cakrasvāmī," she says, "that Gaṅgā Valley is burning with red flames" (chapter 199). More humorously, Nāthobā defecates on a treasure chest he finds, angry that it would turn up too late to be put to use in the service of Cakradhar (chapter 223).

But, for all the pain of separation from Cakradhar, Bhaṭobās resists attempts to find Cakradhar or to fabricate a substitute for him. Twice in *Smṛtisthaḷ* (chapters 132 and 232) Cakradhar is reported to have been sighted in Ujjain—the last place where his biography, the *Līḷācaritra,* reports him to have been seen. But both times Bhaṭobās refers to Cakradhar's words, "Now we will meet anew" (*Sūtrapāṭh* 11.139; 12.262; *Līḷācaritra,* "Uttarārdha," chapters 646 and 655),[11] takes these as a prohibition against searching out Cakradhar in this lifetime, and discourages the eager disciples from rushing off to Ujjain. Similarly, when an imposter, a man who looks like Cakradhar, appears in Ṛddhipur (chapter 192), Bhaṭobās has another disciple, Mhāībhaṭ, subject the man to a test of his identity; the man fails the test and is led away. Furthermore, even though there are other divine incarnations—Bhaṭobās mentions that one of them is a parrot in a prostitute's house in Devgiri (chapter 210)[12]—Śrīprabhu (Guṇḍam Rāüḷ) is the only one whom Cakradhar's disciples have been commanded to serve, says Bhaṭobās; and since Śrīprabhu's death there have been no more.

Thus, artificially contrived means of ending the disciples' state of *viraha* are rejected. *Viraha* becomes the determining condition of Cakradhar's followers' religious lives. And, having begun as a grim necessity, it develops into a virtue. On two occasions reported in *Smṛtisthaḷ* (chapters 175 and 227), Bhaṭobās praises members of the next generation of disciples, those who have become followers "for the sake of a God they have never seen"—unlike Bhaṭobās and Māhādāïsē, who, in her words (chapter 175), "followed the Gosāvī [Cakradhar] because he caressed us and fondled us."

Devotional Practices

This lifelong separation from God *(asannidhān),* which characterizes the experience not only of the first generation after Bhaṭobās and Māhādāïsē, but of subsequent generations of Mahānubhāvs up to the present, is mitigated by a number of religious practices whose early forms are portrayed in *Smṛtisthaḷ.* Prominent among these practices are recollection, pilgrimage, and the veneration of relics.

Recollection *(smaraṇ)* of the names, looks, and acts of the divine incarnations is a practice enjoined in the *Sūtrapāṭh,* the collection of Cakradhar's aphorisms (9.4 and passim). According to the *Sūtrapāṭh, smaraṇ* is to be performed daily,[13] constantly,[14] and with faithful adherence to the incarnation's name, deeds, appearance, and movements.[15] In *Smṛtisthaḷ,* several disciples are shown practicing *smaraṇ:* most notably, Bhaṭobās himself, on his sickbed (chapter 257) and later his deathbed (chapter 260); and Māhādāïsē, on her deathbed (chapter 254). Bhaṭobās and others refer to *smaraṇ* (or to thinking of or remembering God) in a variety of contexts (e.g., chapters 33, 85, 110, 124, 131, 176, 213, and 221). And in several episodes, various disciples, including Bhaṭobās, are shown using the name "Śrī Cakradhar!" as a cry for help (chapter 105), an expletive (chapter 23), a begging call (chapter 4 and, presumably, chapter 62), a meal prayer (chapter 131), and a shout of victory (chapter 257).[16] *Smaraṇ* of the deeds, the *līḷās,* of Cakradhar also seems to have provided a major motivation for the composition of Cakradhar's biography, the *Līḷācaritra.* This text serves to sharpen and supplement the recollections of those who witnessed the *līḷās,* and to preserve an account of the *līḷās* for future disciples. Chapters 139 to 142 of *Smṛtisthaḷ,* however, which show Mhāībhaṭ researching the *līḷās* and, in consultation with Nāgdev, editing the book, do not explicitly mention this or any other motive for Mhāībhaṭ's work.[17]

In addition to the purely mental practice of *smaraṇ, Smṛtisthaḷ* makes reference to two external ritual practices that can also serve to link the devotees to their absent God. These practices are, first, going on pilgrimage to places the divine incarnations visited, and, second, revering things they touched. Neither of these practices is explicitly enjoined in the *Sūtrapāṭh,* but both appear to be referred to with approval in *Sūtrapāṭh* 12.186: "Whatever pedestals *(oṭe)* and pebbles *(ghoṭe)* have come into contact with me are objects of reverence for you. . . ."

Smṛtisthaḷ depicts the beginnings of what was to become a lively pilgrimage tradition.[18] Several pilgrimages are recorded in *Smṛtisthaḷ,* including a number of trips between the Mahānubhāvs'—and medieval Maharashtra's—two focal regions, the Godāvarī ("Gaṅgā") Valley and Varhāḍ (chapters 5, 63, 115, 178, 190–192, and 224). Bhaṭobās and others are shown bowing or prostrating themselves to places where Cakradhar or Guṇḍam Rāüḷ lived or walked (chapters 5, 6, 63, 115, 178, and 191). And several of Bhaṭobās' discourses and statements have to do with pilgrimage to and reverence for such holy places (chapters 39, 57, 115, 178, and 224).

In *Smṛtisthaḷ,* pilgrimage is clearly portrayed as the external expression of internal devotional attitudes. The first pilgrimage recorded in the text—what may have been the first Mahānubhāv pilgrimage ever—is one that was undertaken by Bhaṭobās, along with a number of other disciples, six of whom are named (chapter 5). This group sets out to visit a series of places along a stretch of the Godāvarī River more than a hundred miles in length. They set out after the death of Guṇḍam Rāūḷ, and the text specifies that it is "out of grief" over his death *(teṇeci dukhẽ)* that they start their journey. Thus this first pilgrimage is motivated by *viraha.* Besides *viraha, smaraṇ* is also closely connected with pilgrimage. The connection is made explicit in the instructions of Bhaṭobās recorded in chapter 39: "Go to holy places (*tīrthas*), and recollect the deeds (*līḷās*) that were done at them. That is the way one practices recollection *(smaraṇ)* there." Thus, pilgrimage provides an occasion for the practice of *smaraṇ,* and *smaraṇ* is the appropriate mental concomitant of pilgrimage.

The importance that Bhaṭobās attached to pilgrimage, and its connection for him to devotional attitudes, is indicated in his conversation with Rāmdev in chapter 57. Rāmdev, a young and ardent disciple who was a particular favorite of Bhaṭobās', is elsewhere (in chapters 56 and 59) portrayed as exceptionally thoroughgoing in the performance of religious austerities. But, for some unexplained reason, Rāmdev balks at the thought of visiting all the Mahānubhāv holy places. "No, Bhaṭ! No!" he says. "Why should you show me the places where the Gosāvī [primarily Cakradhar, but also Guṇḍam Rāūḷ] slept and sat? Can I go and pay homage to them all?" Bhaṭobās' reply indicates that he thinks of pilgrimage as essential to the practice of discipleship: "If you are not going to go and pay homage to them, why have you opened the door to the Gosāvī? Listen! Listen to what I say! You have to wade through a thicket for only a couple of steps. Then there is sovereignty before you. A lame man using a blind man's legs attains God (Īśvar). A blind man using a lame man's legs attains Caitanya."[19] The phrase "you have to wade through a thicket" seems to refer to the actual, physical difficulty of getting to some of the holy spots. Bhaṭobās uses the image of the blind man and the lame man to indicate the felicity of a combination of knowledge and action in religious life. Implicitly, Bhaṭobās is saying that the actions of pilgrimage, which he is trying to cajole Rāmdev into performing, are most effective in combination with a knowledge of the significance of the places one visits: that is, in combination with *smaraṇ.*

The other sort of devotional act described in *Smṛtisthaḷ* is the veneration of relics—that is, of objects considered holy because they have been touched by a divine incarnation. In *Smṛtisthaḷ* such objects are most often called *prasāds*. Whereas the biography of Guṇḍam Rāūḷ[20] points to the existence of and reverence for a tooth, a fingernail, and a lock of hair of this divine incarnation, the *prasāds* mentioned in *Smṛtisthaḷ* do not include parts of the divine persons' bodies. The *prasāds* in *Smṛtisthaḷ* do include food that the incarnations have tasted (a sweet ball, in chapter 142; and a piece of bread, in chapter 140); their spittle (chapter 6); dishes that they have used (chapter 197); furniture on which they have sat (a stool, in chapter 216; and a cot, in chapter 156); clothes (unspecified "garments," in chapters 8 and 22; a shawl, in chapters 69 and 70; and two blankets, in chapter 8) and jewelry (an anklet and a chain, in chapter 8; and a ring—or metal that was subsequently fashioned into a ring—in chapter 153) that they have worn; and other objects (a stick and a camphor box, in chapter 8) that they have given to the disciples.

The fact of having been *given* by a divine incarnation seems to be essential to the identity of a *prasād;* the basic meaning of the term *"prasād"* is "a gracious gift." Other relics are also mentioned in the text—a rock, a threshold, pillars, doors, and a door frame, all of which have been touched by Cakradhar (chapter 8)—but these are not called *prasāds*. They are holy because Cakradhar touched them, but they are not his gift. Hence, it seems, it is all right for Bhaṭobās to have them removed, and to have the wooden threshold made into bowls and beads (chapter 8). But the bowls thus made are called *tīrthas*,[21] not *prasāds*. By contrast, when a disciple named Bhānubhaṭ makes necklaces and a pair of earrings out of the wood of a *prasād* cot (chapter 156), Bhaṭobās points out that Bhānubhaṭ has thereby destroyed something essential to the cot's identity as a *prasād (prasādatva),* to its character as a gift (*prasannatā:* literally, the "graciousness" with which it was given). The fact of having been in contact *(sambandh)* with a divine incarnation is not destroyed, but the new objects are not called *prasāds*. Similarly, the ring in chapter 153 was not, according to the variant reading we have translated, one that Cakradhar had worn, but rather one made of metal that he had touched *(sambandhācīye dhātūcī mudī);* the term *prasād* is not used for the ring, either, or for the metal out of which it was made.

The relics, both those that are called *prasāds* and those that are not, are treasured and handled with reverence and care—one disciple, for example, is warned against traveling around alone with his shawl relic in his possession (chapter 70)—and there seems to be a good deal of interest in tracing the relics' transmission within the group of disciples (e.g., chapters 8, 69, and 156). Cutting up larger wooden relics into beads and so on seems not to have been perceived as inherently disrespectful, but rather to have had as its purpose the widest possible dissemination of the holy objects among the members of the group. Bhaṭobās' tearing of the shawl relic that Indrabhaṭ had been selfishly keeping to himself (chapter 69) clearly has such a distribution of the relic as its aim. Even when Bhānubhaṭ cuts up the cot relic and thereby destroys its identity as a *prasād,* his action is not entirely condemned by Bhaṭobās (chapter 156). And when Māhādāïsē rips up a *prasād* garment to bandage a sore on Bhaṭobās' foot (chapter 22), she silences his objections by saying, *"Prasād* has been tied to *prasād"*—in other words, Bhaṭobās, too, is Cakradhar's gracious gift to the other disciples. The relics are thus seen in *Smṛtisthaḷ* not as inviolable sacred objects, but as objects whose holiness is to be subordinated to human needs.[22]

Although it is clear from *Smṛtisthaḷ* that the relics were objects of great respect, it is not clear whether they were objects of actions or attitudes that might be called worship. When Bhaṭobās tells a Brāhmaṇ that he feeds rice to the relic ring on his finger (chapter 153), he seems to be making a joke, but there are indications that more was done to the relics than simply keeping them carefully, bickering over them, and passing them around. Of the food relics, we see bits of the sweet ball *(prasādācā lāḍu)* being eaten in chapter 142; and in chapter 140, water is poured over the bread relic *(prasādācī roṭī)* and then drunk. Āüsẽ, who lives in Ṛddhipur and thus has access to numerous objects that were touched and used by Guṇḍam Rāüḷ, can serve a meal in a relic dish (*prasādācaṃ pātrīṃ,* chapter 197); this seems to be a mark of respect for the guest, while his presumed pleasure in being so served is a sign of respect for the dish. Perhaps the bowls made out of the threshold of the Rājmaḍh at Ḍombegrām (chapter 8) were also used for eating, but, if they were, the text does not tell us so. The most extreme respect for a holy object (or rather, place) is to be seen in Bhaṭobās' kissing, and Bāïdevbās' licking at, Cakradhar's spittle (or rather, a place where Cakradhar once spat) in Ḍombegrām (chapter 6). In his agony over Cakradhar's absence, Bāïdevbās licks at the spittle (or rather, the spot) until he scrapes his tongue and Bhaṭobās has to tell him to stop. A more ritualized expression of reverence may be hinted at in Bhaṭobās' instructions to do "twice as much *prasādsevā*" on a festival day as normally (chapter 176). This may mean twice as much recitation of the text entitled *Prasādsevā,*[23] but more likely it means "twice as much *sevā* ('worship' or 'service') of *prasāds*." Something quantifiable to the point that one can "do" twice the amount of it on special days would have to be a rather highly formalized action or set of actions—something far removed from Bāïdevbās' unrestrained outpouring of emotion.[24]

3. Asceticism

BESIDES DEVOTIONAL attitudes and practices, the other major component of the religious way of life detailed in *Smṛtisthaḷ* is asceticism. The way of life of the ascetic renunciant, the *sannyāsī,* is an old, honored, and elaborate institution in India.[25] Ascetic renunciation is also an essential element of the teachings of Cakradhar. The aphorisms collected in the "Ācār" ("Practice") chapters of the *Sūtrapāṭh* prescribe for Cakradhar's followers a life of strict asceticism and extreme detachment. The ideal is to spend one's life—or, rather, to "throw it away" *(janma kṣepaṇē)*—"at the foot of a tree at the end of the land" (*Sūtrapāṭh* 12.26, 72, 202; 13.219).[26] *Smṛtisthaḷ* shows Bhaṭobās and the other disciples of Cakradhar attempting to live up to this ideal and to follow Cakradhar's prescriptions. It shows Bhaṭobās interpreting Cakradhar's commands, and sometimes supplementing them with legislative decisions of his own; and it records the often heroic attempts of Bhaṭobās and many others to live the life of ascetic renunciation.

Renunciation of Family and Sexual Relations

The first rule of ascetic renunciation, the most basic thing one must do to become a renouncer, is to leave home and break off relations with one's family, including one's husband or wife. The first *sūtra* of the *Sūtrapāṭh* chapter entitled "Ācār" commands: "Renounce your attachment to your own land *(svadeś);* renounce your attachment to your own village *(svagrām);* renounce especially your attachment to your relatives" (*Sūtrapāṭh* 12.1).

Smṛtisthaḷ narrates the stories of several individuals who worked at putting this precept into practice. One of the most dramatic stories is that of Kesobās, the man who would later edit the *Sūtrapāṭh.* In chapter 12 of *Smṛtisthaḷ,* Kesobās comes to Bhaṭobās and takes initiation as an ascetic. In chapter 13, Kesobās' relatives come and take him home. They try in a variety of ways to make him give up his ascetic initiation. Finally they say, "We cannot win him over. If he is to be won over now, it is his wife who will do it. Now lock up the two of them in the same room." But, locked in alone with his wife, Kesobās sleeps on the ground when she lies on the cot, and he sleeps on the cot when she lies on the ground. After several nights of this, Kesobās' wife says, "Let him go now. He has become a *yogī* now. It is a sin for me to interfere." And Kesobās is allowed to return to Bhaṭobās.

Another heroic renunciant in *Smṛtisthaḷ* is Lukhāïsē. Her story is told in chapter 97:

> Lukhāïsē was from Bābuḷgāv. She had received instruction from Bhaṭobās. She withdrew from all pleasures. She was dispassionate. She would eat buttermilk and rice. By vow, she gave up everything but her wedding necklace. She ceased to have sexual relations with her husband. She would go to the river, take a bath, sit for a while, and perform her religious exercises *(anuṣṭhān)*. This is how she lived. On her own she went and found a nice young woman for her husband to marry. She got her husband married.
>
> Then one day she came to the river to bathe, and without returning, she went directly to Bhaṭobās at Nimbā.
>
> She met Bhaṭobās. She took initiation as an ascetic. Before initiating her, Bhaṭobās had inquiries made [about her]. She told him about her previous observances and vows.

After initiating Lukhāïsē, Bhaṭobās sends her away to Ṛddhipur for a year, thus ensuring that her relatives will not find her when they come to take her home. But eventually he sends her back to visit her village:

> Bhaṭobās said, "Lukhāïsē, now you go straight to Bābuḷgāv. Go begging there and come back."
>
> So Lukhāïsē went to Bābuḷgāv. When it was time to go begging, she went to that same house [where she had lived]. [Her husband] was sitting at the door. Without recognizing her, he said, "[I] prostrate [myself to you], Mother."
>
> Lukhāïsē said, "Do you recognize me?"
>
> And he recognized her and said, "Yes, I recognize you. Now [I] prostrate myself again." And he came forward [to receive her]. He took off his turban. And, with great feeling, he placed his head on her feet. He spread out a cloth for her to sit on. He washed her feet over a plate. He drank the water from washing her feet. He applied it to his forehead.
>
> Then Lukhāïsē returned and told Bhaṭobās what had happened. Bhaṭobās was very happy.

Thus, like Kesobās' wife, Lukhāïsē's husband becomes convinced of the firmness of his spouse's renunciation, and, in the end, consents to it. A story similar to Lukhāïsē's is that of the Śūdra man who, after taking initiation as an ascetic, goes by chance to his former wife's new home to beg. She recognizes him and is frightened, but he gives her his blessing and quickly leaves (chapter 53). The case of Queen Kāmāïsē, the wife of the Yādav king, indicates that a woman cannot be a renouncer if she cannot leave her husband's land (chapter 148): Nāgdev refuses to initiate her as an ascetic because the land in which Cakradhar commanded his followers to stay[27] belongs to her husband, the king.

In chapters 54 and 58 of *Smṛtisthaḷ,* a couple, Hīrāïsē and her husband, Paṇḍit, both become renouncers—she more readily than he. And chapters 94–95 tell of a couple who, though they both take initiation as ascetics, do not break off sexual relations. The incident causes a major, but temporary, rupture within the group of disciples.

Besides renouncing husband or wife, the ascetic is also to avoid sexual relations with others. Kesobās' amusing escape from seduction is narrated in chapter 105. This chapter tells of a moneylender's daughter who is attracted to Kesobās when he comes to her house to beg. At night she enters the temple where Kesobās is planning to sleep. She sits on his lap. Kesobās escapes by promising to do whatever she wants, but saying that he needs to go outdoors first to urinate. When he gets out of the temple, Kesobās sets off straightaway, leaving his belongings behind.

When Kesobās arrives at the place where Bhaṭobās is staying, Bhaṭobās praises him for having extricated himself from the situation. Later Bhaṭobās tells of a similar experience of his own (chapter 106). But he also tells Kesobās to return to the village where the woman tried to seduce him: "Kesobās agreed. Kesobās said to himself, 'My body is the cause of this [problem].' So he returned to his wandering. His body became emaciated. He practiced stringent fasting. Then he went to that same village and went to beg at that woman's house. Just then, she was standing there. She saw Kesobās and spat contemptuously, naturally taking him to be a wretched beggar. And she went into the house." Kesobās congratulates himself. The best way to avoid seduction is to prevent oneself from being sexually attractive. Similar reasoning seems to lie behind Bhaṭobās' command to Kavīsvarbās to wear less handsome clothes (chapter 122). "You look too good," Bhaṭobās tells him.

Smṛtisthaḷ shows people breaking not only the bonds between sexual partners, but also the often even more poignant bonds between a mother and her children. In chapter 79, Hīrāïsē—this may be either Paṇḍit's wife or another woman with the same name—serves a meal to Bhaṭobās and her other guests, and then eats her own meal, without revealing the fact that her daughter died just as the guests sat down to eat.

Two other mothers in *Smṛtisthaḷ* try to weaken their sons' commitment to the ascetic life. In chapter 56, Ākāïsē, the mother of the young and zealous ascetic Rāmdev, gets Bhaṭobās to help her make Rāmdev eat food she has cooked; the attempt meets with little success. The other mother at first appears to be more successful, but her story takes something of a tragic turn (chapter 75): when the young ascetic Anantdev's widowed mother threatens suicide, Bhaṭobās sends Anantdev home with her. Anantdev later dies, taunting his mother that she cannot threaten Death as effectively as she could Bhaṭobās.

Bhaṭobās' own mother, Ābāïsẽ, is also an ascetic, as are his widowed sister, Umāïsẽ; his paternal cousins Māhādāïsẽ and Āplo; his maternal cousin Mahādevobā; his son Maheśvarpaṇḍit; and his granddaughter, Maheśvarpaṇḍit's daughter Nāgāïsẽ. Some of these relatives of Bhaṭobās' live with him, sometimes even for extended periods. Presumably they do so not as family members but as fellow disciples, but the text does not make any such distinction, nor does it even seem to see a problem with family members staying together as disciples. But when, during a time of political turmoil, Bhaṭobās tells Ābāïsẽ to stay in his brother Vaijobā's village (chapter 83), she objects. "The Gosāvī has forbidden [us to stay with] our relatives," she says, referring to the *sūtra* "Renounce your attachment . . . to your relatives."[28] From the fact that he belongs to a particular village that can be called "his," Vaijobā seems to be a householder and *not* an ascetic;[29] this may be what causes Ābāïsẽ to object to staying with him, when she has not objected to traveling with Bhaṭobās. Bhaṭobās convinces her that their present situation is an emergency, and that, in any case, she is exempt from the rule: "You have had contact with both Gods,[30] and you have served them in their presence, and you have a son like me. And for whom is [the rule about] relatives? It is for those who are weak."

In several instances that have already been mentioned, ascetics visit their former spouses as a test—or, rather, as proof—of their renunciation. In another case, after Demāïsẽ from Kaṭak has been initiated as an ascetic (chapter 133), Bhaṭobās sends her back to stay in Kaṭak for a while, to disarm her relatives' criticism (chapter 134). But when Gaurāïsẽ from Vihīṭā, who has also been initiated as an ascetic, goes back to her village, Bhaṭobās sends for her and gives her further instruction—"primarily about relatives" (chapter 206).

Renunciation of Money and Possessions

Chapter 151 tells of a test of ascetic resolve that is initiated not by Bhaṭobās, nor by the ascetic in question, but by an official of the ascetic's former village. The ascetic is a newly initiated man called Pāṭhak.[31] Pāṭhak's son is told by the village official in charge of such matters that Pāṭhak's hereditary income *(vṛti,* = Sanskrit *vṛtti)* cannot be transferred to the son until Pāṭhak returns to the village, presumably to see to the arrangements. The son searches out his father, only to be told by him, "Whether he transfers it to you or not, I cannot go [back to my earlier] connections.[32] Go away." On reporting this to the village official, the disappointed son finds out that this was, after all, the correct answer. Convinced that Pāṭhak's resolve is firm, the official transfers the hereditary income to Pāṭhak's son.

Besides being unkind to his son, and thus denying his former family ties, Pāṭhak is also, more specifically, refusing to take part in financial affairs. He is thus obeying the *Sūtrapāṭh*'s command, "Do not [even] look at anything having to do with wealth,"[33] as well as a cardinal rule of Indian asceticism generally. This precept is explicitly enunciated by Bhaṭobās in chapter 41 of *Smṛtisthaḷ* ("[Ascetics] should not handle money"), and its application is elaborated in chapter 50: even the money (in the form of cowries and betel nuts) that the head *(ācārya)* of the group of ascetics must of necessity control should be kept for him not by any of the ascetics, but rather by a lay attendant.

Bhaṭobās expresses pleasure when he hears that Nāthobā has defecated on the treasure chest (chapter 223; see above); conversely, he expresses displeasure with two disciples who fail to relinquish their familial wealth completely. One of these is Dīṇḍorī Gondobā, who, after having taken initiation as an ascetic, returns home at his parents' death and claims his share of the inheritance; Bhaṭobās makes him give it back (chapter 152). Another is Kheibhaṭ, who brings a portion of his own considerable wealth along with him when he comes to be initiated as an ascetic. When Kheibhaṭ places the money in front of Bhaṭobās, Bhaṭobās kicks it away, saying, "Am I some kind of false Mahātmā, that you have brought this to me?" Kheibhaṭ protests that his village is too far away for him to carry the money back. So finally, at Bhaṭobās' instructions, Kheibhaṭ abandons the money, placing it in the corner of a temple (chapter 99).

Not just money, but all unnecessary material possessions are to be avoided. When Kesobās hears a passing stranger comment that Kesobās must not be a member of the order because he is not barefoot, he rips up his sandals and throws them away (chapter 218). In chapter 41, Bhaṭobās warns not only against money but also against keeping needles and against sewing more than is absolutely necessary. And in chapter 231 he instructs, "Do not put on new clothes. You never get tired of patched clothes or of food obtained by begging. They save you from much [harm]."

Food and Begging

Food obtained by begging is the ideal food for ascetics. In large part this is because begging for food obviates the domestication, and the large number of possessions, involved in setting up a kitchen. Bhaṭobās' instructions in chapter 41 begin, "Mahātmās should not set up stoves or kitchens. If the necessity arises, they should arrange three bricks [around a fire for cooking]." Bhaṭobās goes on to specify some simple kinds of food that an ascetic may prepare for guests, and some elaborate kinds of food that ascetics should not waste time preparing.

Another reason for begging for one's food is to avoid having a *choice* about what one is to eat. This is the reason that one should normally not beg at the homes of one's acquaintances (chapter 34).[34] Certain foods are singled out as foci for particular criticisms: onions in chapter 160; salt in chapter 36; and ghee in chapters 72 and 135.[35] But, more than avoiding particular foods, the point seems to be not to pay much attention to one's food at all, to be indifferent toward it. In chapter 213, Bhaṭobās chides "the women"—presumably the women ascetics, who seem to have been preparing a meal for the whole group of disciples—for throwing out the leaves and stalks and saving only the best parts of the vegetables they are preparing. Such fastidiousness is inappropriate for ascetics. Says Bhaṭobās of the discarded food: "If my Mahātmās eat this they will get good at practicing *smaraṇ*."

Bhaṭobās himself illustrates his own indifference to food when a prominent new disciple, Demāïsẽ from Kaṭak, serves him safflower oil by mistake for ghee (chapter 93). Demāïsẽ later realizes her error and is intensely embarrassed, but Bhaṭobās assures her, "I cannot distinguish the taste of safflower oil or any other flavors." On another occasion (chapter 81), when a nervous ascetic asks Bhaṭobās if it is all right to eat a sweet food that he has been given, Bhaṭobās tells him to eat it. Then Bhaṭobās explains that *desire* for a food is what makes it an object of sense pleasure, not any inherent qualities of the food.

Hence asceticism with respect to food is relative. Eating begged food is much more difficult for someone accustomed to rich and luxurious meals than for someone whose normal diet is simple and plain. Bhaṭobās tells Demāïsẽ from Kaṭak—who, the text remarks, is "a bit fastidious" about food—to eat the warm food she has received as alms first, and to save the cold for later (chapter 136). And when another disciple makes the formerly wealthy ascetic Kheibhaṭ throw out some *kuhīrī* pods the two of them have been given as alms, Kheibhaṭ cannot get the *kuhīrī* pods off his mind (chapter 101). Bhaṭobās chides the other disciple for failing to recognize the relativity of asceticism: "How can *kuhīrī* pods be an object of sense pleasure for him? For whom are they an object of sense pleasure? Only for someone who does not [even] have salt to put on his mash."

Smṛtisthaḷ does show Bhaṭobās and others of the ascetics eating in the homes of lay disciples (26, 43, 56, 64, 79, 93, 131, 135, 140, 142, and possibly also 45 and 69) or allowing a lay disciple to give a meal for the group (in chapter 108, for example). We also see the women ascetics preparing meals for the group to eat together (as in the episode of the vegetables, chapter 213; and in chapter 160), and once Bhaṭobās even hires a cook (chapter 110). But the ideal is to beg for one's food and then to eat it on the bank of a river. The command of *Sūtrapāṭh* 13.59, "Go begging and then eat your meal on the bank of a river," is reflected repeatedly in the actions of the ascetics portrayed in *Smṛtisthaḷ*. *Smṛtisthaḷ* tells with approval of several instances in which ascetics go to great lengths to beg and eat at a river despite the rudeness involved in refusing to eat a meal to which they have accepted an invitation (chapter 142), despite the meagerness of the alms obtained during a famine (chapter 107), or despite the fact that they have already eaten in seven lay disciples' homes (chapter 26). It is high praise of the ascetic Lakhudevobā when Bhaṭobās says to him, "You have gotten married to your begging bag" (chapter 181).

Solitude

Begging, and eating begged food, then, is an important and formalized aspect of the ascetic life portrayed and recommended in *Smṛtisthaḷ*. Another important, formalized aspect of that life is to spend long periods of time in solitude. "Get off by yourself at the foot of a tree" *(jhāḍātaḷīṃ vijan kīje),* instructs *Sūtrapāṭh* 13.43, and several other *sūtras* (9.3; 12.56, 67, and 278; and 13.1, 131, 188, and 189) recommend solitude and independence. In *Smṛtisthaḷ,* going off for periods of solitude seems to be a regular part of the ascetics' routine. Chapter 209 uses the habitual past tense to tell of Bhaṭobās and others going out to solitude and returning "one and a half watches," or four and a half hours, later. Several chapters tell of Bhaṭobās (chapters 90 and 124) or Māhādāïsē (chapters 166 and 169) checking on other ascetics' practice of solitude. Chapter 109 tells of an ascetic who does not like solitude and must be urged again and again to go out to solitude. Chapter 161 tells of a quarrelsome disciple, Rambhāïsē, whose disposition is improved by a period of solitude. And in chapter 33, when Sākāïsē, the devoted grandmother of Golho, says to Bhaṭobās, "Whenever I play in my house with Golho, I think of God," Bhaṭobās rejoins, "It is better to sit daydreaming under a tree than to practice *smaraṇ* at home."

But daydreaming is not the recommended way to spend a period of solitude. To Sākāïsē, Bhaṭobās immediately adds, "And sleeping [under a tree] is better than daydreaming there"—but he is clearly not recommending sleeping during solitude either. Neither is working recommended, nor eating(?): Māhādāïsē criticizes a woman who has left behind *kuhīrī* seeds and scraps of cloth at the place where she was sitting in solitude (chapter 166). On another occasion (chapter 124), Bhaṭobās criticizes Kesobās and Paṇḍit for having a discussion when they are supposed to be practicing solitude: "If you just have discussions all the time," he says to them, "when will you think of God?"

Thinking of God, *smaraṇ,* is the best way to spend one's solitude. When Māhādāïsē criticizes Mhāībhaṭ for having chosen too nice a place to practice solitude (chapter 169), she refers implicitly to *viraha* as the motivating impulse for an ascetic's solitude: "Such places are not appropriate for solitude for a man suffering from separation from God." Thus, the ascetic practice of solitude is linked for the Mahānubhāvs with the devotional practice of *smaraṇ* and the devotional attitude of *viraha.* When Kavīśvarbās finds his meditation repeatedly interrupted—by ants, by grazing cattle, and so on—he gives up his practice of solitude for that day; Bhaṭobās does not criticize him, but agrees with his decision (chapter 74).

The term we have translated "solitude" is *vijan,* a "lack of" or "being apart from" *(vi-)* people (*jan*[*a*]). The chapter of *Smṛtisthaḷ* that describes Bhaṭobās' habitual practice of solitude (chapter 209) states that he would usually spend his periods of solitude sitting alone under a tree. But the same chapter also states that Bhaṭobās and his fellow disciples would sometimes sit together and hold a discussion of religious matters *(dharmavārtā).* They are still considered to have "gone out to solitude," because they have left their lodgings and are sitting away from other people on a rocky stretch of ground: they are alone together, it seems.

But then why are Kesobās and Paṇḍit criticized for having a discussion with each other when they are supposed to be practicing solitude (chapter 124)? Perhaps Kesobās and Paṇḍit's discussion is not a religious one: the text uses the terms *carcā* and *jijñāsā* for their discussion rather than *dharmavārtā,* the term it uses for Bhaṭobās' discussions with his companions in solitude.[36] Or perhaps the underlying rule is the one expressed by Bhaṭobās in chapter 235: a person living the religious life becomes tarnished *(maiḷe)* without an alternation between periods of practice *(ācāra)* done alone *(ekākī)* and periods spent in the company of others. Some variety is necessary to keep one fresh and awake.

Wandering

It is not just parts of days but weeks and months at a time that the ascetic is to spend essentially alone, wandering through the countryside. This is true of non-monastic Indian ascetics generally, as well as of the ascetic followers of Cakradhar in particular. *Sūtrapāṭh* 12.1 commands that one give up one's connection, not simply with one's relatives, but with one's land *(svadeś)* and one's village *(svagrām)* as well. *Sūtrapāṭh* 13.132 commands, "Practice constant peregrination" *(nityāṭan kīje),* and *Sūtrapāṭh* 13.40 specifies that the peregrination should be aimless *(aṭan tẽ niraüdes* [*niruddeśa*] *karāvẽ).* In addition to these general commands, the *Sūtrapāṭh* includes numerous specific prescriptions designed to assure that the ascetic, having become detached from home, does not become habituated or attached to any other place.[37]

As with begging and the practice of solitude, *Smṛtisthaḷ* provides numerous examples of Cakradhar's and Bhaṭobās' disciples living the life of wandering ascetics, as well as an account of Bhaṭobās' elaborations of Cakradhar's prescriptions for the peregrinatory life. When Kesobās complains of dullness of mind, for example (chapter 71), Bhaṭobās prescribes for him a month of wandering: "You should go wandering for a month. Don't put a bowl in your begging bag. Be in solitude for three watches a day.[38] Go begging during the third watch.[39] Eat your meal at a river. Sleep in a dilapidated temple or at the foot of a tree. Then your wrongdoing will be done away with, and you will be able to think again." This is Bhaṭobās' most complete description in *Smṛtisthaḷ* of the practice of wandering. Other details are added when a woman setting out to wander asks Bhaṭobās how wandering is to be done (chapter 212). He replies, "Go from one village to another. In one village they will tell you about another village. As you beg, at one house they will tell you about another house."

Both of these statements by Bhaṭobās are based firmly on the *Sūtrapāṭh;* in fact, four of the sentences are quotations from, or close paraphrases of, *Sūtrapāṭh sūtras.*[40] In chapter 214, when someone asks Bhaṭobās about the length of time to stay in one place while wandering, his answer consists of two *Sūtrapāṭh* quotations: " 'One night in a village; five nights in a town' " (13.133);[41] and " 'Stay as long as no one realizes your good and bad qualities' " (13.9).

Elsewhere in *Smṛtisthaḷ,* Bhaṭobās' instructions go beyond the *Sūtrapāṭh*'s commands, commenting on them or supplementing them. In chapter 51 Bhaṭobās explains the terms used in the *Sūtrapāṭh* for types of places for the wanderer to stay in or avoid; and in chapter 206 he gives a definition of the *Sūtrapāṭh*'s repeated phrase, "the end of the land." In chapter 30, Bhaṭobās has the ascetics begin to wear distinctive clothes that will make them recognizable as wandering mendicants and will prevent their being taken for malefactors. Bhaṭobās is careful to say that this is an arrangement that Cakradhar had prescribed for the time when he would be absent—and hence, by implication, that it is not Bhaṭobās' innovation. But chapter 106 shows Bhaṭobās initiating on his own authority the arrangement that the male ascetics should wander in pairs and the female ascetics in groups of four. This rule, which Bhaṭobās makes in response to the attempted seduction of Kesobās and an earlier attempted seduction of Bhaṭobās himself, might be seen as an extension of the *Sūtrapāṭh*'s command, "Women should have company in their solitude" (12.269). However, *Smṛtisthaḷ* makes no allusion to this *sūtra.*

The most significant adjustment that Bhaṭobās makes to the rules for the life of wandering is his institution of the four-month rainy season (Cāturmās) retreat (chapter 29). The suspension of peregrination during the period when the roads are most impassable is customary among Buddhist, Jain, and other Indian ascetics generally, but is not mentioned—not recommended, prohibited, permitted, or discouraged—in the *Sūtrapāṭh.* It seems to be opposed to a strict, literal interpretation of the *Sūtrapāṭh*'s command to "practice constant peregrination" (13.132). Similarly, Bhaṭobās' instructions to Bāïdevbās, "You should direct your wandering to the holy places (*sthāns*). You should bow to all the places" (chapter 115), constitute a distinct innovation, as they transform the aimless wandering prescribed by the *Sūtrapāṭh* (13.40) into pilgrimage travel.

When the ascetic Upādhye falls ill, Bhaṭobās gives him leave to stay in one place (his home?) and thus to give up his peregrination (chapter 182). But when Bhaṭobās, finding that young Rāmdev has a fever, suggests that he not go out wandering as planned (chapter 59), Rāmdev snaps back at him, "Bhaṭ, should I do what you say, or should I do what the Gosāvī [Cakradhar] said?" Bhaṭobās accepts the rebuke and lets Rāmdev go; in the course of his wandering, Rāmdev succumbs to the fever and dies (chapter 61).

In the sixteen years after Guṇḍam Rāüḷ's death and Bhaṭobās' departure from Ṛddhipur, Bhaṭobās spends a good deal of time at Nimbā. He first begins to stay in Nimbā to take care of Sādhē, a disciple of Cakradhar's who has become too sick to wander—but who can still keep her ascetic vow *(saṅgraho),* it seems, by living in Nimbā in the hut that Bhaṭobās builds for her (chapter 65). Bhaṭobās flees Nimbā to escape the army of the Sultan of Delhi (chapters 83–87); he makes a pilgrimage from Nimbā to Ṛddhipur (chapters 190–198) and Pratiṣṭhān (chapters 199–204) and back (chapter 205); and he comes and goes from Nimbā on numerous other wanderings (chapter 205 and passim). Significantly, the establishment that Bhaṭobās sets up in Nimbā is not called a "home" (*gṛha, ghar,* etc.) or a monastery, but "lodgings" or "the place where they were staying" *(birhāḍ).* Thus, although Nimbā served as a headquarters or center for Bhaṭobās and other disciples, several of whom seem to have spent long periods in residence there, they did not think of it as a permanent abode. They still considered themselves wandering ascetics.

The ascetics portrayed in *Smṛtisthaḷ* are involved in a complex pattern of comings and goings and meetings and partings. Bhaṭobās seems to know where each ascetic is at any given time: he can tell Pāṭhak's son where to find Pāṭhak, for instance (chapter 151); and several times he predicts the arrival of guests or of ascetics who have been out wandering (chapters 105–106 and 184, for example). In addition, several chapters of *Smṛtisthaḷ* narrate the wanderers' adventures during their travels. Kesobās' and Bhaṭobās' escapes from seduction (chapters 105 and 106) have been referred to above. Before Bhaṭobās has the ascetics begin to wear distinctive clothes, Mhāībhaṭ and Lakṣmīdharbhaṭ (chapter 20) and Kāḷe Kṛṣṇabhaṭ (chapter 30) get arrested as thieves as they pass through villages where they are strangers. Kāḷe Kṛṣṇabhaṭ suffers a whipping before being released, and Mhāībhaṭ and Lakṣmīdharbhaṭ escape physical harm only narrowly. Umbarī Gaurāïsē is helped by a kindly horseman when she gets a thorn in her foot and is unable to walk; the same man's warning saves her from going to a village where there has just been a raid (chapter 77).

Meeting during wandering is one of the greatest pleasures of the ascetic life, and *Smṛtisthaḷ* portrays the ascetic followers of Cakradhar as eager to obey his rules for such meetings. When Māhādāïsē and Mhāībhaṭ meet, in chapter 169, the text says simply that they do "the whole ritual *(avaghī krīyā)*" of meeting—that is, presumably, they follow the *Sūtrapāṭh*'s directions for such meetings:

12.128. You meet in the course of wandering, or you meet by prearrangement.
129. Those [of you] who have met one another have as good as met me.
130. Ease [one another's] weariness.
131. Eat and drink together.
132. Exchange your ragged clothes.
133. Talk about what I have said and done.
134. Stay together for seven, five days; then you must go your own ways.
135. The first and last moments [of meeting] are precious.

Chapter 177 of *Smṛtisthaḷ* tells of a complex meeting of Bhaṭobās, Māhādāïsē, and Kothaḷobā, and of their conversation about how to interpret the phrase "seven, five days *(sāt pāṃc dīs)*" in *sūtra* 12.134. In normal Old Marāṭhī usage, this phrase would mean "five *or* seven days," but in Bhaṭobās' generous interpretation it comes out meaning twice or three times as long:

> Kothaḷobās said, "Bhaṭ, how many days may we stay together?"
> Bhaṭobās said, "The text *(pāṭh)* says twelve days; but the meaning *(artha)* is eighteen days." *Addendum:* "The final answer *(si[d]dhānta)* is that you may stay together as long as you do not become [aware of one another's] faults, and as long as nothing but new attainments comes of it."

Such meetings punctuate the lives of the wandering ascetics, just as, even when they are not wandering, periods of solitude alternate with periods spent in the company of other members of the group.

4. The Structure of the Group

SMṚTISTHAḶ provides us, then, with a richly detailed account of two primary substantive elements of the religion of the early followers of Cakradhar: devotion and asceticism. In addition, *Smṛtisthaḷ* gives us a good deal of information about some of the more formal aspects of the group's identity. It gives us insight into the early followers' understanding of their group's boundaries and an account of their relations with outsiders. It gives us many details about the relations of the group's members among themselves: their closeness and their quarrels, the distinctions among them, and the role of the chief of them, Bhaṭobās. And finally, it provides an account of the composition of some of the principal Mahānubhāv scriptures.

The Name of the Group

The name "Mahānubhāv," the name the group now uses most frequently for itself, means "one who has a great experience." The term is not used in the *Līḷācaritra,* and it occurs only twice in *Smṛtisthaḷ,* in chapters 53 and 233. But the context of the second occurrence in *Smṛtisthaḷ* makes it seem that the term is already a name for the group and not simply a description of its members or of something that happens to them: "One day Bhaṭobās was sitting there. All the Mahānubhāvs, from Lakṣmīdhar on down, were sitting in front of him in a tightly packed group. . . ."

The name "Bhaṭmārg" also occurs in one chapter of the text, chapter 218. Here the phrase "Mahātmā of the Bhaṭmārg" is used—not by the voice of the text's narrator, but first by an outsider and then by a member of the group—as a way of referring to the group's members. Later in the same chapter, Bhaṭobās echoes the name, calling someone a "Mahātmā of my *mārg.*" This suggests that the "Bhaṭ" in the name "Bhaṭmārg" may refer to Bhaṭobās or Nāgdev, who is often in the text called simply "Bhaṭ."[42]

"Mārg" means "path" or "way," and, by extension, "order" or "the

group of people following a particular religious path or way." In this extended meaning the term is used relatively frequently in *Smṛtisthaḷ* to refer to the group of Cakradhar's disciples. The term "Mahātmā"—"great soul" or "great-souled one"—is also used alone, in the plural, as a way of referring to the ascetic disciples.[43] But most often the text, which was, after all, written by members of the group for members of the group, does not bother to call the group by any name at all. Often it simply refers to "everyone," or to "Bhaṭ and all the others," without any need for further clarification.

Group Boundaries and Relations with Outsiders

There are many indications in *Smṛtisthaḷ* that the early followers of Cakradhar perceived themselves as a group distinct from and opposed to others. The principal indications of this are the accounts of individuals' conversions to the group (for example, in chapters 23, 102, 116, 138, 145, 163, 188, 215, 228, 239, and 244), the accounts of group members' arguments with outsiders (for example, in chapters 116, 119, 138, 145, 172, 188, 202, 204, 215, 239, and 244) and their concern about outsiders' view of them (for example, in chapters 159 and 218), and the accounts of group members' disagreements among themselves about the standards of the outside world (for example, in chapters 157, 193, and 196–197).

The obligation, in undertaking the ascetic life, to sever one's connections with one's land, one's village, and one's relatives (*Sūtrapāṭh* 12.1) is complemented for many of the disciples portrayed in *Smṛtisthaḷ* by the experience of joining a new group and following a new leader. A verb used frequently in *Smṛtisthaḷ* for the act of becoming an ascetic disciple, or for the decision to become one, is *anusaraṇẽ*. This means, literally, "to go after" or "to follow"; the cognate noun is *anusaraṇ*. The numerous accounts in *Smṛtisthaḷ* of disciples who perform *anusaraṇ* make it clear that this act is a decisive one, one that marks—and makes—a radical and permanent change in one's life. Implicit in the radical nature of the change from the old life to the new is the radical separation, the distinct boundary, between one's former connections, who now form the outside world, and the new group of insiders of which one is now a member.

We have already cited a number of *Smṛtisthaḷ* stories illustrating early Mahānubhāv ascetics' thoroughness and determination in cutting themselves off from family and home. This thorough rejection of the old life was but the negative complement of an absolute, positive commitment to the new. Thus Bhaṭobās praises Anantkocā, for example, by saying that he "has followed *(anusaralā)* me completely, from his ears to his hooves" (chapter 187).

A halfhearted commitment, or one dictated by convenience, is not acceptable. Bhaṭobās speaks with scorn of those who turn to asceticism only in their old age: "To take up the begging bag at the end of your life is what I call a half measure" (chapter 24). On another occasion (chapter 100), Bhaṭobās allows that Kheibhaṭ is an exception to this rule—or rather, more precisely, to Cakradhar's statement in *Sūtrapāṭh* 10.257, "One who is very old is not qualified for *dharma.*" But he is careful to say that Kheibhaṭ is a completely random exception—as random as the chance that an insect eating away at wood may carve out a holy syllable—and hence to imply that allowing Kheibhaṭ to become an ascetic may not be considered to set a precedent.

The case of women ascetics poses a particular problem for Bhaṭobās. In this case, his preference for a renunciation undertaken while one is still young enough for it to be inconvenient seems to be tempered by his fear that women may not be capable of a permanent renunciation of family life. In chapter 49, Bhaṭobās pronounces himself "afraid to initiate as an ascetic a married woman or a woman with children," and accordingly he prescribes a period of postulancy lasting two or three months before a married woman may be initiated as an ascetic. Lukhāïsẽ, the story of whose ascetic resolve (chapter 97) we have cited above, is an example of a married woman who becomes—and remains—a renouncer while her husband is still alive; Hīrāïsẽ (chapter 54) is another.[44] But a striking number of the women who become ascetics in *Smṛtisthaḷ* do so only as widows. Remāïsẽ, whose husband beat her, becomes a renouncer only after he has died (chapter 137). Umāïsẽ (chapter 216) and Kamaḷāïsẽ (chapter 183) are also both recently widowed, and Dhānāïsẽ (chapter 216) recently orphaned, when they take initiation as ascetics.

It is not just the individual ascetics in *Smṛtisthaḷ,* however, who must renounce their particular ties to the outside world; and it is not just family life and property, and home-cooked food, that they must reject. The group as a whole sees itself opposed *as a group* to the values and standards of the world it finds around it.

The world to which the group portrayed in *Smṛtisthaḷ* sees itself opposed is primarily that of Brāhmaṇical Hinduism. This is despite the fact that Bhaṭobās, Kesobās, Mhāībhaṭ, Kavīśvarbās, Paṇḍit, and several other leading members of the group were Brāhmaṇs by birth. Even the particles *bhaṭ, bās* (from Sanskrit *vyāsa*), *paṇḍit,* and so on, that are appended to their names or that serve as their nicknames are indicators of Brāhmaṇical status. Moreover, Guṇḍam Rāüḷ was also a Brāhmaṇ by birth,[45] as was Cāṅgdev Rāüḷ, the previous incarnation of Cakradhar[46]—although Cakradhar himself probably was not.[47] But a verse that Guṇḍam Rāüḷ speaks in *The Deeds of God in Ṛddhipur* (chap. 281) and Cakradhar in both the *Sūtrapāṭh* (11.a61) and Kolte's edition of the *Līḷācaritra* ("Uttarārdha," chap. 527) indicates that, as the supreme God, Guṇḍam Rāüḷ and Cakradhar cannot be defined by, or confined to, any of the categories of human or other beings:

I am not a man, nor a god or Yakṣa,
Nor a Brāhmaṇ, a Kṣatriya, a Vaiśya or a Śūdra.
I am not a celibate; I am not a householder or a forest hermit.
Neither am I a mendicant, I who am innate knowledge.

Smṛtisthaḷ clearly illustrates that even the Brāhmaṇs among the followers of this God who is beyond such social categories are concerned to ignore not only caste, but also other aspects of the Brāhmaṇical religion in which they have been raised. Chapter 118 shows Bhaṭobās becoming furious with Keśavācārya, a Brāhmaṇ convert who suggests, using synecdoche, that what Bhaṭobās is teaching him is not opposed to Brāhmaṇism:

One day, when [Bhaṭobās] was teaching him "Mahāvākya,"[48] [Keśavācārya] said, "Bhaṭ, if you think about it, this fits in with our tuft and thread."

Bhaṭobās said, "Burn up your topknot and thread! Burn it up! Throw it in water! You go away now. Give me my things." And he took back the [relics] he had given him to reverence. Then he dismissed him.

Elsewhere it is not Brāhmaṇical inclusivism or "tolerance" but Brāhmaṇical exclusivism that attracts Bhaṭobās' scorn. A clear example is found in chapter 188, when a Brāhmaṇ refuses to bow to Bhaṭobās because Bhaṭobās has no Brāhmaṇical tuft or thread. Bhaṭobās says to the man, "You prostrate yourself to your mother and sisters. Do they have tufts and threads?" The man bows to Bhaṭobās and accepts initiation from him.

In chapter 138, Remāïsẽ, nicknamed "Princess" Remāïsẽ by Bhaṭobās, makes a similar retort to some Brāhmaṇ boys who refuse to give her alms on the grounds that she is not a member of their group:

One day Princess Remāïsẽ went to Taḍasmukh to go begging. In the course of her begging, she went to Paṇḍit Vāṅkuḍe Dāïmbhaṭ's house. Boys were studying there. They said to Remāïsẽ, "O Mahātmā, spread out this bundle of grass for the calves. Then we will give you alms. Otherwise we can't give you anything."

She said, "Why can't you give me anything?"

The boys said, "You have not received the initiation *(upadeśu)* that we have."

Remāïsẽ said, "Have the sparrows to whom you give water received the initiation that you have?"

They replied, "If that is how you feel about it, why do you come to our door?"

Remāïsẽ said, "The god whose order *(mārg)* this is said, 'If you want food, go to a Brāhmaṇ's house; if you want shoes, go to a leatherworker's house.' "

And with that they kept silent.

It is not clear whether the "initiation" the boys refer to is that of some particular sect, or simply the ceremony in which high-caste men are invested with the Brāhmaṇical thread. But in either case it is the boys' childish snobbery to which Remāisē objects.

In a rather cryptic exchange between Mhāībhaṭ and an adult Brāhmaṇ man he meets somewhere (chapter 173), Mhāībhaṭ proves just as quick as Bhaṭobās and Remāīsē in repartee. When the man says, "There's nothing auspicious about a Śūdra," Mhāībhaṭ, himself a Brāhmaṇ, snaps back, "And so much the less about a Brāhmaṇ."

On occasion the rules governing separation among castes intrude on relations within the group of Cakradhar's disciples. In both such cases that *Smṛtisthaḷ* reports, however, the intrusion is quickly repulsed. In chapter 193, Umāīsē, who is Bhaṭobās' sister and thus herself too a Brāhmaṇ, upbraids Kothaḷobā, a Śūdra, for drinking from her cup:

> One day when Kothaḷobā was thirsty, he drank some water from Umāīsē's cup without asking her permission. And Umāīsē got angry. "You are a Śūdra. Why did you drink water from my cup?"
>
> Mhāībhaṭ heard that, and said, "What is this, Umāīsē? You have had contact with both gods, and you have a mother like Ābāīsē and a brother like Bhaṭobās. But still you have not lost your ignorance? What has happened to you? If someone as worthy as Kothaḷā drinks water from your cup, is that not your good fortune?" He admonished her this way.
>
> Then she felt remorse. Mhāībhaṭ said, "Prostrate yourself to Kothaḷā."
>
> "All right." And Umāīsē prostrated herself to Kothaḷobās. "I am ignorant. I did wrong. I am a sinner."
>
> *Addendum:* Then Kothaḷobā lifted her to her feet.

Mhāībhaṭ, who is here shown chiding Umāīsē for what he calls her ignorance, is himself guilty, in a subsequent episode (chapters 196–197), of a similar transgression. He refuses a meal offered to him by Āūsē, a tribal—that is, casteless or low caste—woman who was a particular favorite of Cakradhar's and Guṇḍam Rāūḷ's.[49] When Bhaṭobās hears about this, he remonstrates with Mhāībhaṭ: "If you don't accept food from the Āū who would run ahead while the Gosāvī would run after her to pacify her, the Āū without taking whose food [the Gosāvī] would not eat a meal, whom he indulged this way—if you don't accept that Āū's food, it is the same as not accepting God's." Mhāībhaṭ listens to this. He returns to Āūsē, begs her forgiveness, and asks her to serve him a meal. She does so.

Besides the rules against a high-caste person using dishes that have been used by a low-caste person, or accepting food prepared or served by a low-caste person, other pollution rules too are intentionally violated by Bhaṭobās and the other disciples portrayed in *Smṛtisthaḷ*. In chapter 157, when Bhaṭobās is traveling with a young Brāhmaṇ disciple named Bhānubhaṭ, he instructs Bhānubhaṭ to do something that the young man finds quite shocking:

Bhaṭobās said, "Bhānu, crack this betel nut."

He took it. When he looked, he could not find a stone. Bhānubhaṭ said, "Bhaṭ, there's no stone. How can I crack it?"

Bhaṭobās said, "Crack it with your teeth."

"Bhaṭ, how can I crack it with my teeth? It will get polluted by my saliva *(usītẽ hoil)*."

Bhaṭobās said *(addendum)*: "In service, there is no sense of saliva pollution."

So Bhānubhaṭ cracked it. Bhaṭobās took [some] as a mouth-freshener.

On another occasion, when a disciple slips some of his food into Bhaṭobās' bowl, the others are scandalized (chapter 27). But Bhaṭobās says, "Where there are good intentions there is no sin. Didn't the Gosāvī say, 'Where there is love there are no restrictions'?"

Provoking and permitting such violations of the rules of purity and pollution are some of the methods that Bhaṭobās uses to encourage his Brāhmaṇ followers to separate themselves from their orthodox heritage. Another important method is the preference Bhaṭobās exhibits for the regional language, Marāṭhī, over Sanskrit, the more prestigious language of orthodox, Brāhmaṇical, textual Hinduism.

Bhaṭobās and several of Cakradhar's other Brāhmaṇ disciples are portrayed in *Smṛtisthaḷ* as being familiar with Sanskrit, and not averse to using it on occasion. The exchange between Mhāībhaṭ and the Brāhmaṇ who says, "There's nothing auspicious about a Śūdra" (chapter 173, cited above), for example, takes place in Sanskrit; and Mhāībhaṭ and Lakṣmīdharbhaṭ use their knowledge of Sanskrit to good purpose when they have been mistaken for thieves in an unfamiliar village (chapter 20). Bhaṭobās himself speaks in Sanskrit verse on two occasions reported in *Smṛtisthaḷ* (chapters 42 and 86), and so, on one occasion, does Kavīśvarbās (chapter 204)—whose skill in learned, probably Sanskrit, argument, and in eloquent, possibly Sanskrit, expounding of texts is made a point of in several chapters (116, 119, 120, 121, 202, and 204).

But when Bhaṭobās says that Kesobās is fluent in Sanskrit and Paṇḍit in Sanskrit and Marāṭhī (chapter 88), he probably considers what he says of Paṇḍit to be higher praise. When Paṇḍit and Kesobās try to question Bhaṭobās in Sanskrit, Bhaṭobās replies that he does not understand their *"asmāt"* and *"kasmāt,"* their fancy Sanskrit pronouns (chapter 66). "Śrī Cakradhar taught me in Marāṭhī," he tells them. "That's what you should use to question me."

Bhaṭobās' specific objection to Sanskrit is made clear when he discourages Kesobās from composing Sanskrit texts. "Don't do that, Keśavdev," Bhaṭobās says. "That will deprive my old ladies *(mājhiyā mhāṃtārīyā nāgavatil)*" (chapter 15). The use of Sanskrit is another aspect of Brāhmaṇical exclusivism, for it makes the religious texts written in it inaccessible to women, to low-caste men, and to other uneducated people.

The early Mahānubhāvs were socially more inclusive than the orthodox Brāhmaṇs to whom they found themselves opposed; but their group had distinct boundaries, of which *Smṛtisthaḷ* shows Bhaṭobās and other members of the group to have been clearly aware. In large part, these boundaries were theological. The early Mahānubhāvs recognized the existence of the numerous gods of India, and even their power within their limited domains, but they also made an absolute distinction between these gods and Parameśvar, the one supreme God incarnated in Cakradhar, Guṇḍam Rāüḷ, Cāṅgdev Rāüḷ, Dattātreya, and Kṛṣṇa.[50] Thus when Māhādāïsē's brother Āplo converts (chapter 23), the first thing he must do is to throw his gods into the water:

> Āplo was Māhādāïsē's brother. He had had the Gosāvī's [Cakradhar's] presence. Then, after the Gosāvī had departed, [Āplo] used to become possessed [by various deities] and would worship them ostentatiously.
>
> One day in the course of her wandering, Māhādāïsē went to ask after him. As she started to enter his house, she saw the deities directly in front of her. And she said, "Śrī Cakradhar!" and left.
>
> This name fell on [Āplo's] ears. And immediately he left. He put all the gods into a basket, and went and threw them into water. Then Māhādāïsē took him to Bhaṭobās. He received enlightenment *(bodh)* from Bhaṭobās. Then he became a follower. He was with [Bhaṭobās] until the end. Māhādāïsē was very happy.

Another chapter tells of the conversion of Nāmdev, a prominent devotee of the god Viṭhobā of Paṇḍharpur. The devotees of Viṭhobā identify their god with Kṛṣṇa. According to chapter 244 of *Smṛtisthaḷ*, it was one of the early Mahānubhāvs who was responsible for turning Nāmdev's thoughts to Kṛṣṇa and causing him to compose his famous song of repentance.[51] In chapter 113, the Mahānubhāv poet Narendra urges his two brothers, both of whom are also poets, to choose Kṛṣṇa as the subject for their poetry, rather than other subjects from the Hindu epics. And in chapter 120, when the popular Mahānubhāv rhetorician Kavīśvarbās is expounding a Sanskrit text in public, Bhaṭobās exhorts him to expound one of the great Sanskrit texts of Kṛṣṇa devotion, the *Bhāgavata Purāṇa* or the *Bhagavadgītā,* and to expound it to Bhaṭobās rather than to the public.

Bhaṭobās' objection in this last instance is not just to the text of Kavīśvarbās' sermon, but to its forum. The exclusivism of the early Mahānubhāvs, though at root theological, is certainly also social as well. In *Smṛtisthaḷ* we do not see the extreme exclusivism and emphasis on secrecy that led later generations of Mahānubhāvs to such measures as writing the manuscripts of their scriptures in secret codes.[52] But we do see, for instance, that when Sākāïsē wants to give a meal in memory of her recently deceased father, Bhaṭobās discourages her. The disciples will not accept a meal in honor of her father, Bhaṭobās tells her, because, although she is a disciple (a lay disciple, *vāsanik*), her father was not. They will, he says—and later they do—accept a meal she offers them on her own behalf (chapter 108).

On two occasions we see Kesobās concerned to keep the good opinion of outsiders. His concern implies a sharp distinction between insiders' and outsiders' points of view. Insiders already hold the group in high esteem; it is outsiders who need to be convinced. On the first of the two occasions, Kesobās has seen an ascetic eating begged food directly from his begging bag (chapter 159). Kesobās censures the man—not, apparently, because there is anything inherently wrong with what he has done, but because it *looks* boorish. "Just as I saw you, others will see you too," Kesobās tells the man, "and they will denigrate the *mārg*." On the other occasion, Kesobās is distressed that a stranger fails to recognize him as a member of the group (chapter 218):

> Once Kesobās, Paṇḍitbās, Kavīśvarbās, and a few others were going along the road. Kesobās had on sandals, while all the rest of them were barefoot.
>
> A passerby saw them and said, "These are all Mahātmās of the Bhaṭmārg—all except for this one. He has on sandals."
>
> Kesobās heard this. "So because of these sandals I am not a Mahātmā of the Bhaṭmārg!" he said, and he ripped them up and threw them away on the spot.

Although the opinion of outsiders is important, their friendship is not. Economic relations, for instance, are to be kept strictly businesslike. Hence Bhaṭobās chides the female disciple Gaurāïsẽ on two occasions: once when she gives the hired cook some food in addition to the sum of money that had been agreed upon as wages (chapter 110), and once when she asks someone selling ghee to give her some for free (chapter 82). In his list of types of people to whom not to tell lies (chapter 211), Bhaṭobās mentions friends, relatives, dependents of the order, and others, but he does not explicitly mention outsiders. Here, as elsewhere in *Smṛtisthaḷ,* the question of the moral obligations of the members of the group toward outsiders remains unaddressed.

Relations within the Group

Within the group, by contrast, relations are to be marked by love and affection. "Those who have the same God and the same *dharma* should have the highest love for one another," commands *Sūtrapāṭh* 13.36; and 12.136 exclaims, "You are [or are of] the lineage of Acyut [Kṛṣṇa]! You should have the highest affection for one another." *Smṛtisthaḷ* provides numerous illustrations of the early Mahānubhāvs' love and affection. Beginning with Mahādāïsẽ's searching for Bhaṭobās, reviving him, and carrying him on her back from Bhānkheḍe to Ṛddhipur, there are many demonstrations of love among the followers of Cakradhar.

Some of the most revealing scenes occur at the deaths of various disciples. When Kesobās, Paṇḍit, and Amṛte Māyāmbā [Māïdev] come to tell Bhaṭobās that young Rāmdev has died, for example (chapter 61), Bhaṭobās knows from their demeanor what has happened: "When Bhaṭobās saw them coming, he said, 'Māïdev, Keśavdev, and Paṇḍit have come. Paṇḍit's step is faltering. Rām has died.' " Bhaṭobās is present at Mhāībhaṭ's deathbed (chapter 198), and is able to provide him with some final reassurance:

> Then one day Mhāībhaṭ said to Bhaṭobās, "Bhaṭ, will I attain God?"
> And Bhaṭobās, wondering, Why has he said this? remained silent for a moment.
> That made [Mhāībhaṭ] feel even worse. "I am a sinner," said Mhāībhaṭ. "How can I attain God?" he lamented.
> Then Bhaṭobās said, "Mhāībhaṭ, you have had the presence *(sannidhān)* of both Gods[53] and the opportunity to serve them. So why are you talking this way?"

Bhaṭobās then reminds Mhāībhaṭ of an occasion on which Cakradhar expressed his confidence in Mhāībhaṭ. Bhaṭobās concludes, "That is how the Gosāvī described you. If you do not attain God, no one will attain God. Therefore, you will attain God."

Māhādāïsẽ too has the benefit of a deathbed conversation with Bhaṭobās (chapter 254). After she dies, Bhaṭobās gives her a simple but eloquent eulogy: "Bhaṭobās said, 'The old woman was a protector of the religion *(dharma),* a protector of love. She was my friend, and so I feel bad.' He mourned her with these words." Bhaṭobās' own illness and death are reported almost immediately after this (chapters 256–260), along with a more elaborate eulogy, a poem composed by Paṇḍit shortly after Bhaṭobās' death (chapter 261). Like Mhāībhaṭ, Bhaṭobās too makes a deathbed request for forgiveness: "If I have offended anyone in carrying out the Gosāvī's work, you must all forgive me," he says (chapter 259).

These deathbed scenes are narrated with a simplicity and restraint that make them quite moving, even at a distance of several centuries, and leave no doubt as to the bonds of affection that joined the early followers of Cakradhar. Other passages in *Smṛtisthaḷ* show the disciples protecting one another from danger (chapters 84 and 103) and temptation (? chapter 234), caring for one another in sickness (chapters 60, 65, 198, 221, 254, and 256), easing one another's hunger (chapters 27, 107, and 162) and thirst (chapter 200), washing one another's feet (chapter 21), cleaning one another's clothes (chapter 73), and swearing by one another (Bhaṭobās by Māhādāïsẽ, chapter

111; Kesobās, and once Paṇḍitbās also, by Bhaṭobās, chapters 94, 159, 160). In one of the text's most striking examples of service, the normal relationship between householders and ascetic mendicants is reversed when a mendicant gives alms to a poverty-stricken lay woman (chapter 112):

> Vināyakdā . . . went to beg at the house of someone who sympathized with the order *(mārgīcā anukuḷ)*. He asked about him but he was not in town.
>
> The man's wife was at home. She had no decent clothes to wear. Her baby was lying on the rough wood of its cradle. It was crying. Nothing would quiet it.
>
> She saw Vināyakbās. And immediately she prostrated herself to him in her ragged clothes. . . .
>
> "Why is the baby crying?"
>
> She said, "It's on the rough surface of the cradle; that's why it's crying."
>
> Then Vināyakbās gave her the food from his begging bag, and he gave her a cloth he had to put under the baby. And it stopped crying.
>
> And he left.

Besides examples of service like this one, *Smṛtisthaḷ* also reports several of Bhaṭobās' exhortations to the disciples to serve one another. In chapter 46, Bhaṭobās uses the image of an ambitious cow-dung collector to express the all-embracing enthusiasm with which the disciples should serve one another: "There was a woman collecting cow dung. One lump of dung she claimed with her foot; another she claimed with her hand; another by saying, 'It's mine'; and another she claimed by looking at it. This is how one should perform service." And on a few occasions (chapters 38, 63, and 185), Bhaṭobās rebukes, with words or in silence, disciples who are remiss in serving meals or providing water for other members of the group.

In particular, in two chapters Bhaṭobās makes it clear that asceticism, though praiseworthy when voluntarily undertaken, must not be imposed on others. To a disciple who is washing some guests' clothes, Bhaṭobās explains that Cakradhar's command, "Take off the stench of dirt; put on the stench of water" (*Sūtrapāṭh* 13.74) applies only to washing one's own clothes (chapter 73): "Rām, when you wash your own clothes, you should just get rid of the dirt, but when you wash others', you should wash them bright and clean and dry them in the sun. That is kind service." To another disciple Bhaṭobās explains with some humor that whatever water one might force *oneself* to drink, one should not impose it on someone else (chapter 28):

> One day Bhaṭobās was thirsty. He asked someone for some water. The man got some water from a puddle and strained it. He gave it to Bhaṭobās.
>
> Bhaṭobās drank it; then he said, "Don't give anyone else the sort of water that you have given me."

And the man said, "Bhaṭ, [the Gosāvī] said that a puddle and the Gaṅgā are the same."[54]

Bhaṭobās said, "That is for oneself. When you are giving it to someone else, a puddle is a puddle, and the Gaṅgā is the Gaṅgā. You should realize that what lacks feeling *(bhāv)* lacks God *(daiv)*."

Although one should not force acts of asceticism on another, one may certainly admonish others and encourage them in their practice of the ascetic life. In chapter 61 Bhaṭobās remarks, "It is an act of kindness to be as hard on someone else as you are on yourself." And in chapter 101 he says, "You should not praise those from whom you receive generosity and respectful treatment, but you should take as your benefactors those who [lead you to] *dharma.*" Indeed, one of the principal kinds of service that *Smṛtisthaḷ* shows the disciples performing for one another is to correct one another's faults and mistakes. Māhādāïsē is shown doing this in chapters 104, 166, 167–168, and 169; Hīrāïsē in chapter 241; Gaurāïsē in chapter 255; and Bhaṭobās in numerous chapters, including 90 and 124. But in admonishing one's fellow disciples one is not to be supercilious or arrogant. Chapter 45 tells of one ascetic who taunts the others when they return from a meal that he has been so dispassionate as to refuse. As they are drinking water afterwards, he jeers, "Drink it, fellows. Drink it in gulps." Bhaṭobās finds this man's attitude wrongheaded. "If you had come along," Bhaṭobās says to him, "you might have eaten a cupful of ghee, but you would have kept the rule of love."

Other occasions on which "the rule of love" is broken are also reported in *Smṛtisthaḷ.* Relations among the early followers of Cakradhar were not without their moments of strife and conflict, it seems, and *Smṛtisthaḷ* does not hesitate to tell of these moments as well. Another ascetic who refuses to eat on another occasion when the ascetics are invited somewhere for a meal (chapter 43) is not trying to prove anything; he is simply in a bad mood. This makes everyone unhappy, and Bhaṭobās says to the man, "Even though you are in a bad mood, should you miss digesting your food?" Rambhāïsē is so quarrelsome that Bhaṭobās sends her away for a while (chapters 161–162). Bhānubhaṭ of Kaṭak leaves Bhaṭobās for a longer time, on his own initiative, and then returns when Bhaṭobās goes and finds him and makes peace with him; eventually he leaves again, apparently forever (chapter 158). Keśavācārya, whom Bhaṭobās hesitates to admit to the group in the first place (chapter 117), is eventually, as we have seen, banished entirely (chapter 118). We have also seen two conflicts over caste-based rules about purity and pollution: Umāïsē's with Kothaḷobā, in chapter 193, and Mhāībhaṭ's with Āüsē, in chapters 196–197. In these and other episodes, conflicts between members of the group are mediated by a third member, as when Bhaṭobās makes peace between Govindpaṇḍit and Apar Rāmdev in chapter 64, and when Kaṭak Demāïsē maneuvers a reconciliation between Kesobās and Vaṅki in chapter 131.

The most serious rift reported in *Smṛtisthaḷ* (chapters 94–95) pits Bhaṭobās against almost everyone else in the group. The text does not hesitate to show Bhaṭobās in the wrong:

> A couple took ascetic initiation from Bhaṭobās, but they continued to be passionate. Seeing their inappropriate behavior, Kesobās and Paṇḍitbās said to Bhaṭobās, "You should send these two away, Bhaṭ. They are sinful."
>
> Because they were in a large group, Bhaṭobās could not see the problem. Bhaṭobās said, "They'll improve gradually; or, if not, their vices will cause them to leave. Don't you be the cause [of their leaving]."
>
> Kesobās and Paṇḍitbās said, "Bhaṭ, send them away, or we will all leave."
>
> Bhaṭobās got angry and said, "Go ahead."
>
> Then both [Kesobās and Paṇḍitbās] swore to everyone, "May Bhaṭobās' curse be on anyone who does not leave here."
>
> So everyone left. . . .
>
> Then when everyone had left, only those two remained. So their behavior became evident. They would look at each other and make amorous gestures. They would behave suggestively.
>
> At that, Bhaṭobās said, "These two are the reason that my mendicants left. My people have left for nothing."
>
> To the [couple] he said, "Now you leave. For your sake, I have cut myself off from many."
>
> So they left.
>
> When they heard about this, Kesobās, Paṇḍitbās, and all the others returned. They said to Bhaṭobās, "Bhaṭ, we are sinners. We left you!" and they prostrated themselves. They began to express their remorse.
>
> Then Bhaṭobās made them get up, and he comforted them, saying, "Paṇḍit, Keśavdyā, can one see with one's whole body? One can see only with one's eyes. In the same way, Paṇḍit and Keśavdyā, you are my eyes."

Smṛtisthaḷ includes enough such episodes of strife and conflict to suggest that its authors were remarkably immune to apologetic and idealizing tendencies. This in turn lends greater credence to the text's more numerous accounts of the disciples' love of and care for one another.

Distinctions within the Group

The love that prevailed among the early followers of Cakradhar did not make of them an undifferentiated or amorphously egalitarian group. *Smṛtisthaḷ* categorizes the disciples in various ways, some explicitly stated and others assumed.

The most important distinction within the group depicted in *Smṛtisthaḷ* is that between householders or lay disciples and mendicant ascetics. These two types of followers are sometimes distinguished as, respectively, *pravṛt*

(Sanskrit, *pravṛtta*), or "active [in the world]," and *nivṛt (nivṛtta),* "withdrawn [from the world]" (chapter 58; cf. chapter 11, note 34). This usage is not unique to the Mahānubhāvs. More frequently in *Smṛtisthaḷ,* and more distinctively, the lay disciples are called *vāsaniks*, "those who have desire *(vāsanā)*."

The "desire," or *vāsanā,* referred to in the term *vāsanik* probably means desire for God, or desire to become an ascetic eventually. It might also be sensual desire. This interpretation could be supported by Bhaṭobās' teaching in chapter 37, where he takes the term "one who enjoys sense pleasure" in *Sūtrapāṭh* 12.14 to apply to the Mahānubhāv *vāsanik:*

> One day Bhaṭobās said, "Mahātmās should not eat from lay disciples' (*vāsaniks*') plates, and lay disciples should not eat from Mahātmās' bowls. Our faults destroy their *dharma,* and theirs destroy ours. Why? Because [Śrī Cakradhar] said, 'One should not sit in the same place as one who enjoys sense pleasure.' "

But the term for "sense pleasure" in this—and other—*Sūtrapāṭh* passages is *viṣaya,* not *vāsanā.* And elsewhere in *Smṛtisthaḷ* the term *vāsanik* is used to contrast Mahānubhāv lay disciples with ordinary householders: as, for instance, when Sākāïsē is told that she should not give Bhaṭobās and his companions a meal in honor of her dead father because he was not a *vāsanik* (chapter 108). Since ordinary householders are also involved in the world of sensual desire, this cannot be the type of desire that distinguishes Cakradhar's lay followers from ordinary householders.

If the term *vāsanik* alludes to the lay disciples' desire to become ascetics eventually, it provides an indication of the subordination, among the early followers of Cakradhar, of the householders' way of life to that of the renouncers. The "Ācār" sections of the *Sūtrapāṭh* are completely focused on the ascetic life; the life of a householder disciple is not even considered as a possibility. In *Smṛtisthaḷ,* numerous lay disciples are mentioned, but the principal characters in the text all are—or become—ascetics, and the main interest of the text is in describing, and prescribing for, the ascetic life, not that of householders.

It is possible that the terms discussed above as referring to the group as a whole or to all members of the group are in fact reserved by the text for the ascetic members. In chapter 37, which has just been quoted, the term "Mahātmā" is used exclusively for the ascetic disciples, as contrasted with *vāsaniks*. In the title of chapter 37, the past participle of the verb *anusaraṇē,* "to follow," replaces "Mahātmā": "He forbids followers *(anusaraleyā)* and lay disciples (*vāsaniks*) to eat from one another's dishes." Similarly, in the one passage of *Smṛtisthaḷ* that uses the term "Mahānubhāvs" (chapter 233, quoted above), the individuals it refers to are quite possibly all ascetics. If "all the Mahānubhāvs" included laymen and—more to the point—lay women along with ascetics, they would not be likely all to be sitting together "in a tightly packed group" to hold a discussion about religion. The phrase "Mahātmās of the Bhaṭmārg" in chapter 218 clearly refers to ascetics, since Kesobās' sandals are what prevent him from being recognized as a "Mahātmā of the Bhaṭmārg." But the context does not enable us to determine whether the term "Bhaṭmārg" refers to a group all of whose members are Mahātmās (ascetics), or to a broader group that includes lay disciples as well as ascetics.

Another term that the text sometimes uses, and that it definitely uses only for ascetics, is *bhikṣuk,* "mendicant." We have already discussed the importance of begging, and of food obtained by begging, to the ascetic life portrayed in *Smṛtisthaḷ.* A further indication of this importance is perhaps to be found in the term the text most frequently uses for initiation into the ascetic life. This term is *bhikṣā,* a cognate of *bhikṣuk* that sounds like the much more commonly used term for initiation or consecration, *dīkṣā.* The more common meanings of *bhikṣā* are "begging" and "alms." *Bhikṣā* is also used with these meanings in *Smṛtisthaḷ;* fortunately, the context always makes it clear which sense the term has in a given passage.

Smṛtisthaḷ does not provide a description of the *bhikṣā* ceremony, nor does it indicate whether there is an initiation into the life of a lay disciple corresponding to *bhikṣā* for the ascetic life. There is, before ascetic initiation or *bhikṣā,* another step, which the text calls *śravaṇ.* This term, which literally means "hearing" or "listening," we have generally translated "instruction," "receiving instruction," or "being instructed." The step of *śravaṇ* may precede *bhikṣā* by a period of weeks, months, or perhaps even years, as seems to have happened with Paṇḍitbās in chapters 54 and 58, Vaṅki and Kaṭak Demāïsẽ in chapters 92, 131, and 133, Lukhāïsẽ in chapter 97, Bhānubhaṭ from Kaṭak Devgiri in chapter 155, and Ānobās in chapter 234. Alternatively, *śravaṇ* may be followed almost immediately by *bhikṣā,* as seems to have happened in the cases of Lakṣmīdharbhaṭ in chapter 10, Kesobās in chapter 12, Kavīśvar in chapter 55, Kamaḷāïsẽ in chapter 183, and the unnamed Brāhmaṇs in chapters 102, 215, and 239.[55] It may be that lay disciples are those who have had *śravaṇ* but not *bhikṣā,* but this cannot be determined with certainty from *Smṛtisthaḷ.* The text's lack of clarity on this point is consonant with its generally weaker interest in lay disciples than in ascetics.

Unlike the *Sūtrapāṭh, Smṛtisthaḷ* does give us some bits of information about the duties of lay disciples. Complementary to the ascetics' duty to practice mendicancy is the lay disciples' duty to give alms. "The rule for lay disciples is to give time, hospitality, and clothes to those who yearn [for God —that is, to ascetics]," says Bhaṭobās in chapter 176. In this passage, Bhaṭobās is answering a question about what special observances are to be performed on a festival day, but the rule must surely apply to ordinary times as well. Elsewhere (chapter 125) Bhaṭobās explains the benefits of donations made to the ascetics. "By offering a single grain of food in these mendicants' bowls," he says, "one gets the benefit of giving a mountain of food."[56]

Another duty of lay disciples is analogous, rather than complementary, to a corresponding duty of ascetics. From two passages in *Smṛtisthaḷ* we can conclude that lay disciples too, like ascetics, are to practice solitude *(vijan)*. When Māhādāïsẽ tells Mhāībhaṭ in chapter 169 that places as pleasant as the orchard he has chosen "are not appropriate for solitude for a man *(puruṣ)* suffering from separation from God," and then adds, "They are for the solitude of men who have attachments," we may reasonably surmise that the "men who have attachments" are lay disciples, while those "suffering from separation from God" are ascetics. If this surmise is correct, Māhādāïsẽ's statement implies that lay disciples too are to practice solitude. Similarly, Sākāïsẽ is identified as a lay disciple in chapter 33, and she is shown playing with her grandson at home. Nevertheless, it is to her that Bhaṭobās says, "It is better to sit daydreaming under a tree [that is, to practice solitude, *vijan*, even without meditating] than to practice recollection *(smaraṇ)* at home."[57]

Although the distinction between lay disciples and ascetics is the one most actively used in *Smṛtisthaḷ*, the text also refers to other distinctions among disciples. It begins and ends, for instance, with typologies of disciples that do not exactly correspond to this simple dichotomy—or, for that matter, to each other. At the beginning of the text, before chapter 1, three types of disciples who had Cakradhar's presence *(sannidhān)* are distinguished: *anusarale, bodhavant,* and *darśanīe*. We have translated the terms for these three types as follows: "those who became followers" *(anusarale),* "those who received enlightenment" *(bodhavant),* and "those who had the sight of him" *(darśanīe)*. V. N. Deshpande's edition of the text gives the names of disciples who belong to each of these three types: 110 of them for the third type, two for the second, and fifteen for the first. These lists are found in the Appendix to this volume. In addition, Deshpande's edition gives the names of nine more disciples of the *anusarale* type who became followers after Cakradhar's departure *(gosāviyāṃmāgāṃ),* in his absence *(asannidhānī)*. These are also found in the Appendix.

This typology could be outlined either as follows:

- I. *sannidhān*
    - A. *anusarale*
    - B. *bodhavant*
    - C. *darśanīe*
- II. *asannidhān*

or in this way:

I. *anusarale*
  A. *sannidhān*
  B. *asannidhān*
II. *bodhavant*
III. *darśanīe*

In either case, the two axes along which the typology is ordered are, on the one hand, the progression from the sight *(darśan)* of Cakradhar, to enlightenment *(bodh),* to discipleship *(anusaraṇ);* and, on the other hand, the opposition between the presence *(sannidhān)* and the absence *(asannidhān)* of Cakradhar.

The typology of disciples at the end of *Smṛtisthaḷ,* after chapter 261, is organized not only according to the presence or absence of Cakradhar and the presence or absence of discipleship (*anusarauni* and *nanusarauni,* which we have translated in this context as "initiated" and "not initiated"), but also according to the disciples' relationship to Bhaṭobās: whether they were Bhaṭobās' fellow disciples *(gurubhāvaṇḍe);* his own disciples, instructed and initiated by him *(bhaṭobāsāṃjavaḷī śravaṇ houni anusaralīṃ);* or both his fellow disciples *(gurubhāü)* and his own disciples (*siṣya* [Sanskrit, *śiṣya*]). We have not been able to work out a consistent outline of this typology. The disciples named as fitting its various categories coincide only partly with the disciples listed in the beginning of Deshpande's edition (our Appendix). Whatever the precise logic of these typologies of disciples, it is clear at least that they were thought, either by the text's original author(s) or compiler(s) or by a subsequent editor, to be a fitting frame for *Smṛtisthaḷ*—a text that is, after all, not just the story of Bhaṭobās but that of his companions and disciples as well.

The distinction between disciples who had the presence *(sannidhān)* of Cakradhar and those who had to do without it *(asannidhān)* is referred to elsewhere in the text as well as in these initial and final typologies. We have discussed Bhaṭobās' and Māhādāïsē's admiration for those who have become followers of "a God they have never seen" (chapters 175 and 227). The distinction between those who have become followers *(anusarale)* and those who have not is almost certainly the familiar and important one between ascetics and lay disciples. And it seems that the "enlightened" *(bodhavant)* ones mentioned clearly in the typology at the beginning of the text, and less clearly at the end,[58] have received something like the instruction *(śravaṇ)* that is discussed above as a step preceding ascetic initiation. What they have received is called *bodhu,* "enlightenment," though, and not "instruction," because they have received it from Parameśvar himself—that is, from Cakradhar—and not from a mere human being.[59]

Another typology of disciples that is referred to in a few passages of the text is a psychological one. This typology is based on the three *guṇas* ("qualities") of Sāṃkhya thought: *rajas* ("passion"), *tamas* ("darkness"), and *sattva* ("goodness," "purity"). In chapter 31, Bhaṭobās teaches that disciples characterized by *rajas* and *tamas* should imitate those characterized by *sattva.* In chapter 208 he discusses whether one should keep company with people characterized by *rajas* and *tamas.* And in chapter 46 he assigns different duties for the different types of people: those characterized by *rajas* and *tamas* should go wandering, while those characterized by *sattva* should take care of other people. Nowhere in *Smṛtisthaḷ* does Bhaṭobās explain how to tell which psychological type a given person belongs to, nor does he or the text identify any particular disciples as belonging to one or another of these types.

A distinction between people that is remarkable for the lack of stress placed on it in *Smṛtisthaḷ* is the distinction between male and female. Among the early Mahānubhāvs, women as well as men could take initiation as ascetics, and even instruct and initiate others, and many women in *Smṛtisthaḷ* do these things. This arrangement is relatively unusual among Hindu ascetic orders,[60] but *Smṛtisthaḷ* does not seem to find the position of the female ascetics it portrays something calling for explanation or defense, or even for comment. Readers searching the text for a gender-based division of duties within the group will notice "the women" (chapter 213) or a particular woman, Gaurāïsẽ (chapters 110 and 160), most often in charge of the cooking, and the young woman Nāgāïsẽ (chapter 209) left behind to take care of the lodgings while Bhaṭobās and the others go out for solitude or for discussions about religion. But women as a class are singled out for mention on only two occasions, both having to do with teaching the scriptures to women. In telling Kesobās to write in Marāṭhī rather than Sanskrit, as we have seen (chapter 15), Bhaṭobās cites the "old ladies" *(mhāṃtārīyā)* as those who will be deprived by the use of Sanskrit. And in chapter 171 he recommends a special method for teaching women, urging that they not be made to memorize a whole text before its meaning is explained to them: "Women cannot retain a [whole] sermon. Teach them the words and their meanings together."

Much more prominent in *Smṛtisthaḷ* than distinctions based on gender are distinctions based on seniority. When Bhaṭobās says in chapter 96, "*Dharma* should bring about equality. . . . So through *dharma* even one who is senior *(vaḍilẽhīṃ)* should do what his junior *(dhākuṭā)* says," he is commenting on the episode of the couple whose amorous behavior he had failed to recognize in chapter 94. Although Bhaṭobās' statement is ostensibly an assertion of equality, the wording ("even . . .") betrays an underlying assumption of the principle of seniority. Similarly, in chapter 21, although Bhaṭobās rules that a senior disciple *(guru)* may wash his junior's (*siṣya*'s) feet, the junior disciple's shocked reaction to the incident that prompts Bhaṭobās' ruling reveals with what seriousness the principle of seniority was generally taken.

Elsewhere Bhaṭobās' statements make more direct use of the principle of seniority (in chapters 189, 217, and 234, for example); in one chapter (226), Bhaṭobās provides a detailed set of rules for determining seniority: seniority is to be based on priority of ascetic initiation, on appointment by Bhaṭobās, or on maturity of knowledge. Finally, chapter 80 shows Bhaṭobās enforcing the rule of seniority based on priority of ascetic initiation:

> Once when Bhaṭobās was sitting along with everyone in a row to eat, Virūpākhya Mahādevobā had taken a seat higher than Rūpdevobā's. Seeing him, Kesobās said, "You get up from here. Sit over there."
>
> And [Mahādevobā] got up, but he was a little upset. He made a face.
>
> Seeing this, Bhaṭobās said, "If you are going to make a face like that, why didn't you take initiation before him? Seniority must be followed."
>
> And [Mahādevobā's] mood changed. He felt remorse.

Bhaṭobās' Role

The seniormost member of the group portrayed in *Smṛtisthaḷ* is Bhaṭobās himself. Indeed, Bhaṭobās' status is not merely special: it is unique.

A number of passages in *Smṛtisthaḷ* describe or refer to Bhaṭobās' extraordinary personal characteristics: his brightly shining body, for instance (chapter 102), or his sonorous voice (chapter 219):

> Bhaṭobās used to go begging. Bhaṭobās' sonorous call for alms would fill the air. When a baby who was crying heard the sound, it would give up its demands; it would take its mouth from its mother's breast and start looking at Bhaṭobās. Someone who was suffering would forget his misery. Others would be made happy by the sight *(darśan)* of him. People who were quarreling would lose their anger.
>
> So on both banks of the Gaṅgā [the Godāvarī] they called Bhaṭobās "the charismatic *(vedhavantī)* Nāgdev Bhaṭ." He was known by this name.

The term *vedhavantī,* whose meaning we have tried to approximate with the translation "charismatic," means "profoundly attractive"; Bhaṭobās is called "*vedhavantī*" at several other places in the text as well (chapters 146, 204, and 239).

Besides Bhaṭobās' attractive voice and looks, *Smṛtisthaḷ* also illustrates his extraordinary knowledge. He knows, for example, that one disciple carries a pouch of salt around with him (chapter 36), and that another has been surreptitiously indulging in eating ghee (chapter 72). He knows that for six months yet another disciple has been secretly carrying a sealed coconut shell full of water, until finally it is put to use to slake Bhaṭobās' thirst (chapter 200). He knows where to find missing objects (Queen Kāmāïsē's toe ring, in chapter 146; his own sandal, in 179). He interprets a dream (chapter 258). He knows that his mother and brother have escaped capture by an invading army (chapter 85), and he can predict such events as the arrival of guests (chapter 184), the return of an ascetic who has been out wandering (chapters 105–106), the future success of a newly initiated disciple (chapter 180), and the fate of the Yādav king (chapter 86).

Neither the text itself, nor Bhaṭobās as portrayed in the text, makes the claim that such extraordinary powers are innate to him. On many occasions when someone expresses surprise at Bhaṭobās' miraculous knowledge, he says, "I know by the grace of Śrī Cakradhar," or "Can I not know even so small a thing by the grace of Śrī Cakradhar?" The source of Bhaṭobās' powers is Cakradhar. Similarly, the source of his authority among Cakradhar's disciples is the fact that Cakradhar appointed him their leader.

Several passages in the *Līḷācaritra* (for example, "Uttarārdha," chaps. 606, 620, and 623) and several *sūtra*s of the *Sūtrapāṭh* (10.153, 155, 156, 158–162, 240; 12.137) attest to Cakradhar's singling out of Bhaṭobās. A number of these passages and *sūtra*s are referred to, directly or indirectly, in *Smṛtisthaḷ*. When Mhāībhaṭ, for example, on his deathbed, says to Bhaṭobās, "Bhaṭ, nothing untrue comes from your mouth" (chapter 198), he is paraphrasing *Sūtrapāṭh* 10.159: "Nothing contrary to the scripture leaves your mouth." This is something Cakradhar says to Bhaṭobās in both "Uttarārdha," chap. 325 and "Uttarārdha," chap. 622 of Kolte's edition of the *Līḷācaritra*.[61] Three chapters of *Smṛtisthaḷ* (1, 3, and 111) repeat the assertion that Māhādāïsẽ was "entrusted" *(nirovilẽ)* to Bhaṭobās by the Gosāvī (Cakradhar and/or Guṇḍam Rāüḷ). This same distinctive verb, *nirovinẽ*, is used in the *Līḷācaritra* ("Uttarārdha," chap. 625) when Cakradhar tells Āüsẽ that he has "entrusted" her (and, by implication, the others) to Bhaṭobās, and Bhaṭobās to Śrīprabhu. And the same verb, this time *nirovīṇẽ*, is used in *The Deeds of God in Ṛddhipur*, chap. 322 when Guṇḍam Rāüḷ (Śrīprabhu) is dying. Bhaṭobās says to him, "Lord, King Śrī Cakradhar entrusted us to you. Now you are leaving, Gosāvī. So to whom have you entrusted us?" Guṇḍam Rāüḷ answers, "I have entrusted all these others to you, and I have entrusted you to Śrī Dattātreya Prabhu."[62] Finally, in chapter 111 of *Smṛtisthaḷ*, Bhaṭobās repeats a conversation he had with Cakradhar that is also found in *Līḷācaritra*, "Uttarārdha," chap. 623:

> . . . Bhaṭobās answered, "Once the Gosāvī said to me, 'I will make Vānares my deputy *(adhikaraṇ)*. [Through him,] five or six [literally, seven or five] will be given enlightenment. One or two will get it from me, and five or six from Vānarā.'
>
> "At that, I said, 'What is this? One or two will get it from the Gosāvī, and five or six from me?'
>
> "And the Gosāvī said, 'What? Are you the giver of enlightenment? God (Parameśvar) is the giver of enlightenment. A *jīva* gives [only] the syllables.' "[63]

The term used in this and several other passages in *Smṛtisthaḷ*, the *Līḷācaritra*, and the *Sūtrapāṭh* for the position to which Cakradhar appoints Bhaṭobās is *adhikaraṇ*. We have translated this term "deputy." The word *adhikaraṇ* is not generally used with this meaning in non-Mahānubhāv Marāṭhī, but its basic meaning in Sanskrit is closer: "the act of appointing or placing at the head [of government, etc.]." In Sanskrit, *adhikaraṇa* is a nominal form of the verb *adhi* √*kṛ*, "to place at the head," "to appoint." The notion of appointment seems then to be essential to the meaning of *adhikaraṇ*. *Adhikaraṇ* is also related to the Marāṭhī and Sanskrit word *adhikār(a)*, which means "authority," "office," "right," and so on. In *Sūtrapāṭh* 10.113, *adhikaraṇ* is used in conjunction with a form of its cognate Marāṭhī verb *adhikaraṇẽ* as follows: *adhik[a]raṇātẽ adhikarūni paramesvarūci udharīti*, "[Even when] relying on [literally, having appointed] an *adhikaraṇ*, Parameśvar alone uplifts [that is, gives salvation]." Thus, an *adhikaraṇ* is an appointee of God, God's instrument in saving people and enlightening them.

Smṛtisthaḷ gives us a concrete image of what this means in practice. Throughout the text we are shown Bhaṭobās, the *adhikaraṇ*, in his many and varied interactions with Cakradhar's other disciples. We see him portrayed as the preferred teacher and the preferred bestower of ascetic initiation. We see him as the legislator for ascetic practice, and as the interpreter and final arbiter of scripture. We see other disciples sharing in his work. And we see his and their delicate negotiations over the degree and kind of respect that they are to pay to him.

Teaching is central to the role of the *adhikaraṇ* as it is portrayed in *Smṛtisthaḷ*. Toward the end of the text, when Bhaṭobās reviews his life's work from his sickbed (chapter 257), it is his performance as a teacher (the *evenhandedness* of his treatment of his disciples?) that he singles out for mention: "Since the Gosāvī made me his deputy *(adhikaraṇ)*, I have finally told the old woman [Māhādāïsẽ] the same thing that I told Paṇḍit and Keśavdev." Earlier in the text, Bhaṭobās instructs the others, "When you are with the deputy *(adhikaraṇ)*, you should question him. Either you should study the scriptures or you should wander in strange lands. You should not waste your time doing anything else" (chapter 47). And numerous chapters of *Smṛtisthaḷ* show the disciples asking Bhaṭobās questions, or listening to his teachings. In several places he is called a *guru* (chapters 93, 145, and 146, for instance), and once, at least (chapter 50), *ācārya*, "preceptor."

The *adhikaraṇ*'s teachings are the teachings of God himself. Bhaṭobās uses the image of the Gandharvas, the celestial musicians of Hindu mythology, to imply that God takes pleasure in hearing the *adhikaraṇ* teach, and to state that the *adhikaraṇ*'s teachings are God's own (chapter 48):

> One day Bhaṭobās said, " God (Parameśvar) gives his divine knowledge *(brahmavidyā)* and prepares a deputy *(adhikaraṇ)*; then He himself listens

> to his own knowledge. The Gandharvas provide an analogy to this: the Gandharvas teach their Gandharvas' art and then listen to it themselves. God listens the same way."

In explaining to Kaṭak Demāïsē that she should not go searching for Cakradhar in Ujjain (chapter 132), Bhaṭobās repeats what Cakradhar told Māhādāïsē—that he will meet her "anew," in her next rebirth. Then Bhaṭobās adds: "What he said to her is the same thing he says now to those who do not have his presence. Whether he said it with his own holy mouth or said it through a deputy *(adhikārdvārē),* they should accept it." During the period of Cakradhar's absence, the teachings of the *adhikaraṇ* have the same authority that Cakradhar's did during the time of his presence. In one passage (chapter 67), Bhaṭobās is even said to speak with *parā vāc,* the divine speech with which, according to *Sūtrapāṭh* 8.21 *(parā gīrā),* Parameśvar himself reveals his own existence.

On several occasions the other disciples invoke Bhaṭobās' appointment as *adhikaraṇ* to justify their preference for having Bhaṭobās teach what others of them also know perfectly well. After the episode in which Umāïsē gets angry with Kothaḷobā for drinking out of her cup, Mhāībhaṭ asks Bhaṭobās to teach Umāïsē "Mahāvākya," chapter 6 of the *Sūtrapāṭh.* Asked why he does not teach it to her himself, Mhāībhaṭ replies, "The Gosāvī made *you* his deputy *(adhikaraṇ)*" (chapter 194). Similarly, after Upādhyabās has given instruction to his niece Kamaḷāïsē, he still asks Bhaṭobās to instruct her again and to give her ascetic initiation (chapter 183). Bhaṭobās asks him, "Did you tell her about one God, while I will tell her about another?" Upādhyabās replies, "No, Bhaṭ. The Gosāvī made *you* his deputy *(adhikaraṇ).* You will tell her about the God that God told you about."

After Remāïsē has silenced Paṇḍit Vāṅkuḍe Dāïmbhaṭ's snobbish pupils (in chapter 138, quoted above), she convinces Vāṅkuḍe Dāïmbhaṭ that God cannot be attained through works *(karma).* But when Dāïmbhaṭ asks her how God *can* be reached, she replies, "That I do not know. Bhaṭobās knows that." Although she finally lets Dāïmbhaṭ convince her to give him instruction, she brings him to Bhaṭobās for initiation as an ascetic. In chapters 163–164, by contrast, Māhādāïsē gives both instruction and ascetic initiation to Nāïkbāï, with no mention of Bhaṭobās.

Queen Kāmāïsē first meets Ānobās, and is impressed by his erudition. When she asks him how he has gotten so much knowledge, he answers, "I have a *guru* to instruct me." Later she goes to meet Bhaṭobās, and Ānobās gives her a letter of introduction (chapter 145). But when Demāïsē, the wife of the Yādav minister Hemādri, has converted, she does not go to meet Bhaṭobās; rather, Bhaṭobās is brought to the capital (Kaṭak Devgiri) to meet her (chapter 92):

> Once, in the course of his wanderings, Nāthobā went to Kaṭak Devgiri. There he gave instruction to Demāïsē from Kaṭak and to Vaṅki.

> They offered Nāthobā some payment, but he would not accept it. Then they insisted. So Nāthobā said, "Give it to me, and I will give it to Bhaṭobās." And he took it.
>
> Demāïsē asked, "Who is Bhaṭobās?"
>
> "He is the seniormost *(vaḍil)* among us."
>
> She said, "Then you should introduce him to me."
>
> Nāthobā agreed. Then he went from there to Nimbā to see Bhaṭobās. He met Bhaṭobās. He told him what had happened. Then he invited Bhaṭobās [to come there].
>
> Bhaṭobās agreed. Then he brought Bhaṭobās to Kaṭak. Demāïsē was introduced to Bhaṭobās.

The subsequent chapter tells of a meal that Demāïsē gives for Bhaṭobās and the other ascetics. Afterwards, the text continues,

> Both Kaṭak Demāïsē and Vaṅki became Bhaṭobās' disciples. Nathobā entrusted [them to him].
>
> Then Bhaṭobās said to everyone, "It is only because the Gosāvī made me his deputy *(adhikaraṇ)* that I am everyone's *guru*. Otherwise all [of you] are Śrī Cakradhar's frontrunners, and my criers. Now no one should laugh at this Nātho." This is what Bhaṭobās said.
>
> In the same way Upādhye and Kānhopādhye would bring anyone who asked them questions to Bhaṭobās. Bhaṭobās called them too his criers.

This passage addresses rather directly the question of who is the new converts' *guru*. It is Bhaṭobās. But in the case of Demāïsē and Vaṅki, Bhaṭobās has become their *guru* at least in part because Nāthobā "entrusted" *(nirovilīṃ)* them to him. In chapter 183, Upādhyabās' niece Kamaḷāïsē stays with Bhaṭobās for some time after Upādhyabās brings her to him for instruction and initiation. "But," the text remarks, "the group of disciples used to call her Upādhyabās' disciple." This sentence might be seen as revealing a certain amount of competition over the new converts, a kind of competition that is otherwise not in evidence.

Just as in chapter 93 Bhaṭobās calls the other disciples "Śrī Cakradhar's frontrunners, and my criers," so in chapter 91 he says, "Paṇḍit's song is my call." This is after a Brāhmaṇ who hears Paṇḍit singing is inspired by the song to take initiation as an ascetic. Paṇḍit brings the man to Bhaṭobās and tells Bhaṭobās "everything that had happened"—but only *after,* it seems, Paṇḍit has already himself initiated the man into the ascetic life. Elsewhere, too, Bhaṭobās seems to conceive of the other senior disciples as his agents. After the episode in which Paṇḍit and Kesobās organize the other disciples to leave Bhaṭobās alone with the troublesome amorous couple (chapter 95), a chastened Bhaṭobās says to Paṇḍit and Kesobās, "You are my eyes." Of Māhādāïsē, whose checking on others' practice of the ascetic life is reported in several chapters of *Smṛtisthaḷ* (104, 166, 167–168, and 169), Bhaṭobās says in chapter 168, "The old woman is the protection of my religion *(dharma).*" Later Bhaṭobās says of Gaurāïsē (chapter 255), "Since Māhādāïsē died, Gaurāïsē keeps up the standards in the order." The text, and the people in the text of whom Bhaṭobās makes such statements, seem to conceive of them as high praise.

When a paṇḍit whom Kavīśvarbās has tied in verbal knots (chapter 204) exclaims that Kavīśvarbās must be a god, he replies, "I am not a god. I belong to the charismatic Nāgdevbhaṭ." Bhaṭobās himself never goes so far as to say that the disciples *belong* to him, but he does on two occasions (reported in chapters 162 and 206) call himself a particular disciple's *dharma* —that is, her duty, or her religion.

Although Bhaṭobās was the preferred teacher among the early Mahānubhāvs, it seems that neither Bhaṭobās nor the others viewed his teaching authority as absolute. On the one hand, his authority was limited by its dependence on his knowledge of the teachings of Cakradhar, and, on the other hand, his authority was tempered by the frequent discussions and debates in which Bhaṭobās and other members of the group took part. When, in *Sūtrapāṭh* 10.160, Cakradhar says of Bhaṭobās, ". . . he will speak nothing of his own; everything he will speak is mine," Cakradhar is giving Bhaṭobās' teachings the authority of his own. But it is also the case that a good deal of what Bhaṭobās teaches consists of quotations, paraphrases, or interpretations of words collected in the *Sūtrapāṭh* as the sayings of Cakradhar.[64] To cite only one of the most extreme examples, in chapter 214 Bhaṭobās' answer to a question consists entirely of two quotations from the *Sūtrapāṭh*. Chapter 144, of which only the title, and no contents, has been preserved, has to do with a matter of practice about which Bhaṭobās forgot to ask Cakradhar: the implication seems to be that information on this point has been lost forever.

If Bhaṭobās' authority as a teacher is limited on the one side by its dependence on Cakradhar's teachings, it is limited on the other side by the independent knowledge and judgment of Cakradhar's other disciples. In chapter 217, Bhaṭobās explains how to apply his teachings about the amount of time to devote to different religious activities: "The deputy *(adhikaraṇ)* has explained the number of years. Then when a man is in another land, he should adjust them for himself. If there is something he does not understand, he should come and ask the deputy, or he should ask those who are senior to him."

The other disciples are not only to use their own judgment in applying Bhaṭobās' teachings; they also participate in the formulation of the teachings. In chapter 68, Bhaṭobās says that the scripture gets "illuminated" when he discusses it with Paṇḍitbās and Kesobās.[65] And in chapter 253 he praises these two and a third disciple for constantly being engaged in scripture discussion: "I challenge anyone to show me Keśav, Paṇḍit, or Rām standing or sitting idle, not engaged in a discussion of scripture," Bhaṭobās says.

Numerous passages in *Smṛtisthaḷ* report the lively religious discussions that took place among Bhaṭobās and other disciples. The word the text uses for these discussions is *dharmavārtā*. Sometimes *Smṛtisthaḷ* uses this term for what appears to be a monologue by Bhaṭobās (for example, in chapters 150, 208, 211, 217, 235, and 252); but often others take part as well. Several such sessions are described by the text in enthusiastic detail.[66] Chapter 233, for example, begins as follows: "One day Bhaṭobās was sitting there. All the Mahānubhāvs, from Lakṣmīdhar on down, were sitting in front of him in a tightly packed group. During the discussion about religion *(dharmavārtā)*, Lakṣmīdharbās said. . . ." On another occasion (chapter 228), the *dharmavārtā* is so engrossing as to lead an eavesdropper to convert:

> One day Bhaṭobās was sitting in a temple having a discussion about religion *(dharmavārtā)* with his disciples. There was much give and take. A certain paṇḍit was standing outside the temple listening. He would listen, and immediately say, "Bhaṭ has said this, so now what will Bhaṭ's disciples say?" Then when they had given their answer he would nod to himself.
>
> He was engrossed in their conversation this way for several hours, nodding his head. Then the discussion was over.
>
> So he came inside. He prostrated himself completely to Bhaṭobās. He became his disciple, and said, "Bhaṭ, for you it was a search for knowledge, but for me it was instruction *(upadeśu)*."
>
> Then immediately he took initiation as an ascetic.

And, on one occasion reported in the text (chapter 237), one of the disciples argues so heatedly with Bhaṭobās that another disciple takes offense:

> Once Bhaṭobās was holding a discussion about religion *(dharmavārtā)*. During the discussion, Bhaṭobās and Kavīśvarbās did most of the talking. They had a huge debate, with objections and answers.
>
> Kesobās spoke to Kavīśvarbās about it: "Bhaṭ, it is wrong to argue that much with the deputy *(adhikaraṇ)*. The deputy *(adhiṣṭhān)* gets displeased. Can any understanding emerge from this? What Bhaṭobās says is the word of God *(īśvarvāṇi)*. You should bow your head and accept it as you have heard it. If you cannot accept it, then think it over to yourself. Then in time, when your unworthiness has gone away, you will come to understand."
>
> Kesobās spoke angrily to Kavīśvar this way.

Significantly, it is Kesobās, not Bhaṭobās, who chides Kavīśvarbās in this passage. Bhaṭobās himself is never shown stifling discussion or squelching disagreement the way that Kesobās does here.

Several passages in *Smṛtisthaḷ* show Bhaṭobās insisting on a clear distinction between himself and God. When Mhāībhaṭ comes to Ṛddhipur to die (chapter 198), Bhaṭobās is there and comes out to receive him. Mhāībhaṭ takes Bhaṭobās' foot in his hands and asks Bhaṭobās to place it on his forehead. Bhaṭobās says, "It is the Gosāvī's holy foot that should go on one's forehead. I should put my *hand* on your forehead." And he does so. In chapter 129 a stranger asks Bhaṭobās if he is God (Īśvar); Bhaṭobās replies clearly, "No. I am a devotee of God." And in chapter 126 another stranger expresses surprise that Bhaṭobās' disciples address him simply as "Bhaṭ," rather than as "Bhaṭ, Lord" *(hāṃ jī bhaṭo)*. To this man Bhaṭobās explains that he himself has told the disciples to use the simpler form of address: " 'Lord, Lord' should be used only for God (Īśvar). It cannot be used for a *jīva*."

The question of whether Bhaṭobās should be paid special reverence, homage, or worship seems to have been a particularly difficult one. Many of the disciples, it seems, wanted to make toward Bhaṭobās the gestures of ritual homage that in India are traditionally made to a deity or a godlike human being—a saint, a divine incarnation, a *guru*, or a parent. Several passages in *Smṛtisthaḷ* show Bhaṭobās objecting to such treatment. The principal basis for his objection seems to be that making such gestures to a human being blurs the clear-cut distinction between God and all other beings, a distinction that is the hallmark of Mahānubhāv theology.[67] But on at least one occasion, Bhaṭobās also expresses a fear that receiving worship is incompatible with the practice of asceticism. Chapter 40 of *Smṛtisthaḷ* describes a sumptuous ceremony of worship that a disciple performs to Bhaṭobās, using gold, silk, pearls, and incense. With tears in his eyes, Bhaṭobās stops the man who is doing the worship, and reminds himself as well as the man of "Asatīparī." This is a chapter of the *Sūtrapāṭh* (9) that summarizes the life of devotion and asceticism prescribed by Cakradhar for his followers: "To one who, free from passion and error, with his nature restrained, independent, spends his life in recollection of God, Parameśvar again gives union with himself."

Bhaṭobās' reference to this scriptural passage silences the disciple in chapter 40, but on two other occasions in *Smṛtisthaḷ,* it is Bhaṭobās who is silenced. On both of these occasions, Bhaṭobās objects to being worshipped not on the grounds that such worship poses a danger to his practice of asceticism, but on the grounds that worship should be given only to God. And in both cases, the disciple who has been making the gestures of worship to Bhaṭobās explains that it is not Bhaṭobās who is being worshiped, but God who is being worshiped, through Bhaṭobās. This seems, at least, to be the point of chapter 127:

> One day a certain lay disciple washed Bhaṭobās' feet and drank the water. Seeing that, Bhaṭobās said, "You should drink the water from washing only God's feet. And you should eat only God's leftovers as *prasād*."[68]
>
> The man said, "Yes, Bhaṭ. It is as God's that I am taking it."
>
> Bhaṭobās remained silent.

Chapter 130 is the other chapter in which Bhaṭobās is shown becoming convinced that gestures of ritual worship made to him do not necessarily imply that he is God. This chapter must be read in conjunction with chapter 128, in which Bhaṭobās forbids the disciples to prostrate themselves to him. In chapter 128 Bhaṭobās says, "You should prostrate yourself this way to the Gosāvī's holy feet. You should not do this to me." In chapter 130, Ākāïsē forgets this restriction, and finally convinces Bhaṭobās to lift it:

> One day when Bhaṭobās was sitting there, Ākāïsē arrived. She bowed to him repeatedly, and then, absentmindedly, she placed her head on Bhaṭobās' feet and prostrated herself lovingly to him.
>
> Bhaṭobās said, "Ākāï, don't prostrate yourself to me this way. I have told you over and over again not to do this, but you keep on doing it." And he got angry. He threw her out.
>
> The next day she returned. She bowed to him, and went and sat down near Paṇḍitbās. Softly she said to Paṇḍitbās, "Paṇḍit, religion *(dharma)* means going toward God, but Bhaṭ gets upset when we do homage to him. Though I [try to] do what is right, I end up doing wrong, and that makes me sinful. So ask Bhaṭ, 'May we or may we not do homage to Lord Cakradhar's connection *(sambandh)* [with him]?' "

Paṇḍitbās asks Bhaṭobās Ākāïsē's question, and Bhaṭobās answers, "You may." So Ākāïsē prostrates herself to Bhaṭobās.

After this, it seems, Bhaṭobās came to accept prostrations and other gestures of homage, as well as such simpler services as putting away his sandals (chapter 179). In chapter 188 he even helps convince a reluctant Brāhmaṇ to prostrate himself to him. And in chapter 201 he gives as one of his reasons for not wanting to stay in Pratiṣṭhān, the town that once served as Cakradhar's headquarters, "I cannot stand to accept homage here. So I cannot stay here for too many days." As uncomfortable as Bhaṭobās may have felt about it, accepting homage became one of the obligations of his position as *adhikaraṇ*.

Scriptures

As *adhikaraṇ*, then, Bhaṭobās had a special authority that had been conferred on him by a divine incarnation, Cakradhar, and a special status that placed him higher than other human beings. His status was never as high, however, as that of an incarnation of God, and so he could not appoint a successor with an authority as great as his own, the authority of divine appointment. Nor was Cakradhar understood to have intended for anyone after Bhaṭobās to hold the position of *adhikaraṇ*. The position died with Bhaṭobās.

Certainly numerous Mahānubhāv *gurus* have succeeded Bhaṭobās. But—as with the Sikhs, whose tenth *guru* was succeeded by a book, the *"Guru"*

Granth Saheb—Bhaṭobās' real successor is the Mahānubhāv scriptures. In chapter 225 of *Smṛtisthaḷ,* Bhaṭobās says this to Kesobās, the editor of the *Sūtrapāṭh:*

> One day Bhaṭobās said, "Keśavdyā, there is no doubt about what I myself say, but you have arranged that the scripture *(śāstra)* will not be lost after I am gone. This scripture will settle arguments within the order *(mārg)* in the future."
>
> In this way Bhaṭobās praised Kesobās' editing of the scripture.

After Bhaṭobās, then, the Mahānubhāvs are to become a scriptural tradition, one in which the authority of a book is at least as important as the personal authority of any living *guru.*

Smṛtisthaḷ shows this scriptural tradition in the process of formation. It describes in some detail the methods by which the principal Mahānubhāv scriptures were composed, and it gives a general picture of a period of intense literary activity. The two principal Mahānubhāv scriptures whose composition *Smṛtisthaḷ* describes are the *Sūtrapāṭh* and the *Līḷācaritra.* The *Sūtrapāṭh* is the collection of the sayings of Cakradhar. As we learn in chapters 16–17 of *Smṛtisthaḷ,* the *Sūtrapāṭh* was edited by Kesobās, under the close supervision of Bhaṭobās. The *Sūtrapāṭh* as we have it now consists of nine[69] short chapters—"Anyavyāvṛtti," "Yugdharma," "Vidyāmārg," "Saṃhār," "Saṃsaraṇ," "Mahāvākya," "Nirvacan," "Uddharaṇ," and "Asatīparī"—and four longer ones—"Ācār," "Ācār Mālikā," "Vicār," and "Vicār Mālikā." *Smṛtisthaḷ*'s account refers to the short chapters (but not by name, and not, except by implication,[70] as totaling nine—chapter 16), and to the chapters "Ācār" and "Vicār" (chapter 17). *Smṛtisthaḷ* also refers to both the *Dṛṣṭāntapāṭh,* a collection of parables that forms an appendix to the *Sūtrapāṭh,* and "Lāpikā," the summary of the *Dṛṣṭāntapāṭh* (chapter 17).

In addition, *Smṛtisthaḷ* makes it clear that even before the *Sūtrapāṭh* had attained the form of a written scripture, its contents were known and reverently repeated by the followers of Cakradhar. The disciples quote to one another numerous individual *sūtras*, and sometimes quote or refer to whole chapters: "Mahāvākya" in chapters 61, 118, 194, 247, and 259; "Nirvacan" in chapter 259; "Uddharaṇ" in chapters 15, 67, and 259; and "Asatīparī" in chapters 40, 76, 195, and 240. In addition, *Smṛtisthaḷ* refers to some early commentaries on the *Sūtrapāṭh.* Chapters 10 and 17 report the composition of *Sūtrapāṭh* commentaries of a type called "Lakṣaṇ"—*Prakaraṇīcī Lakṣaṇē, Ācār Lakṣaṇē,* and *Vicār Lakṣaṇē*—by Lakṣmīdharbā of Rājaur; and chapter 76 refers to another *Sūtrapāṭh* commentary, *Ācārsthaḷ.*[71]

The other principal Mahānubhāv scripture besides the *Sūtrapāṭh* whose composition is described in *Smṛtisthaḷ* is the *Līḷācaritra.* The *Līḷācaritra* is the biography of Cakradhar. It was compiled by Mhāībhaṭ. Mhāībhaṭ's methods of research are described in chapters 139–142 of *Smṛtisthaḷ*. In conformity with Bhaṭobās' advice that in researching the episodes (*līḷās*) of the biography, he should "ask Upādhye about the ones that Upādhye experienced; ask Nātho about the ones that Nātho experienced; ask Sādhẽ about the ones that Sādhẽ experienced" (chapter 141), Mhāībhaṭ traveled around searching out people who had firsthand knowledge of the events of Cakradhar's life. In chapter 139, for example, Mhāībhaṭ berates himself for having missed an opportunity to question Gadonāyak, the treasurer of the Yādav king. And in chapter 140, Mhāībhaṭ follows a busy farmer to his fields to question him about the *līḷās*:

> . . . Mhāībhaṭ went to Kheibhaṭ's village. He met him there. Mhāībhaṭ's purpose was to discover *līḷās* of the Gosāvī.
>
> Kheibhaṭ would go to work in his fields. Mhāībhaṭ would go along with him. Kheibhaṭ would do his farming, and Mhāībhaṭ would follow along with him, asking him about the Gosāvī's *līḷās*. Kheibhaṭ would tell them to him, and Mhāībhaṭ would accept them with reverence. Then he would go begging and eat his meal. . . .

After gathering the *līḷās*, Mhāībhaṭ would confer with Bhaṭobās, who seems to have maintained some form of editorial control over the *Līḷācaritra,* as he did over the *Sūtrapāṭh*. Bhaṭobās' principal corrections to the *Līḷācaritra* consisted not so much in editing or selecting the stories as in sorting out the genuine from the spurious among the words attributed to Cakradhar in the *līḷās* (chapter 141): "Then Mhāībhaṭ told Bhaṭobās everything that had happened. They discussed the *līḷās* of the Gosāvī that Mhāībhaṭ had collected. Bhaṭobās approved the ones that were correct; of those that were wrong, he said, 'These are not the words of his holy mouth. These are.' " When Bhaṭobās had reviewed the *līḷās*, Mhāībhaṭ classified them as belonging to the earlier *(pūrva)* or the later *(uttar)* part of Cakradhar's life. In this way the two halves of the *Līḷācaritra,* "Pūrvārdha" and "Uttarārdha," were created. Although *Smṛtisthaḷ* does not allude to the fact, the dividing point between the two halves of the *Līḷācaritra* is Bhaṭobās' *anusaraṇ,* his becoming a follower, of Cakradhar.

Like the *Sūtrapāṭh,* the *Līḷācaritra* was not just a written document. *Smṛtisthaḷ* shows that the *Līḷācaritra* too was also a living oral text whose episodes (*līḷās*) the disciples knew and recited to one another in various situations. In chapter 61, for instance, Amṛte Māyāmbā brings peace to some of the final hours of young Rāmdev's life by narrating to him some of Cakradhar's *līḷās*.

Besides the *Sūtrapāṭh* and the *Līḷācaritra, Smṛtisthaḷ* describes the composition of a number of other early Mahānubhāv works as well. Some of these are short poems that are included in their entirety as part of the text of *Smṛtisthaḷ:* Kāḷe Kṛṣṇabhaṭ's nine-verse poem about the *gopīs*' complaints to Uddhav in chapter 114, Kavīśvar's extemporaneous verses in chapters 116 and 204, Sākāïsē's *ovī* verses in chapter 33, Māhādāïsē's *ovī* verses in chapter 123, Nāïkbāï's verses about the *gopīs*' lament in chapter 165, and in chapter 261 the *dhuvā* verses composed by Paṇḍitbās in his distress over Bhaṭobās' death. Other Mahānubhāv works whose composition is described or referred to in *Smṛtisthaḷ* are Kesobās' *Ratnamāḷā Stotra* (chapters 13–14), the second half of Māhādāïsē's *Rukmiṇī Svayaṃvar* (chapter 174), Virahe Lakṣmīdhar-bhaṭ's *Jñānbhāskar* (chapter 18), Narendra's *Rukmiṇī Svayaṃvar* (chapter 113), and Haragarva's *Gadya*[*rāj*] (chapter 113). Other Mahānubhāv authors who are mentioned in *Smṛtisthaḷ*, but whose works are not, include Bāïdev, the author of the short works *Pūjāvasar, Prasādsevā, Mūrtijñān,* and *Nāmāce Dahā Ṭhāy;* and Ānobās, the author of a text entitled *Ṛddhipur Māhātmya.*

In addition, *Smṛtisthaḷ* also refers to the contemporary literary world outside the sect. The text mentions the composition of three contemporary non-Mahānubhāv works: Nṛsiṃhakavi's *Nalopākhyān* and Sālkavi's *Rāmāyaṇ* are mentioned in chapter 113, and Nāmdev's poem "My days have passed to no purpose" in chapter 244. With this mention of a poem of Nāmdev's, we see in chapter 244 an attempt to bring into the Mahānubhāv fold one of the major poet-saints in the literary movement connected with the god Viṭhobā of Paṇḍharpur. And in chapter 113 we see the Mahānubhāv poet Narendra being offered—and refusing—royal patronage in exchange for the authorship of his *Rukmiṇī Svayaṃvar.*

Thus *Smṛtisthaḷ* depicts the early followers of Cakradhar as active participants in a lively literary culture. Indeed, most of the major works of Old Marāṭhī literature were composed during the period described in *Smṛtisthaḷ.* The *Līḷācaritra,* to cite only the chief example, is the earliest prose text in Marāṭhī, and the principal text in prose from the Old Marāṭhī period (approximately A.D. 1000 to 1350). For *Smṛtisthaḷ,* though, and for the group it portrays, the *Līḷācaritra* and the other Mahānubhāv texts are not only works of literary merit but also scriptures. That is, they are texts with a certain religious authority.

In *Smṛtisthaḷ,* the authority of the written scriptures is not seen as independent of the oral tradition on which they are based. One cannot learn the scriptures simply by reading them, but must study them with a *guru.* In chapter 207, Bhaṭobās says, "One should not study this scripture *(śāstra)* on one's own. Written words cannot bring about attraction *(vedhu)* or enlightenment *(bodhu).* When the scripture is heard from the mouth of one's *guru,* it comes alive. . . ." The term that we have translated "scripture," *śāstra,* has a double meaning: it refers not just to the written text, like the English word "scripture," but also to the body of knowledge, the "science," that the scripture records. Both sides of this meaning are alive in *Smṛtisthaḷ,* and appropriately so. For *Smṛtisthaḷ* portrays a religious group that, bereft of the personal authority of a divine leader, is on the verge of replacing the personal authority of a divinely appointed successor with the scriptural authority of texts preserving the divine leader's words and recording his deeds. So, although *Smṛtisthaḷ* describes the composition of scriptural texts, neither it nor the group it portrays has as yet come to see those texts as replacing the oral traditions they record.

In this, then, as in other aspects of the identity of Cakradhar's followers, *Smṛtisthaḷ* captures a fluid moment in the history of the group. The members are aware of the boundaries of their group, they are aware of the emphasis on devotion and asceticism that determines their distinctive character as a group, they are aware of role divisions and status distinctions among them, and they are aware of a need for written scriptures. Yet everything is new, and nothing is fixed. *Smṛtisthaḷ* depicts the beginnings of a sect that has perdured through seven centuries. Yet, in its beginnings, the "sect" that *Smṛtisthaḷ* depicts was simply a group of people whose God had left them, and who were trying to muddle along without him.

5. The Text of *Smṛtisthaḷ*

Title

Smṛtisthaḷ not only provides an account of the composition of the Mahānubhāv scriptures; it is also itself a scripture for Mahānubhāvs. Its title indicates this. The name *"Smṛtisthaḷ"* is a compound of two words, *smṛti* and *sthaḷ*. The second element of the compound, *sthaḷ*, means "topic of discourse"; it is found in the titles of such other Mahānubhāv texts as *Vicārsthaḷ* and *Ācārsthaḷ*, commentaries on the "Vicār" ("Doctrine") and "Ācār" ("Practice") chapters, respectively, of the *Sūtrapāṭh*. The first element, *smṛti*, refers to a hierarchy of Mahānubhāv scriptural authority that simulates that of orthodox Hinduism.[72]

Orthodox Hinduism calls the Vedas, as revealed texts, unauthored but "heard" by the seers who first recited them, *"śruti"*; *"smṛti"* refers to another class of texts, still authoritative but with a lesser degree of authority, which are held to have had human authors. In Mahānubhāv terminology, *śruti* is the words of Cakradhar or another of the "Five Kṛṣṇas"—for instance, Kṛṣṇa's words as preserved in the *Bhagavadgītā*—while *smṛti* is the words of Bhaṭobās. In addition, the words of the first generation of preceptors who followed Bhaṭobās are called *vṛddhācār,* and those of the next few generations, *mārgrūḍhī*.[73] These four types of scripture form a hierarchy, with *śruti* the most authoritative, *smṛti* the next, and so on.

The root meaning of the word *smṛti* is "remembrance"; *smṛti* is related to the activity of *smaraṇ* that we have seen to be so important in early Mahānubhāv devotional practice. As a category of scripture, *smṛti* is thus implicitly not just the words of Bhaṭobās, but the words and deeds of Cakradhar as remembered by Bhaṭobās. Ānobās, a contemporary of Bhaṭobās who also appears as a character in *Smṛtisthaḷ*, defines *smṛti* in such terms. He says that it is the biography *(līḷācaritra)* of Cakradhar as seen and remembered by the deputy (the *adhikaraṇ*—that is, Bhaṭobās) and narrated to his disciples.[74] *Smṛtisthaḷ*, though, exists now as a separate text from the

Līḷācaritra, and is in fact much more directly concerned with Bhaṭobās and his contemporaries than with Cakradhar.

Smṛtisthaḷ is about human beings, whereas the other Mahānubhāv biographies are about incarnations of Parameśvar. This difference in subject matter is reflected in a difference in the titles of the works. Although the *Līḷācaritra* and the other biographies of divine incarnations are based on the recollections of Bhaṭobās and other early Mahānubhāvs, these texts do not have the word *"smṛti"* in their titles, as *Smṛtisthaḷ* does in its. The title of the *Līḷācaritra* refers to the divine "deeds," "plays," or "games"—*līḷā*s—that are narrated in it; the other biographies are named for the places where the *līḷā*s of the other divine incarnations were enacted. Thus, for example, the original title of the work that has been edited as the *Govindprabhucaritra*[75] is *Ṛddhipurcaritra* or *Ṛddhipurlīḷā,* since the *līḷā*s, the divine deeds, recorded in it took place in Ṛddhipur. Similarly, the biography of Cāṅgdev Rāüḷ is called the *Dvārāvatīlīḷā,* and that of Dattātreya the *Sahyādrīlīḷā,* for the places where these incarnations lived. And the Mahānubhāv prose biography of Kṛṣṇa is sometimes called *Dvāparlīḷā,* for the world-age *(yug)* in which this incarnation lived. Once, but only once, in chapter 247, *Smṛtisthaḷ* seems to name itself after Nimbā, the place where Bhaṭobās spent most of his time. Otherwise, though, this name is not used. It may have been felt to put *Smṛtisthaḷ* on the same level as the other biographies and thus implicitly to put Bhaṭobās on the level of the divine incarnations.

Smṛtisthaḷ, then, lacks the status of the other Mahānubhāv biographical texts, and it lacks the authority of the *Sūtrapāṭh* or the *Bhagavadgītā.* It is not a biography of a divine incarnation, nor does it record the words of one. However, because much of the text is concerned with *interpreting* the words of Cakradhar, *Smṛtisthaḷ* has an extremely close relationship with the *Sūtrapāṭh.* In fact, it could be said that, like other Mahānubhāv texts with the ending *-sthaḷ* in their titles, *Smṛtisthaḷ* is a commentary on the *Sūtrapāṭh.* Numerous passages in *Smṛtisthaḷ* quote, echo, refer to, or assume the reader's familiarity with *sūtra*s found in the *Sūtrapāṭh.* These *sūtra*s are identified in the notes to the translation, and they are indexed at the end of this volume. The *Smṛtisthaḷ* passages in which *sūtra*s are found generally show the disciples discussing a *sūtra*'s meaning, or Bhaṭobās interpreting one for other disciples, or Bhaṭobās or another disciple attempting to apply a *sūtra* in an effort to determine the correct behavior in a particular situation. *Smṛtisthaḷ* thus serves, at least in part, as a kind of living, narrative commentary on the *Sūtrapāṭh.*

Edition

Our translation of *Smṛtisthaḷ* is based on Vaman Narayan Deshpande's edition. This is the principal scholarly edition of the text. Another edition, prepared by S. G. Tulpule in 1969 and reprinted with revisions in 1990 (Puṇe: Anamol Prakāśan), was intended primarily for university students. Deshpande's edition was first published in 1939; it was revised in 1960. We have used the third edition, a corrected reprint that was published in 1968.[76] Deshpande based his edition on four undated manuscripts. On the basis of their "paper, ink, handwriting, and so on," he judged these manuscripts to be "250 to 350 years old." All of the manuscripts were written in the Mahānubhāv code named *sakaḷ lipī.*[77] In editing the text, Deshpande gave the readings of the oldest looking of the four manuscripts, transcribing it out of *sakaḷ lipī* into ordinary *devanāgarī* script. He standardized the spelling in the Sanskrit passages in the text (but left *ḷ* wherever it occurred instead of *l*) and corrected for the variation between *n* and *ṇ* brought about by the use of *sakaḷ lipī.*[78] Some minor lacunae in the base manuscript were dealt with by supplying the missing word(s) or letter(s) from the other manuscripts. Deshpande gave these words and letters in parentheses in the body of the text; he provided major variants from the other three manuscripts in footnotes.

After his 1939 edition of *Smṛtisthaḷ* had gone to press, Deshpande received seven more manuscripts of the text, one of them dated Śaka 1523 and A.D. 1601, and another dated Śaka 1604 (that is, A.D. 1682). The 1960 and 1968 editions of Deshpande's *Smṛtisthaḷ* were nevertheless still based on the same manuscript that was used for the first edition; for the second edition, Deshpande corrected the printed version by comparing it once again with that manuscript, but for the third edition he corrected only typographical errors.

All of the eleven manuscripts examined by Deshpande were of the same text. The text includes 260 or 261 *smṛti* chapters—the number depending primarily on the presence or absence of chapter 222[79]—and twenty-three[80] chapters of a section entitled "Vṛddhācār" that we have not translated here.

Authorship and Date

This text, entitled *Smṛtisthaḷ,* is but one of three extant Mahānubhāv *smṛti* collections. Deshpande compared the other two to *Smṛtisthaḷ* in the introduction to his edition, and he gave in appendixes materials found in them but not in *Smṛtisthaḷ.* Neither of the other two texts has been published in full. For his excerpts from one of them, *Smṛtisamuccaya,* Deshpande used one of three manuscripts available to him. This manuscript is presumably the one he described in his introduction[81] as the only one bearing a date (Śaka 1662 and A.D. 1740). It contains 357 *smṛtis*, forty-five chapters of "Vṛddhācār," and seventy additional titles for which the *smṛtis* are not given, along with the "usual" list of names of disciples.[82] For the third *smṛti* text, Deshpande had only one manuscript, dated Śaka 1545 and A.D. 1624.

Because the manuscript, which does not name the text, also contains the *Ajñāt Līḷā* ("Unknown *Līḷā*s") of Cakradhar, Deshpande called this *smṛti* text *Ajñāt Smṛti.*[83]

Deshpande compared these three *smṛti* texts in the introduction to his edition of *Smṛtisthaḷ.* He argued that *Smṛtisamuccaya* is more recent than *Ajñāt Smṛti* and *Smṛtisthaḷ,* and that *Ajñāt Smṛti* is either contemporary with or more recent than *Smṛtisthaḷ.*[84] And he pointed out a number of potentially controversial or historically questionable passages in the two other texts that are not found in *Smṛtisthaḷ.* For instance, whereas both *Ajñāt Smṛti* and *Smṛtisamuccaya* include chapters (*Ajñāt Smṛti,* chaps. 18–19; *Smṛtisamuccaya,* chaps. 23–24 and 56) telling of Bhaṭobās and Māhādāïsẽ visiting Mātāpur, *Smṛtisthaḷ* makes no mention of any of the disciples going there. Mātāpur is present-day Māhūr, a major goddess pilgrimage place that is also connected with Dattātreya, one of the Mahānubhāvs' "Five Kṛṣṇas"; Cakradhar is said to have forbidden going to Mātāpur,[85] but Guṇḍam Rāüḷ, on his deathbed, is supposed to have given the opposite command.[86] In addition, a historically unreliable chapter about the Sultan of Delhi (*Ajñāt Smṛti,* chap. 95; *Smṛtisamuccaya,* "Vṛddhācār," chap. 24) is not found in *Smṛtisthaḷ.* And *Ajñāt Smṛti,* chap. 108 and *Smṛtisamuccaya,* chap. 212 make a reference to Śaṅkarācārya that is not found in the otherwise similar chapter (118) of *Smṛtisthaḷ.*[87]

Despite important differences among them, *Smṛtisamuccaya, Ajñāt Smṛti,* and *Smṛtisthaḷ* have a large number of *smṛti*s in common. Deshpande took this to mean that the three texts share a common source. What this source might be is more difficult to say, and Deshpande did not commit himself to a decision as to whether it is one of the three extant texts or another, earlier one.[88]

Mahānubhāv tradition tells of four different early Mahānubhāv authors who made *smṛti* collections. According to the "Anvayasthaḷ" of the Pāramāṇḍalya lineage,[89] the poet Narendra collected 700 *smṛti*s, and the poet Mālobās 500. The poet Narendra, who appears as a character in *Smṛtisthaḷ* (chapters 64 and 113), was a disciple of Bhaṭobās; Raeside[90] dates Mālobās to the late fourteenth century. The Sāḷkar "Anvayasthaḷ" and Rāghavmuni's "Caritra-abāb" name Paraśurām, a disciple of Kavīśvarbās whom Raeside[91] dates to the early fourteenth century, as having made a collection of *smṛti*s. And yet another work, "Anvayasthaḷācī Parī," tells of a collection made by [Gurjar] Śivbās, whom Raeside[92] dates to the early fifteenth century. Dhārāśivkar Oṃkārbās and Nāyābā (or Nyāyavyās), both of whom are dated by Raeside to the middle of the fourteenth century,[93] are also sometimes named as authors of *smṛti*s.[94]

The text of *Smṛtisthaḷ* as we have it now cannot simply be identical with any one of these *smṛti* collections. Rather, our *Smṛtisthaḷ* is the product of several authors and more than one generation of editors. The text itself bears the marks of the long-term, complex process of refinement that brought it to its present form. The most ubiquitous reminder of this process is the term *"śodhu."* This word, found in numerous places in the text,[95] indicates that the words that follow it are an editor's correction made on the basis of further research. We have translated this term as *"addendum."* Another, less frequent editorial comment is to be seen in the phrase *"hẽ yathāpratī."* This phrase, which occurs in chapters 240 and 247, means, "This is the way it is in the original"; we have translated the phrase literally, as *"sic."*

In several places in *Smṛtisthaḷ,*[96] the term *"vāsanā"* is used to introduce a variant version of a piece of information. The term *"vāsanā,"* "desire," seems here to mean, "as so-and-so would have it." We have translated *"vāsanā"* in these contexts as "according to. . . ." Most often, no particular source of this sort of variant is named: the text simply says *"ekī vāsanā,"* "according to some. . . ." In two places, though, a particular person is named as responsible for a *"vāsanā"* version: Kavībās in chapter 200, and Kesobās in chapter 246.

Kavībās (or Kavibās) is also named in the text as the source of the chapters from 225 through 253; of all or part of chapters 63, 202, and 216; of a *śodhu* addendum in chapter 104; of chapters 143 and 144, only the titles of which are given in *Smṛtisthaḷ;* and of the title of chapter 147, a chapter that is said not to be (otherwise) extant.[97] Despite the fact that some of the manuscripts read "Kavīśvarbās" for "Kavībās" at some places, Deshpande argued[98] that this Kavībās is not Kavīśvarbās, but the Mālobās ("Kavi Mālobās") named in the Pāramāṇḍalya "Anvayasthaḷ" as having made a collection of 500 *smṛtis*.

Chapter 208 introduces a variant version of a statement by Bhaṭobās without using the word *vāsanā* or naming a particular source of the variant. Instead, the text says, *"pāṭhāntar,"* "another version." And finally, also without using the word *"vāsanā,"* chapter 106 remarks, "Malekoyābā used to tell this episode *(smṛti)* and talk about *dharma."* Malekoyābā, according to the *guru*-disciple lineage given by Deshpande,[99] was a fifth-generation disciple of Nāgdev (Bhaṭobās).

Another kind of editorial comment is found in chapters 23 and 247. Each of these chapters remarks that it more properly belongs to the time of one of the other Mahānubhāv biographies than to *Smṛtisthaḷ*—chapter 23 to the time of the second half, "Uttarārdha," of the *Līḷācaritra,* and chapter 247 to the time of the *Ṛddhipurcaritra.* Chapter 247 takes place during the period, after the departure of Cakradhar and before the death of Śrīprabhu or Guṇḍam Rāüḷ, that the disciples spent in Ṛddhipur. In the opposite temporal direction from these two chapters, chapter 221 ends with an addendum that it identifies as coming from the *mārgrūḍhi* period. That is, the addendum reflects a later and less authoritative tradition than the *smṛti* traditions recorded in the rest of the text.

The mention of Malekoyābā in chapter 106 and of *mārgrūḍhi* in chapter 221 were Deshpande's principal grounds for suggesting that *Smṛtisthaḷ* took its present shape in the middle of the fourteenth century Śaka—that is, in the second quarter of the fifteenth century A.D.—at the hands of an editor belonging to the *mārgrūḍhi* period,[100] that is, to the first few generations of the disciples of Bhaṭobās' disciples. More tentatively, Deshpande believed that that editor might have been Gurjar Śivbās.[101] In that case, the original *smṛti* materials would have been collected by Narendra and Paraśurāmbās, and the *śodhu* variants would have come from Mālobās (alias Kavibās), Nāyābā, and Dhārāśivkar Omkārbās.[102] Thus, the basic materials in *Smṛtisthaḷ* would date from soon after Bhaṭobās' death in the early fourteenth century, but the text might not have reached its final form until more than a hundred years later.

Whatever the precise details of the composition and editing of *Smṛtisthaḷ*, whatever the names and dates of the disciples who recited, wrote, compiled, selected, arranged, rearranged, and revised its chapters, the text as we now have it is clearly the result of the combined work of generations. Given this fact, the freshness and frankness of *Smṛtisthaḷ* are all the more remarkable. In *Smṛtisthaḷ*, the early Mahānubhāvs sought to preserve the memory of their formative years. It seems that they did this not just with piety, but with a striking degree of honesty as well.

Notes to Introduction

1. For an introduction to the history and thought of the Mahānubhāvs, see I. M. P. Raeside, "The Mahānubhāvas," *Bulletin of the School of Oriental and African Studies, University of London* 39 (1976): 585–600; Anne Feldhaus, *The Religious System of the Mahānubhāva Sect: The Mahānubhāva Sūtrapāṭha* (New Delhi: Manohar, 1983); Anne Feldhaus, "The *devatācakra* of the Mahānubhāvas," *Bulletin of the School of Oriental and African Studies, University of London* 43 (1980): 101–109; and Anne Feldhaus, "Kṛṣṇa and the Kṛṣṇas: Kṛṣṇa in the Mahānubhāva Pantheon," in *Bhakti in Current Research, 1979–1982,* ed. Monika Thiel-Horstmann (Berlin: Dietrich Reimer Verlag, 1983), 133–142.

2. In Mahānubhāv terms, it is incorrect to speak of Cakradhar's death. He did not die, but went away.

3. Chapters 149 and 150 indicate that Bhaṭobās was alive at the time of King Rāmcandra Yādav's death; but we know from other sources that King Rāmcandra died in 1311 (Śaka 1231). Chapter 83 tells of an invasion by the "Sultan of Delhi" that occurred in 1310. And in chapter 86 Bhaṭobās predicts that the "Marāṭhā" (that is, Yādav) kingdom will last as long as he himself lives *(mīṃ vartē tavā marhāṭē vartail).* The Yādav kingdom fell to Muslims in 1312 (Śaka 1234). It seems reasonable to assume that the authors of *Smṛtisthaḷ* remembered and reported Nāgdev's prediction because they understood it to have come true. *Smṛtisthaḷ*'s date for Cakradhar's departure has also been questioned. See V. B. Kolte, *Śrīcakradhar Caritra,* 2d ed. (Malkāpūr: Aruṇ Prakāśan, 1977), 293–318.

4. See Anne Feldhaus, "Maharashtra as a Holy Land: A Sectarian Tradition," *Bulletin of the School of Oriental and African Studies, University of London* 49 (1986): 532–548.

5. See Günther-Dietz Sontheimer, "God, Dharma and Society in the Yādava Kingdom of Devagirī According to the *Līḷācaritra* of Cakradhar," in *Indology and Law: Studies in Honour of Professor J. Duncan M. Derrett,* ed. Günther-Dietz Sontheimer and Parameswara K. Aithal (Wiesbaden: F. Steiner Verlag, 1982), 329–358.

6. The term *viyog,* "separation," is also used in *Smṛtisthaḷ,* and often simply *dukh* (= Sanskrit *duḥkha),* "suffering, grief."

7. There is a vast literature on this subject in English. See, for example, Friedhelm Hardy, *Viraha-bhakti: The Early History of Kṛṣṇa Devotion in South India* (Delhi:

Oxford University Press, 1983), and Edward C. Dimock, Jr., *The Place of the Hidden Moon: Erotic Mysticism in the Vaiṣṇava-Sahajiyā Cult of Bengal* (Chicago: University of Chicago Press, 1966).

8. Dimock, *The Place of the Hidden Moon.*

9. See Feldhaus, "Kṛṣṇa and the Kṛṣṇas."

10. This work appears as no. 125 in I. M. P. Raeside's "A Bibliographical Index of Mahānubhāva Works in Marathi," *Bulletin of the School of Oriental and African Studies, University of London* 23 (1960): 464–507. According to Raeside, the work consists of 124 *ślokas* and is "said to have been published at Lahore by the Datta-prakāśa Press" (p. 481).

11. Feldhaus, *The Religious System of the Mahānubhāva Sect,* 85–169; *Mhāībhaṭ Saṅkalit Śrīcakradhar Līḷā Caritra,* 2d ed., ed. V. B. Kolte (Mumbaī: Mahārāṣṭra Rājya Sāhitya-Saṃskṛti Maṇḍaḷ, 1982).

12. The existence of a parrot incarnation is consistent with Cakradhar's aphorism in *Sūtrapāṭh* 10.106: "God becomes a tortoise, he becomes a fish; he descends among the gods, he descends among men, he descends among animals. When he has descended among men, God becomes a madman, he becomes a possessed man, he becomes a mute; but a walking, talking God is rare."

13. *Sūtrapāṭh* 12.32: "Think of me [at least] once or twice; do not allow a day to go to waste."

14. *Sūtrapāṭh* 12.30: "Keep Parameśvar in mind while you are lying down, sitting, and eating."

15. *Sūtrapāṭh* 12.27–28: "Remember me as you have seen me: [my] name *(nām),* deeds *(līḷā),* appearance *(mūrti),* and movements *(ceṣṭā).*"

16. The term *jāpya,* equivalent to *jap(a),* a term used widely among Hindus for the repetition of the name or names of (a) God, occurs once in *Smṛtisthaḷ,* in chapter 176. It is found in a context indicating that *jāpya* is a standard practice: on a festival day, one should do twice as much of it [as usual], Bhaṭobās tells Māhādāïsẽ.

17. See chapter 4, below, on the structure of the group. In another Mahānubhāv text, "Itihās," *smaraṇ* is more clearly indicated as the motivation for Mhāībhaṭ's composition of the *Līḷācaritra.* Nāgdev tells Mhāībhaṭ the importance of *smaraṇ,* and then Mhāībhaṭ suggests writing down the *līḷās* for their own and future generations of disciples. Y. K. Deshpande, "Mahānubhāvāṃce Caritra-Granth," *Bhārat Itihās Saṃśodhak Maṇḍal Quarterly* 13 (1932): 45–57.

18. See Anne Feldhaus, "*Sthānapothī,* the Mahānubhāva 'Book of Places,' " in *Proceedings of the Third International Conference on Devotional Literature in New Indo-Aryan Languages,* Leiden, December 1985, ed. G. H. Schokker (New Delhi, forthcoming), and "The Religious Significance of Ṛddhipur," in *Religion and Society in Maharashtra,* ed. Milton Israel and N. K. Wagle (Toronto: University of Toronto, Centre for South Asian Studies, 1987), 68–91.

19. Caitanya is the highest of the *devatās,* deities of the relative sort utterly inferior to Īśvar/Parameśvar/the one absolute God. See Feldhaus, "The *devatācakra* of the Mahānubhāvas."

20. *The Deeds of God in Ṛddhipur,* translated by Anne Feldhaus (New York: Oxford University Press, 1984), chaps. 175, 176, 185.

21. The root meaning of this term is "ford" or "crossing place"—for getting from one side to the other of a river, or, by analogy, from this world into the other. The

term is used primarily for holy places, but also for holy persons, and, as here, for holy objects.

22. We will discuss below the question of whether or not the text considers Bhaṭobās an ordinary human being.

23. This text, which probably dates to the last quarter of the thirteenth century, has been edited by Hari Nārāyaṇ Nene in *Nityadīnīlīḷā: Prasād Sevā, Pūjāvasar, Mūrtijñān, Nāmāce Dahā Ṭhāy* (Nāgpur, undated [1930s or 1940s]).

24. Present-day Mahānubhāvs do perform ritual reverence of *prasāds* and of stones (*sambandhī pāṣāns*) believed to have been touched by one or another of the incarnations. Long lines of worshipers sit crosslegged on mats on the ground while the holy objects are passed along the lines, each object being rubbed between the hands, and touched to the forehead and eyes, of each worshiper, before being passed on to the next person in line. For what little information is available in English on contemporary Mahānubhāv ritual practice, see Anne Feldhaus, "The Orthodoxy of the Mahānubhāvas," in *The Experience of Hinduism: Essays on Religion in Maharashtra,* ed. Eleanor Zelliot and Maxine Berntsen (Albany: State University of New York Press, 1988), 264–279.

25. See Louis Dumont, "World Renunciation in Indian Religions," *Contributions to Indian Sociology* 4 (1960): 33–62; the works of Patrick Olivelle, including his edition and translation of *Vāsudevāśrama Yatidharmaprakāśa* (Vienna: Publications of the De Nobili Research Library, 1976–1977); and the works of J. F. Sprockhoff, including "Saṃnyāsa: Quellenstudien zur Askese im Hinduismus I. Untersuchungen über die Saṃnyāsa-Upaniṣads," *Abhandlungen für die Kunde des Morgenlandes* 42 (1976).

26. See Feldhaus, *The Religious System of the Mahānubhāva Sect,* 57–64, for a more detailed discussion of the *Sūtrapāṭh*'s teachings on asceticism.

27. "Stay in Maharashtra" *(mahārāṣṭrīṃ asāvẽ). Sūtrapāṭh* 12.24.

28. *Sūtrapāṭh* 12.1, quoted in full above.

29. Cf. *Līḷācaritra,* "Pūrvārdha," chap. 499, where Vaijobā is referred to as having his own fields.

30. Cakradhar and Guṇḍam Rāüḷ.

31. This is a title, rather than a name. It means "Reader," "Reciter," or "Teacher," and indicates that the man was an educated Brāhmaṇ.

32. The word translated here as "connections" is *sambandh,* the same word that has been translated as "attachment" and "relatives" in *Sūtrapāṭh* 12.1, quoted above.

33. 13.14. Cf. 13.15, "Do not buy or sell"; and 12.12, "Woman intoxicates by being seen; wealth intoxicates by existing."

34. Cf. *Sūtrapāṭh* 12.82 ("Beg without picking and choosing the houses [at which to beg]") and 83 ("Do not go to the houses of your acquaintances").

35. Cf. *Sūtrapāṭh* 13.185 (oil and ghee), 13.253 (salt), 12.98 and 13.210 (flavorful food), 13.61 (sweets), 13.143 (chick-peas), and so on.

36. But cf. the advice of the seventeenth-century non-Mahānubhāv *guru*-saint Rāmdās: "When saints who have spiritual experience *(pratyaya)* come together, it is more than solitude *(yekāntāparīs yekānta).* One should attentively conduct varied discussions *(nānā carcā).*" *Dāsbodh* 20.7.24. *Śrīsamartha Rāmdāskṛt Śrīmat Dāsbodh.* Puṇẽ: Citraśāḷā Press, 1964.

37. For instance, the *Sūtrapāṭh* urges ascetics to go to places where they know no

one and no one knows them (12.22), and to places so desolate that no one learns about their death if they die there (13.189). And, complementary to a number of commands to stay "at the foot of a tree at the end of the land" (12.26, 12.72, 13.219; cf. 13.43), *Sūtrapāṭh* 12.37 cautions: "Do not get used to any one tree; do not get used to any one place."

38. Nine hours.

39. During the late afternoon.

40. 13.53 ("Beg during the third watch"), 13.59 ("After completing your begging, take your meal on the bank of a river"), 13.66 ("Sleep outside a village in an abandoned temple or under a tree"), and 13.41 ("Go from village to village").

41. Bhaṭobās is quoting from the *Sūtrapāṭh* here; but in the *Sūtrapāṭh* this is a quotation from Sanskrit legal sources. In another chapter (42), to explain why he eats unusually early in the day while traveling, Bhaṭobās quotes a Sanskrit legal verse that is not found in the *Sūtrapāṭh*.

42. "Bhaṭ" is a nickname for a Brahmaṇ that is used, even within *Smṛtisthaḷ*, for other Brāhmaṇs too besides Nāgdev. That the "Bhaṭ" in "Bhaṭmārg" refers to Nāgdev is made clear in *Ajñāt Smṛti*, chap. 95 (*Smṛtisthaḷ*, 3d ed., ed. Vaman Narayan Deshpande [Puṇē: Venus Prakāśan, 1968], p. 105), when a non-Mahānubhāv *sannyāsī* named Rāghavcaitanya reports to the Sultan of Delhi about a new group named the "Nāgdevobhaṭ" sect *(mārg)*. On the question of the name of the group, see V. B. Kolte's article " 'Mahānubhāvpanth' kī 'Parmārg'?" in his *Mahānubhāv Saṃśodhan: 1* (Malkāpūr: Aruṇ Prakāśan, 1962), 12–37.

43. A feminine form, "Mahātmī," also occurs once, in the singular, in chapter 137.

44. Hīrāïsē and her husband Paṇḍit do, however, wait to become renouncers until their son is full grown. She becomes a renouncer before Paṇḍit because they agree that he will arrange their son's wedding before taking initiation as an ascetic.

45. Feldhaus, *The Deeds of God in Ṛddhipur*, chap. 1.

46. *Līḷācaritra*, "Pūrvārdha," chap. 2.

47. In *Līḷācaritra*, "Pūrvārdha," chap. 20, when Cakradhar's mother asks his father to allow him to go on pilgrimage to Rāmṭek, his father objects, "We are rulers *(rāje)*. Do rulers ever go anywhere? A king does rituals through his priest *(prohītdvārē)*; he sends a Brāhmaṇ." The phrase "Cakradhar himself" sounds a bit odd in the Mahānubhāv context. In terms of Mahānubhāv theology, Cakradhar "himself" was, like Guṇḍam Rāüḷ and Cāṅgdev Rāüḷ, Parameśvar, the one supreme God, incarnated on earth in a human body. Moreover, as *Līḷācaritra*, "Pūrvārdha," chaps. 16–17 tells it, the Cakradhar incarnation originated when Cāṅgdev Rāüḷ intentionally gave up his body and entered the corpse of a young man named Haripāḷdev. The resurrected Haripāḷdev was Cakradhar.

48. *Sūtrapāṭh* 6.

49. Mhāībhaṭ also refuses most of Kheibhaṭ's invitations in chapter 140 and eats only a token amount of the meal prepared by Sāraṅgpaṇḍit's wife in chapter 142. But in these two chapters the reason for his reluctance seems to be his determination to eat food for which he has gone begging, rather than worries about the caste status of his hosts, who are, in both cases, Brāhmaṇs. In chapter 142, as in the episode described here, Bhaṭobās chides Mhāībhaṭ for having slighted Sāraṅgpaṇḍit and his wife. "You did wrong, Mhāībhaṭ," says Bhaṭobās.

50. See Feldhaus, "The *devatācakra* of the Mahānubhāvas."

51. We doubt the historical validity of this story. See S. G. Tulpule, "Mahānubhāv Panth āṇi Nāmdev," *Navbhārat* (October 1977): 51–53; and S. G. Tulpule, *Marāṭhī Vāṅmayācā Itihās, Khaṇḍ Pahilā* (Puṇe: Mahārāṣṭra Sāhitya Pariṣad, 1984), 229–231.

52. See I. M. P. Raeside, "The Mahānubhāva *sakaḷa lipī,*" *Bulletin of the School of Oriental and African Studies, University of London* 33 (1970): 328–334.

53. Cakradhar and Guṇḍam Rāüḷ.

54. *Sūtrapāṭh* 12.115: "A puddle and the Gaṅgā should be the same to you."

55. That both options are possible is indicated in chapter 99, which remarks that it was "not known" whether Kheibhaṭ received *śravaṇ* at the same time as he received *bhikṣā,* or whether he had received *śravaṇ* at some earlier time.

56. Literally, of offering [Mount] Meru, the highest mountain in the world, at the center of the world.

57. One other duty of lay people that is discussed in *Smṛtisthaḷ* is completely unrelated to the duties of ascetics. It has to do with the conflict between, on the one hand, the duties of a married woman of a princely family, who may be required to immolate herself on her husband's funeral pyre—that is, to be a *satī*—if he dies before she does, and, on the other hand, the general duty not to commit suicide. In chapter 149 Bhaṭobās instructs Queen Kāmāïsē not to become a *satī* willingly and assures her that if she is nevertheless thrown onto her husband's pyre, she will not suffer the punishment for suicide.

58. The passage at the end of *Smṛtisthaḷ* refers to two of three "fellow disciples who were not initiated" as having "lost their enlightenment *(bodhu)*:" these two, Dāïmbā and Demāïsē, are identical with the two *bodhavant* disciples listed in the beginning of Deshpande's edition (Appendix).

59. Cf. *Sūtrapāṭh* 13.121: "A *jīva* gives the syllables; Parameśvar gives enlightenment."

60. But see Lynn Tesky Denton, "Varieties of Hindu Female Asceticism," in *Roles and Rituals for Hindu Women,* ed. Julia Leslie (London: Pinter Publishers, 1991), 211–231.

61. Kolte's edition of the *Līḷācaritra* rests on the principle that each *sūtra* of the *Sūtrapāṭh must* be found in the *Līḷācaritra.* Hence in some instances he has used the readings of manuscripts that include the *sūtras* rather than other readings that, on other principles, might have been chosen instead. In this case, the *sūtra* appears to be better integrated with its context in *Līḷācaritra,* "Uttarārdha," chap. 325 than in *Līḷācaritra,* "Uttarārdha," chap. 622.

62. Śrī Dattātreya Prabhu is another of the "Five Kṛṣṇas," the five principal divine incarnations recognized by the Mahānubhāvs.

63. Of the *mantra. Sūtrapāṭh* 13.121: "A *jīva* gives the syllables; Parameśvar gives enlightenment." In Mahānubhāv thought, a *jīva* is to be distinguished not only from Parameśvar and from material things, but also from the many gods *(devatās)* different from and inferior to Parameśvar.

64. There is a certain circularity involved in this situation, since, according to *Smṛtisthaḷ* 16–17, the *Sūtrapāṭh* was prepared under Bhaṭobās' close supervision.

65. It is not clear why Bhaṭobās singles out Paṇḍit and Kesobās for praise here—except, in terms of the structure of the text and the choice of the order of its chapters, that this praise balances Bhaṭobās' snub of Paṇḍit and Kesobās in chapter 66 (for

speaking Sanskrit)—nor is it clear why Bhaṭobās says that the scripture is *not* illuminated when he discusses it with Mhāībhaṭ or Lakṣmīdharbhaṭ.

66. In addition to the examples quoted here, see especially chapters 184 and 209.

67. See Feldhaus, "The *devatācakra* of the Mahānubhāvas."

68. *Prasād,* here, is food that has been offered to, and presumably tasted by, a deity or holy person.

69. Some manuscripts, and most printed editions, of the *Sūtrapāṭh* add three initial short chapters, "Pūrvī," "Pañcakṛṣṇa," and "Pañcanām" to the nine that form the "Navprakaraṇ," the "Nine Chapters," of the first part of the text. The reasons for excluding these from the Feldhaus edition of the *Sūtrapāṭh* are detailed in the introduction to that edition, *The Religious System of the Mahānubhāva Sect,* 9–12.

70. The implication of calling "Lāpikā" the "tenth chapter" *(dahāvẽ prakaraṇ)* in chapter 17 of *Smṛtisthaḷ* is that there are nine *Sūtrapāṭh* chapters preceding it. Most *Sūtrapāṭh* manuscripts that we have examined include "Lāpikā" between the nine (or twelve) initial short chapters and the four final long chapters of the *Sūtrapāṭh.*

71. *Smṛtisthaḷ* itself might also be considered something of a commentary on the *Sūtrapāṭh,* as so many of its chapters consist of Bhaṭobās' explanations, interpretations, or modifications of sayings of Cakradhar that are found in the *Sūtrapāṭh.* See chapter 5, below, on the text of *Smṛtisthaḷ.*

72. V. N. Deshpande, in the introduction to his edition of *Smṛtisthaḷ,* 6, suggests that the Mahānubhāvs' four-level system of scriptural authority is a modification of the list of four sources of law found in the *Mānavadharmaśāstra* 2.12: Veda, *smṛti,* the practice of good people *(sadācāra),* and what pleases one. With respect to the first two members of this list, the close similarity to the Mahānubhāv list is clear, and is discussed below. In addition, Deshpande is probably pointing to the similarity between "*sadācāra*" and the Mahanubhāv category "*vṛddhācār,*" which means, literally, "the practice of the elders."

73. See Anne Feldhaus, "The Mahānubhāvas and Scripture," *Journal of Dharma* 3 (1978): 295–308, and V. B. Kolte, "Mahānubhāv Panthāce Avaidikatva," in *Mahānubhāv Saṃśodhan: 1* (Malkāpūr: Aruṇ Prakāśan, 1962), 59–76. A fifth class of scriptural authority is sometimes named: *vartamān.* This word means "of the present day." *Vartamān,* the teachings of the successors of the *mārgrūḍhi gurus,* was presumably "contemporary" at the time the list of types of scriptural authority was formulated.

74. *Mahānubhāvīya Paṇḍit Āṇerāj-kṛt Lakṣaṇa-ratnākara,* edited by H. N. Nene (Nāgpur, 1937), notes, 7. Raeside, "Bibliographical Index," 484, dates this work to the early fourteenth century.

75. V. B. Kolte, ed. (Malkāpūr: Aruṇ Prakāśan, 1944; 5th ed., 1972). Translated by Feldhaus as *The Deeds of God in Ṛddhipur.*

76. Puṇẽ: Venus Prakāśan, 1968. Our account of the methods used in preparing this edition follows that of Deshpande in his introduction, 1–2.

77. For descriptions of this code, see Raeside, "The Mahānubhāva *sakaḷa lipī,*" 328–334; V. B. Kolte, *Ravaḷobās-kṛt Sahyādri-Varṇan* (Poona: Poona University Press), 9–26; and Feldhaus, *The Religious System of the Mahānubhāva Sect,* 79–81.

78. *Sakaḷ lipī* substitutes *n* for *ṇ* and vice versa, thus exacerbating the orthographic irregularity of Old Marāṭhī.

79. Manuscripts that omit chapter 222 give the information found in it at the end

of chapter 183. One manuscript that omits chapter 222 nevertheless still has 261 chapters instead of 260, for it divides the chapter numbered 260 in Deshpande's edition (and in our translation) into two chapters, which it numbers 259 and 260.

80. In Deshpande's base manuscript, and hence also in his edition, the chapters of "Vṛddhācār" number twenty-six. But the base manuscript does not in fact include more material than the others. Rather, it assigns chapter numbers to lists of disciples that are found, but not numbered as separate chapters, after chapter 23 in all the manuscripts.

81. Deshpande, *Smṛtisthaḷ,* 3–4.

82. Ibid., 108.

83. Ibid., 3.

84. Ibid., 5–7.

85. *Sūtrapāṭh* 12.25: "Do not go to Mātāpur or Kolhāpur. . . ."

86. Feldhaus, *The Deeds of God in Ṛddhipur,* chap. 322: "Go to Mātāpur, I tell you!"

87. *Ajñāt Smṛti,* chap. 108 and *Smṛtisamuccaya,* chap. 212 read *"śivasūtra"* instead of *Smṛtisthaḷ*'s *"śikhāsūtra"* ("[Brāhmaṇical] tuft and thread").

88. Deshpande, *Smṛtisthaḷ,* 5.

89. According to Raeside, "Bibliographical Index," 470, "Anvayasthaḷ" is "a general descriptive title applicable to several works . . . which enumerate earlier Mahānubhāva writers and their *guru-śiṣya* relationships *(anvaya).*" The Pāramāṇḍalya lineage *(āmnāya)* is one of the thirteen such groups into which the Mahānubhāvs were at one time divided. See V. B. Kolte, "Mahānubhāvāṃce Don Āmnāya," in *Mahānubhāv Saṃśodhan: 1* (Malkāpūr: Aruṇ Prakāśan, 1962), 123–136.

90. Raeside, "Bibliographical Index," 507.

91. Ibid.

92. Ibid., 506.

93. Ibid., 507.

94. Deshpande, *Smṛtisthaḷ,* 3.

95. Chapters 8, 10, 11, 17, 20, 21, 34, 56, 62, 63, 64, 67, 69, 70, 77, 83, 87, 93, 102, 103, 104, 106, 107, 108, 110, 111, 118, 119, 150, 152, 154, 156, 157, 168, 176, 177, 182, 185, 186, 189, 190, 193, 194, 195, 196, 197, 198, 201, 204, 205, 206, 207, 212, 213, 214, 216, 221, 222, 223, 227, 233, 236, 246, 252, 257, and 258.

96. Chapters 4, 9, 11, 12, 26, 101, 165, 200, 233, 244, and 246.

97. This remark is another example of an editorial comment included in the body of the text. Cf. the list of seventy chapterless titles in the manuscript of *Smṛtisamuccaya* from which Deshpande took the extracts given in his edition.

98. Deshpande, *Smṛtisthaḷ,* 8–9.

99. Ibid., 7.

100. Ibid., 7–8.

101. Ibid., 9–10.

102. Ibid., 3, 7–10.

Part Two
Smṛtisthaḷ

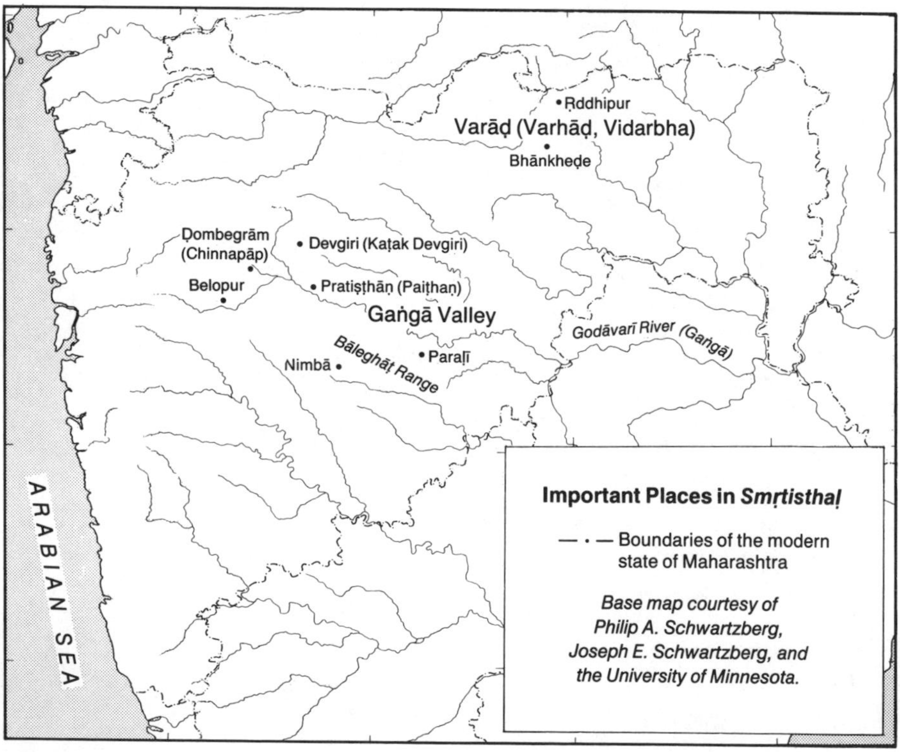

Ṛddhipur
Varāḍ (Varhāḍ, Vidarbha)
Bhānkheḍe
Ḍombegrām
(Chinnapāp)
Devgiri (Kaṭak Devgiri)
Belopur
Pratiṣṭhān (Paiṭhaṇ)
Gaṅgā Valley
Godāvarī River (Gaṅgā)
Bāleghāṭ Range
Paraḷī
Nimbā
ARABIAN SEA
Important Places in *Smṛtisthaḷ*
— · — Boundaries of the modern state of Maharashtra
Base map courtesy of Philip A. Schwartzberg, Joseph E. Schwartzberg, and the University of Minnesota.

Homage to Śrī Pareś.[1]

In the Gosāvī's[2] presence *(sannidhān)* there were three kinds of disciples: (1) those who became followers *(anusarale);* (2) those who received enlightenment *(bodhavant);* (3) those who had the sight of him *(darśanīe).*[3] These were the three types of followers of the Gosāvī. Among them Bhaṭ[4] was especially active, because from the beginning he had been shaped and molded, and made fit for [God's] presence. That [process] will now be described in detail.

1. Bhaṭobās' father was Māhādevbhaṭ. He was from Purī. Bhaṭobās had three siblings: Sāraṅgpāṇibhaṭ, the eldest; Vaijobā; and Umāïsē. Umāïsē became a widow. Sāraṅgpāṇibhaṭ was killed by highway robbers. In her grief over that, their mother, Ābāïsē, built a cell at Sīdhanāth in Rāvasgāv. She was staying there when Dādos[5] came along. Something good happened to all of them through him, and he told them about the excellence of the Gosāvī.

Then Dādos set out to have *darśan* of the Gosāvī. Ābāïsē, Umāïsē, Bhaṭobās, and Māhādāïsē[6] went with him. They came to Srīnagar.[7] They had *darśan* of the Gosāvī. That made them even more attracted to him.

After that, Bhaṭobās met [the Gosāvī] six more times. At their sixth meeting, [Bhaṭobās] received enlightenment; at the seventh, he became a follower. He became a follower when he was thirty-two years old. He was in [the Gosāvī's] presence for four years. Six months of that period he spent in the presence of Śrīprabhu.[8] He had three and a half years in our Gosāvī's[9] presence. He became worthy; he was formed and molded; [the Gosāvī] made him the preceptor *(ācārya)* and entrusted Māhādāïsē to him. Then the Gosāvī changed his inclination [and departed],[10] on Monday, the fourth day of the bright half of the month of Māgh in Śaka 1194, in the Saṃvatsar year Śrīmukh.[11]

2. Bhaṭobās is desolate because of being separated from God.

After the Gosāvī had departed, Bhaṭobās was desolate, and so he went away. His desolation manifested itself.[12] No one could console him.

Then Māhādāïsē went from the Gaṅgā Valley[13] to Parameśvarpur,[14] searching for him. She had *darśan* of Śrīprabhu Gosāvī. Then she said mournfully, "Lord, Śrī Cakradhar has left us, and Nāgdev has disappeared as well."

The Gosāvī responded to her plea. Śrīprabhu Gosāvī said: "O dead one,[15] go to Bhānkheḍe, I say."

And Māhādāïsē said, "All right," and set out immediately. She touched his holy feet.

She went to Bhānkheḍe, but she did not see him. Then she searched in the wilderness and on the hillsides. She asked some cowherds, and they said, "Yes, we have seen him. We used to squeeze *kurandhana*[16] fruits into his mouth."

Then Māhādāïsē found him. She brought him to consciousness, brushed off the mushrooms that had grown on him, wrapped a shawl around him, and carried him on her back to a place near the village. Then, seating him somewhere, she went into the village. She got some milk and fed it to him on a twist of cloth. That revived him some more.

3. When Māhādāïsē reveals that Śrīprabhu is an incarnation *(avatār)*, [Bhaṭobās] says, "My [God] is Śrī Cakradhar."

Then Māhādāïsē said, "Come on, Nāgdev. Let's go to the Gosāvī."

Bhaṭobās said, "Where is the Gosāvī?"

Māhādāïsē said, "Isn't that he, in Ṛddhipur? Śrīprabhu Gosāvī has sent me to get you."

Bhaṭobās said, "I don't recognize your Śrīprabhu. My God *(devo)* is Śrī Cakradhar."

Māhādāïsē replied, "Nāgdev, the Gosāvī has entrusted you to Śrīprabhu,[17] and he has entrusted me to you.[18] Come on!"

And she set out, carrying him on her back.

4. He goes to the presence of Śrīprabhu.

Then they set out from there. (According to some, they began to walk very slowly.) As they walked along the road, people would recognize him and say, "Isn't he the one who used to put out his hands and beg, saying, '[In the name of] Śrī Cakradhar! Give alms!'?"

At that, Māhādāïsē would say, "God's absence has made him go crazy."

In this way, they reached Ṛddhipur. In the early morning, Śrīprabhu Gosāvī had gone to the Five Pīpaḷs. He was playing there when Māhādāïsē arrived with Bhaṭobās. Seeing them, Śrīprabhu said, "O drop dead! Aren't these those [disciples] of Śrī Cāṅgdev Rāüḷ?"[19]

This made Bhaṭobās and Māhādāïsē very sad. Śrīprabhu Gosāvī comforted them: "Drop dead! Stay here! Stay here, I tell you!"

Then [Bhaṭobās] stayed for 14 years in Śrīprabhu Gosāvī's presence. Mhāībhaṭ also came. All the devotees came. They stayed in [the Gosāvī's] presence. They began to serve him.

5. After Śrīprabhu's death, Bhaṭobās comes and bows to the banks of the Gaṅgā.

Thus, after many days, in the Saṃvatsar year Vyaya, on the fourth day of the dark half of the month of Māgh,[20] Śrīprabhu Gosāvī also died.[21] Bhaṭobās and the devotees were very sad.

Then, because of that grief, Bhaṭobās came to the Gaṅgā Valley.[22] With him were Lakṣmīdharbā, Bāïdevobā, Māhādāïsē, Kothaḷobā, Pomāïsē, and Sādhē, and others as well. They bowed to the river bank from Rāvasgāv to Ḍombegrām. They spent five nights in Pratiṣṭhān. They all circumambulated the town and bowed to it. Then they went from Vṛddhāsaṅgam and Jogeśvarī to Khaḍakāḷī. Then they went from Peharāsaṅgam and Neurgāv to Chinnapāp. They bowed to Chinnasthaḷī and to all the other holy places (*sthāns*). They sat for a while at Chinnasthaḷī. Then they left.

6. Bāïdevobā takes *prasād,* and [Bhaṭobās] forbids him to grieve excessively.

Then, along with all the disciples, Bhaṭobās entered Ḍombegrām. He prostrated himself at the gate in the compound wall. Then he came straight to the temple *(maṭh)* that faces east. There Bhaṭobās saw the place where the Gosāvī had once spat on a stone of the dilapidated wall.[23] And he felt very sad. He put his mouth to the place and took *prasād.*

At that point, Bāïdevobās arrived. He had been initiated as a follower by Bhaṭobās, but it is not known when. Bhaṭobās told him about the spittle: "Take this spittle, Bāïdeyā, which is the Gosāvī's *prasād.*"

Seeing it, Bāïdevobās threw himself to the ground. Everyone felt sadder. Immediately he started licking up the *prasād.* He scraped his mouth.

Bhaṭobās stopped him. He comforted him. Bhaṭobās said, "Don't do that, Bāïdeyā. The suffering will make you lose your mind." And he took him by the hand and raised him to his feet.

Then they bowed to both temples *(maḍhs).*

7. He spends seven nights in the Rājmaṭh.

Then, along with all the others, he went into retreat at Chinnasthaḷī. He would beg in Bādāṭhān and Degāv. In the evening he would go to sleep in the Rājmaṭh.[24] He spent seven nights this way.

8. He takes out the threshold and makes it into three *tīrthas.*

Then one day Bhaṭobās sent for a carpenter. He had him make another threshold. The temple *(maṭh)* was made entirely of wood, and the threshold was also wooden. Bhaṭobās took it out. He put another one in its place. Out of the middle part where the holy feet[25] used to step, he made a large bowl. The two ends he made into two smaller bowls. The rest he made into beads and gave them to everyone to reverence.

And he kept the large bowl for himself. Into it he put the cloth he had been given as a relic *(prasād)*, the anklet,[26] the chain,[27] the stick,[28] the two blanket relics, Śrīprabhu Gosāvī's relic *(prasād)* garments, and the camphor box.[29] He reverenced it for as long as he lived.

Addendum: Later, when Cakrapāṇibās[30] was initiated as an ascetic in the name of Bhaṭobās, Kavīśvarbās gave him one of the smaller bowls. No one knows who got the other one.

Further addendum: At the same time, Bhaṭobās took out the Chinnasthaḷī [rock] and kept it. And the pillars, the door frame, and the doors were removed, but it is not known when.

9. Because he sees the extremity of Bāïdeyā's grief, he does not go to Belopur.

Then one day as he was about to set out, Bhaṭobās said, "If I go to Belopur now, Bāïdeyā will die." (According to some, he said this because of the episode of the spittle.) So he did not go. He turned back without leaving.

10. *Addendum:* Lakṣmīdharbhaṭ from Rājaur receives instruction and becomes a follower.

One day Lakṣmīdharbhaṭ from Rājaur had the sight *(darśan)* of Bhaṭobās. It is not known how this came about. He received instruction. He was initiated as an ascetic. Then they began to call him Lakṣmīdharbā of Rājaur.

Then later, during the lifetime of Bhaṭobās, he wrote *Ācār Lakṣaṇẽ, Vicār Lakṣaṇẽ,*[31] and *Prakaraṇīcī Lakṣaṇẽ,*[32] questioning Bhaṭobās repeatedly.

11. He meets Mhāībhaṭ.

Addendum: As Bhaṭobās was setting out for the Gaṅgā Valley, Īśvarnāyak filed a suit.[33] His daughter had refused to get married [again]. So Mhāībhaṭ stayed behind.

The case was decided in Deuḷvāḍā. Īśvarnāyak was outargued.

Addendum: Can anyone understand the Gosāvī's inclination?

(According to some: she was given a share [of his property].)

Then afterwards Mhāībhaṭ came to the Gaṅgā Valley. Āüse stayed on [in Ṛddhipur]. Then Mhāībhaṭ and Bhaṭobās met in the Gaṅgā Valley.[34]

12. He meets Kesobās. Kesobās becomes a disciple.

It is not known what village Kesobās was from. (According to some, he was from Pāpdaṇḍī Rāmpurī.) He was a learned preacher. One day he came to Bhaṭobās and was initiated as an ascetic by him. Bhaṭobās loved him very much. He stayed in Bhaṭobās' presence.

13. When [Kesobās] gives up his connection with his relatives, Bhaṭobās says, "My Keśav is the great *yogī* Śuka."

Then one day Kesobās' relatives, hearing [that he had become an ascetic], came to take him away. His brother, Gopāḷdev, and his father-in-law came to take him away because they were opposed to what he had done.

They took Kesobās away. They tried to make him give up his initiation; but no matter what they did, he would not give it up.

Then they summoned all the learned men and had them argue with him. But he silenced them in argument. And the learned men washed their hands of him. They said, "We cannot win him over. If he is to be won over now, it is his wife who will do it. Now lock up the two of them in the same room."

So they locked them in. If she lay on the cot, he would sleep on the ground. If she lay on the ground, he would sleep on the cot. In this way, the night would pass.

During the daytime, he would go to the river. They would put someone there to watch him. Kesobās would stay alone at the river. He was composing *Ratnamāḷā Stotra*[35] there. Then they would bring him into the village.

Several days passed this way. Then his wife said, "Let him go now. He has become a *yogī* now. It is a sin for me to interfere."

So they all gave Kesobās permission to leave. He left. He met Bhaṭobās. He told him what had happened. Bhaṭobās listened, and then praised him lavishly, saying, "My Keśav is the great *yogī* Śuka."[36]

14. When [Kesobās] shows him *Ratnamāḷā Stotra,* he praises it as worship of God.

Then Kesobās composed *Ratnamāḷā.* He read its verses to Bhaṭobās. In one place he had put "Hanumantvāḍā" instead of "Deuḷvāḍā."[37] When Bhaṭobās heard this, he said, "It's not Hanumant; it's Deuḷvāḍā.

"You have done well, Keśavdev. You have put the unfailing deeds (*līḷā*s) of the Gosāvī into verse. You have worshipped God with verbal flowers."

15. And he forbids him to compose *Uddharaṇa Stotra* in [Sanskrit] verse.

When [Bhaṭobās] had read the manuscript of *Ratnamāḷā,* Kesobās asked Bhaṭobās, "Bhaṭ, may I compose 'Uddharaṇ'[38] in [Sanskrit] verse, the same way?"

And Bhaṭobās said, "Don't do that, Keśavdev. That will deprive my old ladies."[39]

So Kesobās stopped writing Sanskrit verse.

16. And he permits him to edit the chapters of scripture.

Then later Kesobās asked, "So, Bhaṭ, may I arrange the chapters of scripture?"

Bhaṭobās agreed to this. Then he said, "But arrange them by subject according to my idea of which should go where."

Then Kesobās, questioning Bhaṭobās repeatedly, arranged the chapters[40] in order. He gave each of them its proper title.

17. And he permits him to edit the chapter of parables.

Then, after Kesobās had edited all of them, he asked Bhaṭobās, "Bhaṭ, now may I edit the parables (*dṛṣṭāntas*)?"[41]

Bhaṭobās agreed.

Then, questioning Bhaṭobās again and again, Kesobās edited the chapter of parables also. He wrote the inferences (*dṛṣṭāntiks*) for the parables. He prepared a list *(lāpikā)* of all the parables. It is called the "Tenth Chapter."[42]

Addendum: In the same way, questioning Bhaṭobās repeatedly, he edited the 300 [aphorisms of] "Ācār" and the 300 [aphorisms of] "Vicār," together with the "Lāpikā."

Further addendum: Then Lakṣmīdharbā of Rājaur took the order of the aphorisms (*vacans*) according to Kesobās and composed explanations (*lakṣaṇs*) of them.[43]

In this way, the scriptures were codified.

18. He praises *Jñānbhāskar,* which Virahe Lakṣmīdharbhaṭ has composed in a state of pining for God.

Once Virahe Lakṣmīdharbā[44] went out to wander. As he traveled around, he was filled with great pining.

As he wandered around this way, he came to Bābūḷgāv near Pātharī. There was a small temple there in the open area around a well. He sat in that temple and composed *Jñānbhāskar.*[45]

As he was writing, he would faint sometimes from grief. Then he would return to consciousness and go out to beg. Some days he would just lie there. Then the temple priest would come; he would lift him up and bring him to consciousness.

In this way he completed the *stotra.*[46] Then he came to meet Bhaṭobās. He handed the manuscript to Bhaṭobās. Bhaṭobās looked at it, read it, and gave it his hearty approval. He was so delighted that his feelings could not be expressed in words.

19. When Lakṣmīdharbā and Mhāībhaṭ have a discussion, [Bhaṭobās] explains what a *yogabhraṣṭa* is like.

One day Lakṣmīdharbhaṭ asked Mhāībhaṭ, "What is a *yogabhraṣṭa*[47] like?"

Mhāībhaṭ said, "He is like us."

Hearing that, Bhaṭobās said, "Look, he is not even like me, so how can he be like you?"

Then they said, "So, Bhaṭ, what is he like?"

Bhaṭobās said, "When he is pinched it does not hurt him—that is what he is like."

And they understood.

20. He chides Mhāībhaṭ for having kept silent when he was arrested as a thief.

Once Mhāībhaṭ and Lakṣmīdharbā, asking Bhaṭobās' permission, went out to wander. At a certain place, they were arrested as thieves. As the people were about to harm them, Lakṣmīdharbā looked at Mhāībhaṭ. And Mhāībhaṭ said, *"jvaro vā śastro vā."*[48]

And the people said, "Hey, these are learned men!" So they let them go.

Then they came to Bhaṭobās. Someone had already told Bhaṭobās [what had happened].

Then Bhaṭobās said, "Why did you keep silent until things reached that point?"[49]

Addendum: "You should have given whatever explanation you were able to give."

21. In answer to Kṛṣṇabhaṭ's question, [Bhaṭobās] quotes the aphorism *(vākya)* about easing weariness.

Addendum: Once Bhaṭobās came with the disciples to Indrabhaṭ's village. Indrabhaṭ washed everyone's feet.

And when he went to wash Kāḷe Kṛṣṇabhaṭ's feet, [Kṛṣṇabhaṭ] said: "How could you wash my feet?"

Indrabhaṭ replied, "It's all right for me to wash them. Ask Bhaṭ."

So [Kṛṣṇabhaṭ] asked Bhaṭobās, "Bhaṭ, may a *guru*[50] wash a disciple's feet?"

Bhaṭobās said, "Yes, he may."

Kṛṣṇabhaṭ said, "How is it that he may?"

Bhaṭobās said, "He may because of the aphorism *(vacan)* about easing weariness."[51]

Then [Kṛṣṇabhaṭ] let [Indrabhaṭ] wash [his feet].

22. When Māhādāïsē bandages his wound, Bhaṭobās accepts what she says about service.

Once Bhaṭobās had a boil on his foot. Māhādāïsē said, "Nāgdev, you should bandage the boil."

Bhaṭobās replied, "What should I use to bandage it?"

Then Māhādāïsē ripped up a *prasād* garment,[52] wet it, and tied it [on his foot].

And Bhaṭobās said, "What is this, Rūpai? How could you rip up a *prasād* garment and tie it [on my foot]?"

And Māhādāïsē said, "Nāgdev, *prasād* has been tied to *prasād*."[53]

And Bhaṭobās remained silent.

23. He meets Āplo and [Āplo] becomes a follower.

Āplo was Māhādāïsē's brother. He had had the Gosāvī's presence. Then, after the Gosāvī had departed, [Āplo] used to become possessed [by various deities] and would worship them ostentatiously.

One day in the course of her wandering, Māhādāïsē went to ask after him. As she started to enter his house, she saw the deities directly in front of her. And she said, "Śrī Cakradhar!" and left.

This name fell on [Āplo's] ears. And immediately he left. He put all the gods into a basket, and went and threw them into water. Then Māhādāïsē took him to Bhaṭobās. He received enlightenment *(bodh)* from Bhaṭobās. Then he became a follower. He was with [Bhaṭobās] until the end. Māhādāïsē was very happy.

Earlier, at Khaḍakāḷī, the Gosāvī had given him the boon that in the end he would become [a follower].[54] That came true.

This chapter belongs to "Uttarārdha,"[55] and it has been put here as an addendum.

24. He calls it a half measure for lay disciples (*vāsaniks*) to take up the begging bag at the end of their life.

Once, on an appropriate occasion, Bhaṭobās said to Cāṅgdevbhaṭ, "To take up the begging bag[56] at the end of your life is what I call a half measure."

25. When Devatāsambandhī Mahādevobā sees the pain of a scorpion bite and becomes a follower, [Bhaṭobās] gives him a blessing.

Once Devatāsambandhī Mahādevobā was at home, eating a meal. His wife went to get salt for him. She was bitten by a scorpion.

And Mahādevobā said, "If it had been a snake bite instead, to whom would you have gone for help?"

Then the three of them—his mother, Ākāïsē; Mahādevobā; and his wife —came to Bhaṭobās. They took initiation as ascetics. Bhaṭobās said, "Your initiation will be fruitful."

And the group of disciples used to call him "Devatāsambandhī" Mahādevobā,[57] because he had walked back and forth one and one-half times holding Śrīprabhu's hand.[58]

He was Ākāïsē's son, and Bhaṭobās' maternal cousin. He is the one [Śrīprabhu] called "the white woman's white son."[59]

26. When he hears about Cāṅgdevbhaṭ's observance, he says that he knows the right thing to do.

Once Cāṅgdevbhaṭ dined at the homes of seven lay disciples (*vāsaniks*); then he went begging and ate his meal at the river.

Someone told Bhaṭobās about this. Hearing about it, Bhaṭobās said, "That Cāṅgdev knows the right thing to do."[60] (According to some, "That Cāṅgdev is pleasing to me.")

27. He says that where there is love there are no restrictions.

Once there was a famine. Bhaṭobās had gone wandering. In a certain place they mixed everyone's food together and sat down to eat. As they ate, someone put some of the food he was eating into Bhaṭobās' bowl in such a way that Bhaṭobās would not notice.

The others saw this and said, "What's going on? How can you put used food *(usītẽ anna)* on Bhaṭ's plate?"[61]

At that, Bhaṭobās said, "Where there are good intentions there is no sin. Didn't the Gosāvī say, 'Where there is love there are no restrictions'?"[62]

And they kept quiet.

Bhaṭobās ate [the food].

28. When a Mahātmā gives him water, he explains the distinction between a puddle and the Gaṅgā.

One day Bhaṭobās was thirsty. He asked someone for some water. The man got some water from a puddle and strained it. He gave it to Bhaṭobās.

Bhaṭobās drank it; then he said, "Don't give anyone else the sort of water that you have given me."

And the man said, "Bhaṭ, [the Gosāvī] said that a puddle and the Gaṅgā are the same."[63]

Bhaṭobās said, "That is for oneself. When you are giving it to someone else, a puddle is a puddle, and the Gaṅgā is the Gaṅgā. You should realize that what lacks feeling *(bhāv)* lacks God *(daiv)*."

29. He explains what Mahātmās should do during Cāturmās.

Once Bhaṭobās said, "You should wander for eight months of the year; then for Cāturmās,[64] you should choose a few villages in one area. If you cannot manage in one place, stay in another."[65]

30. He criticizes Kāḷe Kṛṣṇabhaṭ for keeping silent when people harass him.

While Kāḷe Kṛṣṇabhaṭ was out wandering, he was arrested as a thief. He was whipped with a switch. He got welts on his body.

Then someone said, "Isn't this a follower of the charismatic *(vedhavantī)* Nāgdevbhaṭ?" So they let him go.

Bhaṭobās heard about this, and said, "Why did Kṛṣṇa keep silent for so long?"

Then Bhaṭobās made for the Mahātmās the garb that the Gosāvī had prescribed that they should wear during his absence. Until then, they had been wearing the garb for [the period of his] presence.[66]

31. After he explains that there are passionate and turbid [disciples], he says that they should act like those established in goodness.

One day Bhaṭ said, "[Among] Śrī Cakradhar's disciples are passionate *(rājas)* and turbid *(tāmas)* ones; but they should behave just the same way as those established in goodness *(satvastha)*."[67]

32. He praises spending [one's life] repeating the five names.

One day Bhaṭobās said, "If a person who gets a little knowledge of injunctions and prohibitions and then spends his life at the foot of a tree repeating these five names[68] goes to waste, then I take the responsibility for it."[69]

33. When he explains the importance of solitude and tells Sākāïsẽ not to practice recollection at home, he says, "Whose is Golho?"

Sākāïsẽ was a lay disciple *(vāsanik)*. She was a widow and a disciple of Bhaṭobās. Bhaṭobās had gone to her village. Golho was her grandson. One day Bhaṭobās said to Sākāïsẽ, "Sākāï, why don't you go off to solitude?"

She said, "Bhaṭ, whenever I play in my house with Golho, I think of God."

Bhaṭobās said, "It is better to sit daydreaming under a tree than to practice recollection *(smaraṇ)* at home. And sleeping [under a tree] is better than daydreaming there."

Bhaṭobās said—it is not known whether in this context or at another time—"Whose is Golho? Whose is Sitī? Think of your own, Sākubāī." He said this and laughed.

Sitī was her granddaughter.

Then one day she sang to Bhaṭobās two verses (*ovīs*) about her son:

> If one's offspring ignore Govind,[70]
>   it is like giving birth to a rock.
> Though I bore a child, O Mother, I'm barren:
>   my son has let go of Govind's feet.

Bhaṭobās listened to these verses.

34. He forbids Mahātmās to enter villages except as prescribed.

One day Bhaṭobās said, "Mahātmās should not go into villages except when it is time to go begging. And on the twelfth day of the fortnight they may[71] go to beg at the homes of lay disciples. And they may go at any time for guests, for the weak, and for the incapacitated."

Addendum: "Otherwise they should not go again and again to the homes of their acquaintances."[72]

This is what he said. There is a good deal [of value] in it.

35. He praises salvation *(uddharaṇ)* by a particular incarnation.

One day Bhaṭobās said, "In this world, anyone who is not saved *(nudhare)* by this incarnation *(avatār),* Śrī Cakradhar, will never be saved, will not be saved, will never be saved."

36. He criticizes Rūpdevobā for having a pouch of salt.

One day Bhaṭobās said, "Rūpdeyā is somewhat dispassionate, but he carries a pouch of salt with him."

At that, someone said, "How do you know this, Bhaṭ?"

"Can I not know such a small thing by the grace of Śrī Cakradhar?"

37. He forbids followers *(anusaraleyā)* and lay disciples (*vāsanik*s) to eat from one another's dishes.

One day Bhaṭobās said, "Mahātmās should not eat from lay disciples' (*vāsanik*s') plates, and lay disciples should not eat from Mahātmās' bowls. Our faults destroy their *dharma,* and theirs destroy ours. Why? Because [Śrī Cakradhar] said, 'One should not sit in the same place as one who enjoys sense pleasure.' "[73]

38. He takes a drinking cup at mealtime, to practice self service.[74]

One day Bhaṭobās' companions forgot to put a drinking cup at his place in a row of people sitting to eat. So, during the meal, Bhaṭobās stood up and left.

The others thought, "Has he gone to vomit?"

And Bhaṭobās went and got his own drinking cup. He drank some water.

They were ashamed. After that his companions were more careful.

39. He says that when one bows to places that have had [God's] contact (*sambandhsthān*s), one should recollect what [God] did at them.

One day Bhaṭobās said, "Go to holy places (*tīrtha*s), and recollect the deeds (*līḷā*s) that were done at them. That is the way one practices recollection *(smaraṇ)* there."

40. When he has accepted a lay disciple's worship, [Bhaṭobās] feels repentance and elucidates "Asatīparī."

A lay disciple worshipped Bhaṭobās with golden flowers. He offered him a silk shawl. He prepared a seat with a design made of pearls. Then he was about to perform *āratī*[75] with incense.

At that point, Bhaṭobās stopped him. There were tears in his eyes.

The lay disciple said, "Bhaṭ, why are you sad?"

Bhaṭobās said, "Was 'Asatīparī'[76] prescribed for my father?"[77]

And [the lay disciple] kept quiet.

41. He teaches about mendicancy, forbidding stoves and kitchens.

One day Bhaṭobās said, "Mahātmās should not set up stoves or kitchens. If the necessity arises, they should arrange three bricks [around a fire for cooking]. If guests come they should make *roṭī* bread and roasted eggplant. They should not spend time making spaghetti *(sevaiyā)* or vermicelli *(saravaḷīyā)*.

"They should not keep on sewing. They should not waste time. They should not keep needles. They should sew with a thorn.

"They should not cut their nails. They should not handle money."

This is what he taught.

42. When a Brāhmaṇ sees him eating at an early hour, he explains that one should act like a Śūdra, and gives him initiation.

Once while Bhaṭobās was traveling, he ate a meal early in the morning. A certain Brāhmaṇ saw this, and said, "What is going on? Why so early?"

And Bhaṭobās said, "In one's own village one should observe all the rules; in another village, half of them; in a town, a quarter of them; and on the road, one should act like a Śūdra."[78]

Then [the Brāhmaṇ] took initiation.

43. To a Mahātmā who is in a bad mood, he says, "You have missed digesting your food."

Once a lay disciple took Bhaṭobās and all the others [home with him] for a meal. One Mahātmā was in a bad mood and would not eat. No one liked that.

And Bhaṭobās said, "Even though you are in a bad mood, should you miss digesting your food?"

And [the Mahātmā] kept silent.

44. And he says that even detachment for the sake of praise is all right.

One day Bhaṭobās said, "Practice detachment even if only for praise, but don't just sit with your legs stretched out."

45. He chides a Mahātmā whom he hears laugh at the disciples for drinking water.

One day someone invited Bhaṭobās and all the others [for a meal]. Bhaṭobās went there, along with all the mendicants. One renouncer was so dispassionate that he stayed behind.

When Bhaṭobās and all the others returned, some of them were drinking water. Thoughtlessly [the one who had stayed behind] said, "Drink it, fellows. Drink it in gulps."

Bhaṭobās heard this, and got angry. Bhaṭobās said, "If you had come along, you might have eaten a cupful of ghee, but you would have kept the rule of love.[79] Now who will protect you? The Gosāvī has said, 'Some fall away while practicing [sensuality]; some fall away without practicing it.' "[80]

Then [the renouncer] felt remorse.

46. He uses the parable of the woman gathering cow dung to illustrate the regular and occasional rules.

One day Bhaṭobās taught: "The passionate *(rājas)* and the turbid *(tāmas)* should primarily wander; and those established in goodness *(satvastha)*[81] should primarily serve others. The regular *(nitya)* rules are one's maternal home, and the occasional *(naimittya)* rules are one's in-laws' house.[82] One should be like a ladle.[83]

"There was a woman collecting cow dung. One lump of dung she claimed with her foot; another she claimed with her hand; another by saying, 'It's mine'; and another she claimed by looking at it. This is how one should perform service."

47. And he praises the occasional rules.

One day Bhaṭobās said, "You should follow the occasional *(nimitya)* rules. The Gosāvī told me more as I was practicing the occasional rules for three and a half years than he told Bhāndārekār in sixteen years.[84] So when the regular observances become mechanical, you should enliven them by following the occasional rules.

"And both joining new companions and taking care of the feeble are difficult. Both are the cause of good things as well as bad. So you should make a good effort to care for the feeble and the incapacitated—as Kothaḷā did for Śrīprabhu.[85]

"When you are with the deputy *(adhīkaraṇ)*[86] you should question him. Either you should study the scriptures or you should wander in strange lands. You should not waste your time doing anything else."

48. He uses the analogy of the Gandharvas to illustrate [God's] gift of knowledge to a deputy.

One day Bhaṭobās said, "God (Parameśvar) gives his divine knowledge *(brahmavidyā)* and prepares a deputy *(adhikaraṇ);* then He himself listens to his own knowledge. The Gandharvas[87] provide an analogy to this: the

Gandharvas teach their Gandharvas' art and then listen to it themselves. God listens the same way. And the Gosāvī used the Gandharvas' art as an analogy to illustrate the production of reverberations."[88]

49. He says that there should be a wait of a certain period before a married woman is initiated.

One day Bhaṭobās said, "I am afraid to initiate as an ascetic a married woman or a woman with children. But a married woman should [certainly] not be initiated for two or three months."

50. He commands that an attendant should take care of the preceptor's belongings.

One day Bhaṭobās said, "Only an attendant should keep the preceptor's (*ācārya*'s) cowries and betel nuts.[89] Do not let an ascetic's hand become polluted."[90]

51. He explains appropriate and inappropriate places.

One day Bhaṭobās said, "A village where there are no clothes to hide your shame and no food to take away your hunger is called a *'sīḍī.'* A village where both of these are found is called a *'gaḍī.'*[91]

"A place where there are inhabited houses, mortars that are in use, and stoves that are in use is called a *'pāḷī.'* A place where there are no plates to eat from and no spoons to serve with is a *'hāḷī.'*[92]

"And a village that is full of passion and error is called a *'pur.'* [A place] where there is error mixed with passion is called a *'pāṭan.'*[93]

"A place without a weekly bazaar is a *'gavhān'*; a place that does have one is a *'gāv.'* "

52. When he hears a Mahātmā praised, he tells about [a disciple who] failed in attainment at the end of his life.

One day, seeing a certain Mahātmā's behavior, everyone began to praise him. Bhaṭobās said, "How can you praise him? He has fallen into a pit."

Then Bhaṭobās told the story of Chardobā.[94]

53. When he hears of the firmness of someone's discipleship, he praises him as one who strives for the transcendent.

A certain Śūdra took initiation as an ascetic from Bhaṭobās. He had given his wife [to someone] in a certain village.

In the course of his wandering, he came by chance to that village. He came [to her house] to beg. And that woman brought alms.

She recognized him and became frightened. She started to go [back] into the house.

And the Mahātmā said, "Don't be afraid. I have become a Mahātmā of the Bhaṭmārg. Live your life happily."

Then that Mahānubhāv left the village. He finished his begging round in another village.

Then his companions told Bhaṭobās what had happened. Bhaṭobās was pleased, and said, "This is how those who strive for the transcendent behave."

54. Hīrāïsē becomes a follower.

Hīrāïsē was Paṇḍitbās'[95] wife. Both of them received instruction from Bhaṭobās. One day Hīrāïsē said to Paṇḍit, "Paṇḍit, you take initiation as an ascetic, or let me take it."

He said, "You take it. I will get our son married, and then I will take initiation. You go on."

Then Hīrāïsē approached Bhaṭobās. She took initiation. She stayed in Bhaṭobās' presence.[96]

55. Bhānubhaṭ from Borī becomes a follower.

Once Bhānubhaṭ from Borī[97] had *darśan* of Bhaṭobās. It is not known how he came to have it. He received instruction from Bhaṭobās, and took initiation as an ascetic from him. Bhaṭobās loved him very much.

His previous *guru*'s name was Keśavācārya.

Later, on an appropriate occasion, Bhaṭobās gave him the name "Kavīśvar"; and sometimes he called him Bhaṭ.

56. When he has tried to help Ākāï [break] Rāmdev's strict renunciation, [Bhaṭobās] refers to [the aphorism about] the fraudulent preceptor *(ācārya)*.

It is not known which Ākāïsē and Rāmdev they were. Rāmdev was very young. He was Ākāïsē's son. He took initiation as an ascetic from Bhaṭobās. Ākāïsē was a lay disciple.

Rāmdev was extremely detached. He practiced strict renunciation. Knowing this, his mother asked Bhaṭobās, "Bhaṭ, please eat my food for a month."

Realizing her intention,[98] Bhaṭobās agreed.

So she prepared fine foods. She prepared a plate for Bhaṭobās. She served Rāmdev in the same row. But he would not eat anything.

Then the next day he avoided [meal]time and went and ate his meal at the river. So Bhaṭobās ate his meal and then said, "Ākāï, put aside these leavings of mine for Rām."

Rāmdev arrived. Ākāïsē said, "Eat this, Rām. When Bhaṭobās ate his meal, he put his leftovers aside for you."

[Rāmdev] took it, but he would not eat it.

Then on the third day, before the meal, Bhaṭobās said, "Rām, let's you and I eat together today. Do this little thing for me. Take [the food]."

Still he would not take it.

So Bhaṭobās ate his meal.

Then on the fourth day, he said, "Rām, today I have been given a little bit too much. So take just this little bite of my leavings." And Bhaṭobās stood up from his meal.

As he was holding [the bite of food] out to him, a grain of rice fell to the ground. Rāmdev put it into his mouth; then he said to Bhaṭobās, "Now I won't take [any more], Bhaṭ. I swear by you yourself that I will not take any [more]." And Bhaṭobās sat down.

Then Kesobās said, "What has happened to this Rām? Why has he pushed aside your hand, Bhaṭ, and you say nothing to him?"

At that Bhaṭobās said, "How can I obstruct the step he has taken? Am I some kind of fraudulent [preceptor]?"[99] And he rinsed his mouth after the meal, sat down, and said, "This Ākāï invited me [to eat, thinking] that although Rām does not eat anything [she prepares], at least he would eat with me. But he would not. Or, [she thought,] at least he would take my leavings. He would not even do that. So why should I break his resolve?"

And Kesobās kept silent.

Addendum: Bhaṭobās would not eat [her food any more] either.

57. And in teaching he praises the goal [of ritual practices].

One day Bhaṭobās was teaching Rāmdev. Rāmdev said, "No, Bhaṭ! No! Why should you show me the places where the Gosāvī slept and sat? Can I go and pay homage to them all?"

Bhaṭobās said, "If you are not going to go and pay homage to them, why have you opened the door to the Gosāvī?[100] Listen! Listen to what I say! You have to wade through a thicket for only a couple of steps. Then there is sovereignty before you. A lame man using a blind man's legs attains God (Īśvar). A blind man using a lame man's legs attains Caitanya."[101]

This is what he taught.

58. Paṇḍit becomes a follower.

Previously[102] Paṇḍit had said to Hīrāïsẽ, "You go become a follower. I will get our son married, and then I will come." So Hīrāïsẽ came and became a follower.

Later he got their son married, and afterwards [Paṇḍit] still remained at home. Then one day Hīrāïsẽ sent a message to Paṇḍit: "Say to Paṇḍit, 'Do you want to eat the ashes of the stove from which you once ate rice pudding?' "[103] Then [the messenger] set out. He went and told him exactly what she had said.

Paṇḍitbās said, "Now she's angry. Now I will have to go." So he set out.

Meanwhile, Bhaṭobās said, "Today nobody should go out for solitude. Today we will have to go to receive Paṇḍit."

Then Bhaṭobās and the mendicants went to receive him. And Paṇḍit arrived. They met. They came to their lodgings.

When it was mealtime, Bhaṭobās said, "Paṇḍit, come on. Let's eat together."

He said, "People who are living in the world *(pravṛt)* should not eat with those who have renounced the world *(nivṛt)*."

Bhaṭobās said, "What you say is true, but by virtue of your intention you may [eat with me]."

Paṇḍitbās said, "I will do so when I have fulfilled my intention."

Bhaṭobās said, "Take it as fulfilled."

So they ate together. [Paṇḍit] took initiation as an ascetic that same afternoon.

59. When Rāmdev is setting out to wander, [Bhaṭobās] talks about his fever.

Then one day Rāmdev said to Bhaṭobās, "Bhaṭ, I am going off to wander."

Bhaṭobās said, "All right. Go on."

So he set out. As he was leaving, Bhaṭobās embraced him. His body felt hot.

Bhaṭobās said, "Rām, you have a fever."

"Yes, Bhaṭ. That's why I am going."

Bhaṭobās said, "Rām, when a *jogī* or a *jaṅgam* dies, the *jogī*s or *jaṅgam*s are the ones who carry him away—the way the ants are the ones who carry off a dead ant."[104]

Rāmdev said, "Bhaṭ, should I do what you say, or should I do what the Gosāvī said?"[105]

Bhaṭobās said, "Do what the Gosāvī said. By doing so you will save me."

With that, Rāmdev set out.

60. He sends Paṇḍit and Kesobās along.

When Rāmdev set out he had a fever. Bhaṭobās said to Kesobās and Paṇḍitbās, "You keep an eye on him, and pay attention to his food."

They said, "All right," and set out after him.

They caught up with Rāmdev. Kesobās would expound Sanskrit verses (*ślokas*) to Rāmdev. Paṇḍitbās would sing him *dhuvās*, *ovīs*, and *caupadīs*.[106] None of this appealed to Rāmdev.

Then he would go begging. Paṇḍit and Kesobās would follow him. They would look out for him as they begged. If someone brought them good food as alms, they would say, "Put this food into the bowl of the Mahātmā who will come here alone." They would insist on this.

When Rāmdev came there, the people would give him warm rice.[107]

The next day Rāmdev would leave that village and go to another village. There too Paṇḍit and Kesobās would arrange for him to get good food. They kept his wandering from being interrupted.

61. When Keśav,[108] Māyāmbā,[109] [and Paṇḍit] return, [Bhaṭobās] says that [Rāmdev] has died.

Then one day Amṛte Māyāmbā met [Rāmdev] and narrated the Gosāvī's unfailing *līḷās*, which flow with nectar. That gave Rāmdev peace both inside and out. And Rāmdev rejoiced and said, "You have done well, Māïdev. You have narrated the Gosāvī's unfailing *līḷās*, which flow with nectar. Wherever I am, one man is going *'rūṃ-rūṃ'* and another is going *'ṭhak-ṭhak.'*[110] You have given me peace."

Then—it is not known whether it was right then or a day or two later—Rāmdev was about to die. As he died, Kesobās expounded "Mahāvākya"[111] to him. And with that, he died.

The three of them[, Kesobās, Paṇḍit, and Māyāmbā,] buried him. Then the three returned to Bhaṭobās. When Bhaṭobās saw them coming, he said, "Māïdev, Keśavdev, and Paṇḍit have come. Paṇḍit's step is faltering. Rām has died."

They arrived. They greeted Bhaṭobās. Paṇḍit and Kesobās told him what had happened. They told him everything Rāmdev had said: " 'Māïdev, you have come. You have given me peace.' "

Bhaṭobās listened to everything, and said, "It is an act of kindness to be as hard on someone else as you are on yourself."

62. Māhādāï hugs a child whom she hears say "Śrī Cakradhar!"

One day, when Māhādāïsẽ was begging with another woman, a child said, "Śrī Cakradhar!"[112]

Hearing that, Māhādāïsẽ was very happy. She patted [the child] and wiped him and held him on her hip and hugged him.

The woman who was with her said, "Why did you do that, Mother?"

Māhādāïsẽ said, "In this world, is God *(dev)* hard to find or is someone who remembers God hard to find?"[113]

Addendum: Then she put [the child] down and did her begging.

63. At Rāmdarā, Bhaṭobās gets angry with his disciples when Paṇḍit and Keśavdev cannot start eating.

Kavībās:[114] Once Bhaṭobās went along with all the others to Rāmdarā.[115] He bowed to Rāmdarā. Then he sat down to eat right there on the rocky ground. Some of Bhaṭobās' disciples served everyone, but they forgot to serve Paṇḍit and Kesobās.

Everyone started eating. Paṇḍit and Kesobās kept silent. Bhaṭobās saw this. Bhaṭobās said, "Why haven't you started eating?"[116]

One of them answered, "We haven't been served, Bhaṭ."

Then Bhaṭobās got angry with the servers. Finally he said, "If you do not practice proper behavior, how can you remember the prescribed act at the appropriate time?"

Addendum: Then [Paṇḍit and Kesobās] were served, and they began to eat.

64. He brings about a reconciliation between two lay disciples.

Ḍīṇḍaurī Govindpaṇḍit and Apar Rāmdev[117] had received instruction from Bhaṭobās. They lived in Rāvasgāv. There was some tension between them.

Once Bhaṭobās went there. He met them both. Govindpaṇḍit invited Bhaṭobās for a meal, and he also invited Apar Rāmdev. Without letting on to Bhaṭobās [about the quarrel, Rāmdev] quietly accepted the invitation. Then all the preparations were made. The guests were seated in rows to eat. Apar Rāmdev too was asked to sit and eat. He ate in the same row with Bhaṭobās.

Then, on another day, Apar Rāmdev also invited Bhaṭobās for a meal. [Rāmdev] invited Govindpaṇḍit, and he too came. He ate in the same row with Bhaṭobās, but he did not let on [to him about the quarrel].

Then Bhaṭobās went to Pratiṣṭhān.

Some days later, there was to be a ceremony in Apar Rāmdev's house. The day before, Rāmdev came to invite Govindpaṇḍit. But he would not accept the invitation. Govindpaṇḍit said, "You and I are at odds. I won't accept your invitation."

Rāmdev said, "But you have already eaten at my house."

Govindpaṇḍit said, "I wasn't eating at your house; I was eating in Bhaṭobās' row. Our quarrel is not over."

So Rāmdev had his ceremony.

Then, some time later, Apar Rāmdev and Ḍīṇḍorī Govindpaṇḍit came to see Bhaṭobās. Narendrakavi was also with them. They met [Bhaṭobās].

Addendum: Then someone told Bhaṭobās [about the quarrel]. (Some say that he had already heard about it.) Then Bhaṭobās spoke to them. He resolved the conflict between them. They were reconciled. Then they left.

65. When Sādhē becomes weak, he makes her a dwelling place in Nimbā.

Sādhē became very weak. Seeing this, Bhaṭobās said, "Sādhē has become weak. Now we will have to build a hut for her; otherwise her vow *(saṅgraho)* will be broken."

Then he built a hut in Nimbā, and Sādhē stayed in it. Bhaṭobās also stayed [in Nimbā].

66. When Keśav and Paṇḍit ask a question, Bhaṭobās tells them not to say *"asmāt"* and *"kasmāt."*

One day Paṇḍit and Kesobās asked Bhaṭobās a question in Sanskrit.

Bhaṭobās replied, "Paṇḍit, Keśavdev, I don't understand your *'asmāt'* and *'kasmāt.'*[118] Śrī Cakradhar taught me in Marāṭhī. That's what you should use to question me."

And they agreed.

67. When Paṇḍit is studying, [Bhaṭobās] praises his understanding.

Once when Bhaṭobās was teaching Paṇḍit "Uddharaṇ,"[119] Paṇḍitbās forgot one of the sentences *(vākya)*. As they were going along the road, Paṇḍitbās said to Bhaṭobās, "Bhaṭ, what is this aphorism *(vacan)?*"

Bhaṭobās said, "Let's sit down; then I will tell you."

A Brāhmaṇ who was sitting at the river said, " 'What is done is *karma.*' "[120] He said all of this [aphorism].

And Bhaṭobās said, "Paṇḍit, this is what you were asking about."

He said, "No, it is not, Bhaṭ. What you will tell me with the transcendent speech *(parā vāc)*[121] is."

At this, Bhaṭobās said, "Paṇḍit has come to understand this path."

Paṇḍitbās said, "Bhaṭ, for a long time I thought I knew everything about your path. But now, Bhaṭ, I have realized that I know nothing about this path."

And Bhaṭobās replied, "Only now have you gained knowledge, Paṇḍit. Didn't the Gosāvī say, 'To the extent that one is knowledgeable, one is ignorant'?"[122]

Addendum: Then [Paṇḍit] memorized what Bhaṭobās himself told him.

68. He praises Keśav and Paṇḍit as better than Mhāībhaṭ and Lakṣmīdharbā.

Once Paṇḍitbās and Keśavbās were having a discussion with Bhaṭobās. Bhaṭobās was pleased, and said, "My scripture is not illuminated by Mhāībhaṭ or Lakṣmīdharbhaṭ. It is illuminated when I discuss it with Paṇḍit and Keśodev."

He rejoiced this way.

69. Indrabhaṭ refuses to give his shawl, and [Bhaṭobās] asks for the shawl, explaining that it was meant to be for the order *(mārg)*.

Once Mhāībhaṭ went to Suregāv to meet Indrabhaṭ with a particular purpose in mind. He met Indrabhaṭ.

Addendum: [Indrabhaṭ] gave him hospitality, and he accepted it.

Then he said to Indrabhaṭ, "Indrabhaṭ, the Gosāvī graciously gave you a shawl.[123] You should be gracious and give it to the community of disciples."

Indrabhaṭ said, "It was to me that the Gosāvī graciously gave it. I am not going to give it away."

Mhāībhaṭ said, "No, give it."

[Indrabhaṭ] said, "I won't give it."

Then Mhāībhaṭ approached Bhaṭobās and told him what had happened.

When Bhaṭobās had heard all about it, he said, "Is the shawl his father's? The Gosāvī gave it to him for the sake of the whole community of disciples. When someone as worthy as Mhāībhaṭ asks him for it, how can he not give it to him?"

Then Bhaṭobās himself went, asked insistently for it, and took all of it. Then Bhaṭobās tore it in half and gave one half to Indrabhaṭ. And he handed Indrabhaṭ the other half too, and said, "Indra, now you be gracious and give this half to us in the order *(mārg)*."

This made Indrabhaṭ happy. Then Indrabhaṭ prostrated himself completely and gave Bhaṭobās one half of the shawl. And Bhaṭobās made pieces of it and distributed them to everyone.

Addendum: Then Bhaṭobās came to Nimbā.

Further addendum: Then, after Indrabhaṭ died, his half also came to the order. (Some say that Kavīśvar brought it.)

70. A Mahātmā is forbidden to go wandering with a relic *(prasād)*.

Once a Mahātmā set out to go wandering. *Addendum:* It was Indrabhaṭ. He set out for his village. He had the Gosāvī's shawl with him.

Bhaṭobās said, "You do not have permission to go wandering alone."

Addendum: He forbade him, saying, "Indrabhaṭ, you should not go alone. You have the Gosāvī's shawl."

He stayed back. [From then on,] he never went alone.

71. When Kesobās asks about illuminating his mind, [Bhaṭobās] tells him what to do.

Once Kesobās lost his ability to think. He could not remember anything at the right time. Then one day he asked Bhaṭobās, "Bhaṭ, these days I have trouble thinking. I can't remember anything at the right time."

Bhaṭobās answered, "You should go wandering for a month. Don't put a bowl in your begging bag. Be in solitude for three watches a day.[124] Go begging during the third watch.[125] Eat your meal at a river.[126] Sleep in a dilapidated temple or at the foot of a tree.[127] Then your wrongdoing will be done away with, and you will be able to think again."

So [Kesobās] did this, and [his mind] was illuminated. He could think [again].

72. He admonishes Vāḷuke Rāmdev, showing him his improper behavior when he refuses tasty food *(ras)*.

Once Vāḷuke Rāmdev went wandering. And he prepared *roṭī* breads in a field in a certain village. He ate them with ghee and roasted vegetables.

Then, some time later, he went to meet Bhaṭobās. He met him. [Bhaṭobās] invited him for a meal. Then, as ghee was being served to the row of people who were eating, Bhaṭobās said, "Have some."

"No, Bhaṭ. No thanks. I can't eat it."

And Bhaṭobās said, "Ha! You can eat as much ghee and bread and roasted vegetables as you want in a field, Rām, but you can't eat mine. Who could understand this?"

[Rāmdev] said, "How did you know, Bhaṭ?"

"Can I not know even such a small thing by the grace of Śrī Cakradhar?"

And [Rāmdev] felt remorse. Then everyone ate the meal.

73. And when [Vāḷuke Rāmdev] is washing clothes, [Bhaṭobās] explains how to serve others.

One day, just as the same man was washing the guests' clothes, Bhaṭobās came there and said, "Rām, when you wash your own clothes, you should just get rid of the dirt,[128] but when you wash others', you should wash them bright and clean and dry them in the sun. That is kind service."

He taught him this way. Then [Rāmdev] washed the clothes carefully.

74. He praises Kavīśvar as having done right in giving up his solitude.

One day Kavīśvarbās went off to be in solitude. A row of ants came to the place where he was about to sit.

So he went to another place. Cattle came there to graze. He went to still another place. There he could not meditate fruitfully.[129]

Then, because his solitude was fruitless, he came back to the place where they were staying. Guests had arrived.

Then he told Bhaṭobās what had happened.

Bhaṭobās listened, then said, "It was a good idea to come back."

75. When he hears that Anantdev has died, he explains what will happen to him [in his next life].

It is not known what village Anantdev was from, but he had received instruction from Bhaṭobās. His village was very close to Nimbā.

He was very young. His father was not living. His mother was alive. One day he came to meet Bhaṭobās, and took initiation as an ascetic. Hearing this, his mother came to take him away. He would not leave.

Then his mother said to Bhaṭobās, "Bhaṭ, send him home. If you don't, I will eat poison, and you will be to blame."

Bhaṭobās said, "Anant, for my sake, leave."

He left. He got a fever. His mother said, "Anant, are you going to live?"

He said, "If you say to Death what you said to Bhaṭobās—'Send him home, or I will eat poison'—then I will live." And with that, he died.

Bhaṭobās heard about it, and said, "Any other *guru* who had a disciple like Anant die would stab himself, saying, 'He died because of me.' "

Then someone asked Bhaṭobās, "What will happen to him?"

Bhaṭobās said, "He will be born as a *puruṣ.*[130] Then he will have the *darśan* [of a divine incarnation]."

This is the explanation he gave.

76. When Kothaḷobā teaches Gaurāïsē, [Bhaṭobās] calls him a medium.

One day Bhaṭobās was teaching *Ācārsthaḷ*[131] to Umbarī Gaurāïsē. But she could not learn it. She did not understand it.

So Bhaṭobās said, "Gaurāï, you are not getting it. You go away. Later a veritable medium[132] will speak to you."

So she went out to wander. As she was wandering, she met Kothaḷobās. He expounded "Asatīparī"[133] to her.

Bhaṭobās heard about this, and said, "What can Kothaḷā say? It was a medium who spoke."

77. And he says that she was helped in her wandering.

As Umbarī Gaurāïsē was wandering, one day she was going to a village, and she got a thorn in her foot along the way. It hurt so much that she could not walk. She sat on the road, holding her foot. Another woman was with her.

A horseman came along the road from the village to which she had been heading. Seeing her sitting there, he said, "Mother, what village are you going to?"

"We were going to that village over there, but I got a thorn in my foot, so I can't walk. So I'm sitting here."

He said, "Mother, there's been a raid on that town. Don't go there. Let's go back now to the village you came from." And he got down from the horse. He invited her to sit on it. And he brought her on the horse to the outskirts of the village she had left. He set her down there, and left.

Some time later, Bhaṭobās heard about this.

Addendum: And he said, "Gaurāïsē was helped greatly."

78. When he eats during the daytime, he does not take pan, because of his vow.

Bhaṭobās used to have his meal during the daytime, but he would not chew pan, because that would have broken his vow of renunciation *(sannyās saṅgraho).*

79. He tells about Hīrāïsē's fortitude.

One day Bhaṭobās told this story about fortitude. Bhaṭobās said, "When we went to meet Hīrāïsē, her daughter was not well. We arrived. [Hīrāïsē] welcomed us. She gave us proper hospitality.

"As we sat down to eat, [her daughter] died. Without anyone realizing what had happened, [Hīrāïsē] just wrapped her up and put her aside.

"Everyone ate; then afterwards Hīrāī ate.
(Kavīśvarbās: "We made her eat with us.")
"Then she said, 'Just now she was alive!' and cried profusely."
This is the story that Bhaṭobās told.

80. He instructs Virūpākhya Mahādevobā about where to sit in the row of diners.

Once when Bhaṭobās was sitting along with everyone in a row to eat, Virūpākhya Mahādevobā had taken a seat higher than Rūpdevobā's. Seeing him, Kesobās said, "You get up from here. Sit over there."

And [Mahādevobā] got up, but he was a little upset. He made a face.

Seeing this, Bhaṭobās said, "If you're going to make a face like that, why didn't you take initiation before him? Seniority must be followed."

And [Mahādevobā's] mood changed. He felt remorse.

81. When a Mahātmā asks a question, Bhaṭobās tells him not to have desire or any other feeling toward foods.

One day a lay disciple brought choice green millet and sugar. When Bhaṭobās had him distribute it to everyone, a Mahātmā asked, "Bhaṭ, can we eat something like this?"

Bhaṭobās said, "First eat it; then ask me."

He ate it, and then he asked.

Bhaṭobās said, "If one desires it, [even] salt is an object of sense pleasure."[134] Then he instructed him.

82. Bhaṭobās admonishes Gaurāī for using the name Māhātmā in asking for ghee.

One day Bhaṭobās sent Gaurāīsẽ to buy some ghee. She went to buy it. After the man who was selling it had ladled the customers' ghee into their pots, two spoonfuls of ghee were left over. Gaurāīsẽ asked for it: "Give this to us Mahātmās."

He gave it to her. She brought it back.

Bhaṭobās made her pour it out. "Do not eat this ghee. You are selling your status as a Mahātmā." He admonished her in these words.

So she poured it out.

83. During a time of political turmoil, he has Ābāīsẽ stay at Vaijobā's house.

Once the Sultan of Delhi invaded.[135] The whole region was in turmoil. Bhaṭobās said to Ābāīsẽ, "Ābāī, you stay in Vaijobā's village."[136]

She said, "No, Nāgdev. The Gosāvī has forbidden [us to stay with] our relatives."[137]

Bhaṭobās said, "You have had contact *(sambandh)* with both Gods,[138] and you have served them in their presence *(sannidhāndāsya),* and you have a son like me. And for whom is [the rule about] relatives? It is for those who are weak."

Addendum: "And this is an emergency."

So Ābāïsē agreed. She stayed in Vaijobā's village.

Bhaṭobās said, "The land will be in turmoil. And you should come to me as soon as the banners of the army appear.[139] I have the younger women with me, so I will go ahead to the Ghāṭ."[140]

And Bhaṭobās set out.

84. He has Sādhē stay in Paraḷī.

As Bhaṭobās was on his way to the Ghāṭ, he reached Paraḷī. There was an army approaching from behind. Then Bhaṭobās said to Sādhē, "Yelho, you stay here. The Gosāvī has promised you his protection."[141]

Sādhē agreed. Then all those who were too weak [to travel further] stayed behind with Sādhē. Bhaṭobās set out to go far away.

Sādhē stayed at Vaijanāth's temple; she put all those who were too weak inside [the temple]. Sādhē sat at the door, leaning on a stick.

The Muslims *(turuk)* arrived. They said, "Who's here?"

Sādhē said, "I am here, King Śrī Cakradhar's maidservant Yelho." She spoke this way, and they looked [at her] and left.

Thus, through Sādhē, as many [of the disciples] as were there were saved, and other people as well.

85. He tells about the breakdown of the cart, and says that Ābāïsē escaped being captured.

After Bhaṭobās had left [Vaijobā's village], the whole land was in turmoil. As soon as the army's banners appeared, Vaijobā set out in a cart. With him were Ābāïsē and Maheśvarpaṇḍit.[142] As they fled along the road, the cart broke down. They stayed right there.

And Muslims came up from behind. They said, "These [must] belong to those [of us] who have gone ahead." Those who were ahead said, "These [must] belong to those who are coming from behind."[143] In this way, [Vaijobā and his party] escaped.

And Bhaṭobās said, "Vaijobā's cart broke down, but they escaped being captured. Why? They escaped because there is no break in my recollection *(smaraṇ)* [of God]."

And someone said, "Bhaṭ, how do you know this?"

Bhaṭobās said, "Can I not know even this little by the grace of Śrī Cakradhar?"

The man was amazed.

86. He predicts the king's future.

Bhaṭobās went away to a distant region. Some say he went to Nilaṅgā.

Meanwhile they arrested Rāmdev.[144] When Bhaṭobās heard this, he made a pronouncement about it. Bhaṭobās said, "Rāmdev has been captured, but he will get free."

Those who were with him said, "How so, Bhaṭ?"

Bhaṭobās said, "Marāṭhā rule *(marhāṭē)* will last as long as I do."

Then Bhaṭobās spoke this verse:[145]

A land in which there lives a knowledgeable *yogī*
who reflects on the Self:
such a region surely becomes holy in a moment.

"And he has been captured because he treated good men (*sants*) and ascetic leaders (*mahants*) badly.[146] But this is just the washing of the hands; the meal itself is yet to come."

87. He returns to Nimbā when the political upheaval has settled down.

Addendum: Then, after some time, when security had been restored, Bhaṭobās returned to the Gaṅgā Valley. He met Sādhē—it is not known where. Then he returned with Sādhē to Nimbā, and stayed there.

88. He tells about the different languages spoken by Kešav and Paṇḍit.

One day Bhaṭobās said, by way of praise, "Kešavdev is fluent in Sanskrit, and Paṇḍit is fluent in Sanskrit and Marāṭhī." That is what he said.

89. He forbids Paṇḍit to sing in solitude.

Paṇḍitbās was very fond of music. He would sit in solitude and sing the *dhuvās*, *ovīs*, *caupadīs*, and *gīts*[147] he liked.

One day he was sitting in solitude singing when Bhaṭobās came to check on [the disciples' practice of] solitude. Bhaṭobās heard him singing, and said, "Paṇḍit, from today onward, don't you sing. The Gosāvī has forbidden it; he said, 'Song is an object of sense pleasure.' "[148]

So from then on Paṇḍitbas made it a rule not to sing.

90. And he gives him permission to sing.

One day Paṇḍitbās was sitting in solitude when Bhaṭobās came there checking on [the disciples'] solitude. [Bhaṭobās] stood behind [Paṇḍitbās], out of sight.

Paṇḍitbās was filled with great grief. He was grieving, and at the same time he was singing this song:

1. Let my ears enjoy no other talk;
let my eyes love your form.

Refrain: You are the supreme god: this is all I know.
Many difficulties afflict me.

2. Grant me this, King Govind:
may I never let go of you.

3. May only this come to my mind, King Govind:
   that I think constantly of you.
4. A child can be comforted by no one else:
   what is wrong with his crying for his mother?
5. Don't forget me, O patron of the afflicted,
   O Lord of Nāgdev, Śrī Cakrapāṇī.

He sang this song with great sadness. Bhaṭobās stood and listened to all of it. Then he came forward and said, "Paṇḍit, from today onward you have permission to sing. The Gosāvī said: 'If this wall can feel emotions, then Dematī can be affected when she sings.' "[149]

Quoting scripture this way, Bhaṭobās gave him permission.

91. And when a Brāhmaṇ becomes a disciple upon hearing a song, [Bhaṭobās] says it is his call.

One day Paṇḍitbās was singing a *dhuvā.* Hearing it, a certain Brāhmaṇ took initiation as an ascetic. [Paṇḍit] brought him to Bhaṭobās. He told him everything that had happened.

Hearing about it, Bhaṭobās said, "Paṇḍit's song is my call."

92. At Nāthobā's invitation, he goes to meet Kaṭak Demāïsē.

Once, in the course of his wanderings, Nāthobā went to Kaṭak Devgiri.[150] There he gave instruction to Demāïsē from Kaṭak[151] and to Vaṅki.

They offered Nāthobā some payment, but he would not accept it. Then they insisted. So Nāthobā said, "Give it to me, and I will give it to Bhaṭobās." And he took it.

Demāïsē asked, "Who is Bhaṭobās?"

"He is the seniormost *(vaḍil)* among us."

She said, "Then you should introduce him to me."

Nāthobā agreed. Then he went from there to Nimbā to see Bhaṭobās. He met Bhaṭobās. He told him what had happened. Then he invited Bhaṭobās [to come there].

Bhaṭobās agreed. Then he brought Bhaṭobās to Kaṭak. Demāïsē was introduced to Bhaṭobās.

93. And when he eats something other than ghee, he explains that he cannot distinguish between flavors.

Then Demāïsē invited Bhaṭobās and all the mendicants for a meal. Bhaṭobās accepted. So Demāïsē made all the preparations. Those who were to eat were seated in rows. Everyone was served.

A plate was prepared for Bhaṭobās. By mistake Demāïsē put safflower oil on Bhaṭobās' plate instead of ghee. Then she prostrated herself.

Demāïsē sat near Bhaṭobās' plate. As Bhaṭobās was eating, Demāïsē smelled safflower oil. She looked and saw that he was eating safflower oil.

And she was humiliated. "Oh, why didn't you tell me? I served it by mistake for ghee." And she began to lament greatly. "Oh, what have I done?" Immediately she served him ghee.

As Bhaṭobās was eating, she again said the same thing: "Alas, Bhaṭ! Alas! If only you had told me."

Then Bhaṭobās explained it away for her. Bhaṭobās said, "I swear by Rūpai[152] that I cannot distinguish the taste of safflower oil or any other flavors."

Then everyone ate the meal. Then both Kaṭak Demāïsē and Vaṅki became Bhaṭobās' disciples. Nāthobā entrusted *(nirovilīṃ)* [them to him].

Then Bhaṭobās said to everyone, "It is only because the Gosāvī made me his deputy *(adhikaraṇ)* that I am everyone's *guru.* Otherwise all [of you] are Śrī Cakradhar's frontrunners, and my criers. Now no one should laugh at this Nātho." This is what Bhaṭobās said.

In the same way Upādhye and Kānhopādhye would bring anyone who asked them questions to Bhaṭobās. Bhaṭobās called them too his criers.

Addendum: Then Bhaṭobās returned to Nimbā.

94. When Keśav and Paṇḍit unite [against him, Bhaṭobās] becomes obstinate.

A couple took ascetic initiation from Bhaṭobās, but they continued to be passionate. Seeing their inappropriate behavior, Kesobās and Paṇḍitbās said to Bhaṭobās, "You should send these two away, Bhaṭ. They are sinful."

Because they were in a large group, Bhaṭobās could not see the problem. Bhaṭobās said, "They'll improve gradually; or, if not, their vices will cause them to leave. Don't you be the cause [of their leaving]."

Kesobās and Paṇḍitbās said, "Bhaṭ, send them away, or we will all leave."

Bhaṭobās got angry and said, "Go ahead."

Then both [Kesobās and Paṇḍitbās] swore to everyone, "May Bhaṭobās' curse be on anyone who does not leave here."

So everyone left.

95. When Keśav and the others return, Bhaṭobās says that Keśav and Paṇḍit are his eyes.

Then when everyone had left, only those two remained. So their behavior became evident. They would look at each other and make amorous gestures. They would behave suggestively.

At that, Bhaṭobās said, "These two are the reason that my mendicants[153] have left. My people have left for nothing."

To the [couple] he said, "Now you leave. For your sake, I have cut myself off from many."

So they left.

When they heard about this, Keśobās, Paṇḍitbās, and all the others returned. They said to Bhaṭobās, "Bhaṭ, we are sinners. We left you!" and they prostrated themselves. They began to express their remorse.

Then Bhaṭobās made them get up, and he comforted them, saying, "Paṇḍit, Keśavdyā, can one see with one's whole body? One can see only with one's eyes. In the same way, Paṇḍit and Keśavdyā, you are my eyes."

96. On the strength of *dharma,* he rejects [the distinction between] senior and junior.

So then Bhaṭobās said, "*Dharma* should bring about equality. *Dharma* is not a disciple; *dharma* is itself the *guru.* So through *dharma* even one who is senior should do what his junior says."

This is what Bhaṭobās taught.

97. Because Lukhāī's discipleship is firm, Bhaṭobās sends her to her relatives to convince them.

Lukhāīsẽ was from Bābuḷgāv. She had received instruction from Bhaṭobās. She withdrew from all pleasures. She was dispassionate. She would eat buttermilk and rice. By vow, she gave up everything but her wedding necklace. She ceased to have sexual relations with her husband. She would go to the river, take a bath, sit for a while, and perform her religious exercises *(anuṣṭhān).* This is how she lived. On her own she went and found a nice young woman for her husband to marry. She got her husband married.

Then one day she came to the river to bathe, and without returning, she went directly to Bhaṭobās at Nimbā.

She met Bhaṭobās. She took initiation as an ascetic. Before initiating her, Bhaṭobās had inquiries made [about her]. She told him about her previous observances and vows.

Then he sent her with Bāīsẽ to Parameśvarpur.[154] Right afterwards, her people came pursuing her. They said to Bhaṭobās, "Bhaṭ, Lukhāī has come here. Let us see her."

Bhaṭobās said, "She is not here. Take a look." And he convinced them [that she was not there]. And they left. They went to their village.

Lukhāīsẽ went to Ṛddhipur. She bowed to Ṛddhipur. For a year or so she practised intense asceticism. She became emaciated.

Then after a year she came to meet Bhaṭobās. She met him. And one day, realizing her great fortitude, Bhaṭobās said, "Lukhāīsẽ, now you go straight to Bābuḷgāv. Go begging there and come back."

So Lukhāīsẽ went to Bābuḷgāv. When it was time to go begging, she went to that same house [where she had lived]. [Her husband] was sitting at the door. Without recognizing her, he said, "[I] prostrate [myself to you], Mother."

Lukhāīsẽ said, "Do you recognize me?"

And he recognized her and said, "Yes, I recognize you. Now [I] prostrate myself again." And he came forward [to receive her]. He took off his turban. And, with great feeling, he placed his head on her feet. He spread out a cloth for her to sit on. He washed her feet over a plate. He drank the water from washing her feet. He applied it to his forehead.

Then Lukhāïsẽ returned and told Bhaṭobās what had happened. Bhaṭobās was very happy.

98. When Kheibhaṭ asks a question, [Bhaṭobās] talks about a solvent.

One day Kheibhaṭ from Segāv had the sight *(darśan)* of Bhaṭobās. He asked Bhaṭobās, "Is there anything that can free a cart that has been tied down with iron chains?"

Bhaṭobās said, "There is. If you find the right solvent, [even] iron will melt."

Bhaṭobās used this analogy. It was fixed in Kheibhaṭ's mind like an inset gem. He said to himself, "Now I will go to my village and arrange my affairs, and then I will come to Bhaṭobās."

So he took his leave of Bhaṭobās, took his family with him, and went to his village.

99. And [Kheibhaṭ] becomes a disciple.

Then Kheibhaṭ went to his village and divided his wealth into three equal parts. One part he gave to his son. One he gave to his wife. Taking his own share, he took leave of them, saying, "I am going to Bhaṭobās. Don't expect me back."

He came to Bhaṭobās. He told him everything that had happened. He placed his money in front of Bhaṭobās.

And Bhaṭobās kicked it away and said, "Am I some kind of false *(coḷikā)*[155] Mahātmā, that you have brought this to me?"

Kheibhaṭ found this difficult. He said to Bhaṭobās, "Then what should I do with it? How can I go back so far?" He began to plead with him.

So Bhaṭobās said, "All right, go throw it into that temple over there. The temple will eat it." So he took it and put it into a corner in the temple.

Then he did a fine, proper ritual. He worshiped Bhaṭobās carefully, and gave him a garment. He prepared good foods and invited him for a meal.

Then [Bhaṭobās] gave Kheibhaṭ initiation as an ascetic. It is not known whether he gave him instruction at that time or had given it to him sometime earlier.

100. And he praises [Kheibhaṭ's] qualifications.

Then Bhaṭobās taught Kheibhaṭ some of the scripture. He was an old man. Seeing that, one day Bhaṭobās said, "A man who is sixty years old is not qualified to become a follower[156]—but no one understands the inclination of God (Īśvar). Similarly, when an insect eats away at wood, it may by chance carve out the syllable *Om*."[157]

101. And he criticizes the discipline of [not eating] *kuhīrī* pods, and explains how an ascetic *(puruṣ)* should behave.

One day Vāḷuke Rāmdev asked Bhaṭobās' permission and set out to go wandering. Bhaṭobās sent Kheibhaṭ along with him. They left.

One day when they went begging, they received *kuhīrī*[158] pods as alms. As they ate, Vāḷuke Rāmdev threw away [the *kuhīrī* pods]. Then they both ate. Then Kheibhaṭ stood up and buried [the pods] in the sandy beach.

They stayed in that place for a day or two. Then every day as he ate [Kheibhaṭ] would say [to himself], "Why can't you swallow [your food]? May I tell you? You keep seeing the *kuhīrī* pods." Kheibhaṭ had lived in a very affluent style.

Then, some time later, they came to see Bhaṭobās. And Rāmdev told Bhaṭobās what had happened. Bhaṭobās listened and said, "Rām, you did wrong. If someone who is used to eating the eighteen different kinds of foods[159] can be satisfied with just one, then he is the one who is great!"

(According to some: "How can *kuhīrī* pods be an object of sense pleasure for him? For whom are they an object of sense pleasure? Only for someone who does not [even] have salt to put on his mash.")

Then Bhaṭobās gave an explanation. Bhaṭobās said: "One should restrain his body, restrain his senses, and restrain his mind according to his qualification or lack of qualification. One who does so is called a *tridaṇḍī puruṣ*.[160] You should not praise those from whom you receive generosity and respectful treatment, but you should take as your benefactors those who [lead you to] *dharma*."

102. When a Brāhmaṇ asks him a question, [Bhaṭobās] says that his light is interior.

One day a certain Brāhmaṇ asked Bhaṭobās, "Bhaṭ, your body looks bright. Do you bathe three times a day?"

Bhaṭobās replied, "When the stars shine in the sky does their abode *(mandir)* shine, or does what is inside them shine?"

"No, Bhaṭ. What is inside them shines."

Bhaṭobās said, "In the same way, the Reality *(vastu)*[161] that is inside my body *(mandir)* is what shines."

Addendum: And with that, the man took initiation.

103. On account of an incident with a bull, he proclaims that [God] has protected Gopāḷpaṇḍit.

Once Gopāḷpaṇḍit came to meet Bhaṭobās. One day Bhaṭobās went out to beg. (*Addendum:* It was the twelfth day of the fortnight.) Ānobās[162] was with him. [Ānobās] held his begging bag the same way that lay disciples do.

At one house, an enormous bull charged Bhaṭobās. As it was about to reach him, Gopāḷpaṇḍit grabbed it by the horns. Bhaṭobās slipped away around its side. Then Gopāḷpaṇḍit pushed it away.

Then he caught up with Bhaṭobās. And Bhaṭobās returned to their lodgings. He told the story and then said, "So today the one who identifies himself with me has protected Gopāḷ."

(*Addendum:* Everyone was amazed.)

104. Māhādāïsẽ admonishes Kesobās for sleeping.

One day Kesobās had slept during the day. (*Addendum:* That had made him waste some time.) Seeing that, Māhādāïsẽ said, "Listen, Keśavdev, someone with even a single enemy doesn't sleep during the day, but you have fourteen enemies."[163] (*Addendum,* Kavibās: "How can you sleep, since the whole circle of deities [*devatācakra*][164] is your enemy?")

Hearing Māhādāïsẽ get angry this way, Kesobās was very happy.

105. He says that by rejecting evil Keśav has protected the whole order.

Once when Kesobās had gone out alone to wander, rain fell out of season. He went to a village to beg. At one house a moneylender's daughter saw him. Kesobās was handsome. He was strong. She felt attracted to him. She gave him alms herself, and asked, "Where do you live?"

He just shook his head and moved on indifferently.

She watched for him until evening. That evening it rained. He went to spend the night in a *liṅga* temple[165] near the village gate. He had a small piece of shawl with him. He placed it in front of him and sat in a corner.

At night the temple priest *(gurav)* went home. He had seen [Kesobās], but he left without saying anything.

After a while, the woman wrapped herself in a thick blanket and came to the temple. She looked around and saw Kesobās. And she sat down on his lap.

Kesobās said, "Get up. I'll do whatever you say," and he made her sit on the ground.

And he said to the woman, "I'm going out to urinate. You sit right here." And he left behind the shawl and some belongings that he had. She believed him.

In this way, he got out of the temple, and immediately he left, saying, "Śrī Cakradhar!"

The woman waited for a while. When she realized that he was not going to return, she got frightened. She went home.

That night Kesobās slept out in the open, and the very next day he set out to meet Bhaṭobās.

That morning, Bhaṭobās and the whole group of disciples *(mārg)* had gathered. They were having a discussion about religion *(dharmavārtā)*. Just then, Bhaṭobās said, "Keśavdyā is coming. He has left his shawl in a temple."

And everyone said, "How do you know, Bhaṭ?"

Bhaṭobās said, "I know through the grace of Śrī Cakradhar."

Kesobās arrived. They all greeted him. They prepared a seat for him in front [of Bhaṭobās].

Then Bhaṭobās said, "Keśavdev, tell us how you have come."

So Kesobās told them everything that had happened.

At that, Bhaṭobās said, "Some people have protected themselves from evil; some have protected some others; [but] Keśavdā has protected the whole order *(mārg)*."[166]

This is how Bhaṭobās praised him.

106. And when [Kesobās] returns again, [Bhaṭobās] tells about the *jogiṇī* and the bag.

Then Bhaṭobās said to Kesobās, "Now you go back there."

Kesobās agreed. Kesobās said to himself, "My body is the cause of this [problem]." So he returned to his wandering. His body became emaciated. He practiced stringent fasting. Then he went to that same village and went to beg at that woman's house. Just then, she was standing there. She saw Kesobās and spat contemptuously, naturally taking him to be a wretched beggar. And she went into the house.

With that, Kesobās patted himself on the arms.[167] "Am I not Śrī Cakradhar's Keśavdyā?" he said, showing pride in his name.

Addendum: Immediately he went to the temple priest's place. The temple priest gave him his shawl and all his other belongings, which he had kept for him.

Then, after some time, [Kesobās] came to see Bhaṭobās. Beforehand, Bhaṭobās said, "Keśodyā is coming, having chased away Death." Then [Kesobās] came and told him what had happened. Bhaṭobās was very happy.

Then after that he went wandering a good bit, and performed many religious exercises *(caryā)*.

Malekoyābā[168] used to tell this episode *(smṛti)* and talk about *dharma*.

Addendum: Then Bhaṭobās told the story of the *jogiṇī*[169] and the bag.

Then Bhaṭobās said, "One should not go wandering alone. Once when I was wandering, I had gone in the evening to a temple to sleep, when a certain *jogiṇī* came there. She said, 'Come on, let's have sex.'

" 'Go away,' I replied, and I left the place.

"She said, 'Why are you running away? You'll lose your bag.'

"I said, 'If I lose my bag that's my business. What is it to you whether I keep it or lose it?' And I went somewhere else to sleep."

In this way, he told about his own experience, [and said,] "So you should not go wandering alone."

So he arranged that the men should [go wandering] in pairs and the women in groups of four.

107. Bhaṭobās offers the order his old-age pension.

Once there was a famine in the land. The mendicants got no alms. When the mendicants went to beg, they would get [only] a few pieces of *bhākrī* bread in their begging bags. For fear that Bhaṭobās would see how little alms they had gotten, and would have something cooked for them, the mendicants would put rags into the bottom of their begging bags. On top they would place the food they had received as alms. Then they would have Bhaṭobās look into their bags,[170] and they would go to the river to eat.

One day when Bhaṭobās put his hand beneath someone's bag and lifted up the alms, it felt light. "What is this? Why is your begging bag so light?" he said, and he fingered through the food. And he saw the rags at the bottom. But he kept silent. He understood that there was a famine.

Then in the evening they were all sitting in their sleeping places, and Bhaṭobās got up from his spot. He stood up, folded his hands, and made a request of them: "If you are all Śrī Cakradhar's heroes, then give me what I ask." And he prostrated himself to all of them.

Then, embarrassed, they all stood up. All of them said, "Get up, get up, Bhaṭ. We will give you what you ask."

Bhaṭobās said, "Put to use the old-age pension that I have received. From now on take alms from me as well." And they all agreed.

So Bhaṭobās would have food cooked. The mendicants would make their begging rounds, and then they would accept alms from Bhaṭobās too. Each of them would take the alms—a flat wheat breat *(poḷī),* boiled split lentils, spiced fried buttermilk, rice, and a leaf vegetable—and go to the river to eat.

Addendum: In this way, Bhaṭobās' money was put to use.

Then when there came a time of plenty, they no longer took [Bhaṭobās' food].

108. When he is told that Sākāī's father has died, he refuses to let her give a funeral meal.

Sākāīsē was a lay follower *(vāsanik).* She was Bhaṭobās' disciple *(siṣya).* Her father died. She performed the rites for him and came to Bhaṭobās. As soon as she arrived, Bhaṭobās said, "What have you done, Sākāī?"

She said, "I have planted a banyan tree and a pipal tree." Then she prostrated herself to Bhaṭobās in greeting.

She had brought some money with her. She asked Bhaṭobās, "Bhaṭ, I have brought some money. So may I give a meal [for my father's funeral]?"

Bhaṭobās said, "He was not a disciple *(vāsanik)*. Who will accept his food? No one will take it."

Addendum: "If you do it on your own behalf,[171] they will accept it after the period of mourning is over."

So she kept silent. After the period of mourning had passed, she again asked Bhaṭobās. Bhaṭobās agreed. Then she invited Bhaṭobās and all the others for a meal. They all accepted it.

109. He talks about a Mahātmā's aversion to solitude.

Someone who took initiation from Bhaṭobās did not like solitude. The mendicants would invite him over and over and lead him into solitude.

Seeing that, Bhaṭobās said, "It is like this for him to go into solitude," and he cited the aphorism about the raised seat.[172]

110. He chides Gaurāïsẽ for giving food to a cook.

Once there was a large gathering. A Brāhmaṇ woman was invited to prepare the food. Bhaṭobās agreed to give her four *rukā* coins. She did the cooking. She was paid the four *rukā*s. He dismissed her.

Then the guests sat in rows to eat. Everyone ate. Then Gaurāïsẽ sent for the woman and presented her with two *veṭh*s, and some *mānḍā*s and *purī*s.[173] Bhaṭobās saw this.

He let the woman leave. Then Bhaṭobās asked, "Gaurāï, what did you present her with?"

"Just some *mānḍā*s."

Bhaṭobās said, "But I had already had her paid four *rukā*s. Why did you give her *mānḍā*s? If my Mahātmās had eaten them, they would have been better able to remember God."

Addendum: Then from then on she would not give anyone anything without asking [Bhaṭobās].

111. When Kesobā asks [Bhaṭobās] about his oaths, he explains them.

Sometimes Bhaṭobās would swear by Māhādāïsẽ, or by the five *gurus*.[174] On one such occasion, Kesobās asked, "Why do you swear by Rūpai and by the five *gurus*?"

Bhaṭobās answered, "Once the Gosāvī said to me,[175] 'I will make Vānares my deputy *(adhikaraṇ)*. [Through him,] five or six[176] will be given enlightenment. One or two will get it from me, and five or six from Vānarā.'

"At that, I said, 'What is this? One or two will get it from the Gosāvī, and five or six from me?'

"And the Gosāvī said, 'What? Are you the giver of enlightenment? God (Parameśvar) is the giver of enlightenment. A *jīva* gives [only] the syllables.[177] For this is the lineage of Acyut.'[178]

"That is why I swear by the line of *gurus*.

"And Rūpai brought me from Bhānkheḍe, and she carried me on her back, and she took me to have the sight *(darśan)* of Śrīprabhu. She dressed me and covered me: she took such trouble for me."[179]

Addendum: "The Gosāvī had entrusted her to me.[180]

"That is why I swear by Rūpai."

With that, Kesobās kept silent.

112. During his wandering, Vināyakbās talks with a sympathizer['s wife].

Vināyakdā was Bhaṭobās' disciple. He was extremely detached and dispassionate. One day he asked Bhaṭobās' permission and set out to wander. In the course of his wandering, he went to beg at the house of someone who sympathized with the order *(mārgīcā anukuḷ)*. He asked about him but he was not in town.

The man's wife was at home. She had no decent clothes to wear. Her baby was lying on the rough wood of its cradle. It was crying. Nothing would quiet it.

She saw Vināyakbās. And immediately she prostrated herself to him in her ragged clothes. Vināyakbās asked about the sympathizer. She said that he had gone out of town.

"Why is the baby crying?"

She said, "It's on the rough surface of the cradle; that's why it's crying."

Then Vināyakbās gave her the food from his begging bag, and he gave her a cloth he had to put under the baby. And it stopped crying.

And he left. He finished begging. He ate at the river.

Bhaṭobās heard about this. The whole community of disciples heard about it. They were all amazed. Bhaṭobās was delighted.

113. Narendrabās meets him and becomes a disciple.

Narendrakavi, Sālkavi, and Nṛsiṃhakavi[181] were brothers. Nṛsiṃhakavi wrote *Nalopākhyān*. Sālkavi wrote *Rāmāyaṇ*.[182] They recited their compositions to King Rāmdev.[183]

Narendrakavi was sitting there. He had received instruction from Bhaṭobās. After he had listened to everything, he said, "If you would describe Rām's[184] court in Dvārkā this well, you would atone for your sins."

He rebuked them this way before the king. [The king] said, "You write a poem. Let's see how well you can do."

So Narendrabās accepted the challenge and wrote the 1800-verse work *Rukmiṇī Svayaṃvar.*[185] When he had written it, he recited it before the king in [his brothers'] presence.

As he was reciting, he came to the verse,[186]

> The seven seas could not bear the heat of God's majesty.
> In fear they receded, and gave up Dvārāvatī as tribute.

Then the king said, "Give me the authorship of this work. I will present you with as many *sonṭak*s and four-layered *āsūs*[187] as there are verses.

Narendrabās said, "No, King. That would tarnish the reputation of our community of poets."

And [the king's] pride was taken away. The king was very astonished.

Then Narendrakavi brought *Rukmiṇī Svayaṃvar* to Bhaṭobās. He met Bhaṭobās. Immediately he took initiation.

Then, from that time on, the work *Rukmiṇī Svayaṃvar* came to belong to the order *(mārg)*.

Some time after Bhaṭobās' death, when Ānobās' [disciple] Haragarva[188] had taken initiation, he heard all this and said, "This poet is more clever than all other poets." Then he himself composed the poem *Gadya.*[189]

114. He praises Kāḷe Kṛṣṇabhaṭ when he sings a song.

Once Kāḷe Kṛṣṇabhaṭ composed some verses *(dasāṅk)* about Uddhavdev going to check up on [the cowherd women in] Gokūḷ. He recited the verses to Bhaṭobās. They were as follows:

1. As the women watched Śrī Uddhavdev, the bearer of gracious gifts,
they were confused for a moment when they saw [Kṛṣṇa's] clothes.
Their face lotuses wilted in their burning grief at separation.
Impatient for Kṛṣṇa, the bevy of *gopīs* spoke.

Refrain: "Why has our beloved Kṛṣṇa abandoned us?," said the young women.
"Why do you check up on us now? Bring Kṛṣṇa to us, Uddhav.

2. "We always remember Gokūḷ, our brothers, companions, the cowherds.
We are Devakī's maidservants; we never forget Govind.
Murārī will abandon us. Gopāl[190] will marry
beautiful women accomplished in all the arts, the daughters of kings.

3. "Without Kṛṣṇa, sandalwood paste and the moon[191] only burn.
Whenever we see Vṛndāvan,[192] we remember [him] all the more.
His merciful glances are meant for afflicted souls (*jīvas*).
To whom can we make our complaint about that beloved one?

4. "We gave up our work for his sake, and danced the *rās*[193] in Vṛndāvan.
How can the pain of remembering that night be expressed? The sight of Kṛṣṇa will take it away.
To whom, generous one, can we express our hearts' anguish?
Don't you know, you omniscient one, who are kind to sufferers and generous?

5. "When will we meet that god? This puts us in a state of misery.
We can tell this to no one but you, a devotee.
May he be everything to our minds and our voices. Our mind is forever attracted.

Put aside this philosophical knowledge *(brahmajñān),* put it aside.
What are you telling us, most excellent *munī*?

6. "Kṛṣṇa is a brother without motive, the giver to those who long, the life of the soul *(jīva).*
Ask the king of the Yādavs[194] to give us his presence.
Tell Gopāl this: that we live in hope that he will return to ask after us—
otherwise we will give up our lives."

7. Hearing this request, Uddhav set off quickly.
Seeing their bodies all tormented by separation from Kṛṣṇa,
he said, "These young women are lucky. How in love they are! What good fortune!"
Praising their loving faith *(bhāv),* holding God in his heart,
[Uddhav] reached the town of Mathurā.

8. He too longed fiercely to see Kṛṣṇanāth.
He would not have spent a moment apart from him, but his orders were firm.
As god and his devotee met, all [other] pleasures were dwarfed.
The love in their hearts was not of this world. How can I describe it, O Mother?

9. Anxious for his *darśan,* in love with his feet, Uddhav came near to [Kṛṣṇa].
With his eyes he saw [Kṛṣṇa], a mass of power, full of bliss.
Embracing Nāgdev's patron,[195] the lord of all,
that servant forgot himself in supreme bliss.

When [Kāḷe Kṛṣṇabhaṭ] had sung these verses, Bhaṭobās, delighted, said, "Kṛṣṇa, were you there at the time?"

115. He tells Bāïdevbās to direct his wandering to the holy places.

Once when Bāïdevbās set out to wander, Bhaṭobās said, "Bāïdev, you should direct your wandering to the holy places (*sthān*s). You should bow to all the places." He made this rule.

Then Bāïdevbās set out to wander, bowing to the holy places as he went.

116. Keśavācārya is defeated by Kavīśvar in argument.

One day Kavīśvarbās went to the river; on the way he met his former *guru,* Keśavācārya. They recognized each other. [Keśavācārya] stopped and said sharply to Kavīśvar, "If you are so learned, why did you leave me and go to Nāgdevbhaṭ? Have you grown a third horn?"[196]

Kavīśvarbās said, "Why don't you see for yourself whether or not I have grown a third horn?"

Keśavācārya said, "How did you grow one?"

So an argument started. Kesavācārya was silenced. All his arguments were refuted.

Then finally, on the spur of the moment, Kavīśvarbās composed an extemporaneous verse propounding devotion *(bhakti)*. Kavīśvarbās said:

> O mind *(cetas)*, think of the one who is beyond consciousness, the destroyer of worry, the vivifier of consciousness, made of consciousness.
> O mind *(manas)*, let go of delusion, which is the great well created in the mind, beyond the beyond, the inner sheath, an unsheathed heap of sheathes, the uprooting of the root of good.
> [Think of] Cakreśvar, the supreme one who gives life to the soul *(jīva)*, the one who gives birth to the world.[197]

Hearing this, Keśavācārya said, "Yes, you have grown a third horn. Now come on, let's go to Nāgdevbhaṭ. You ask him, and then I too will take initiation as an ascetic."

Kavīśvarbās agreed to that. The two of them set out.

117. And, at [Kavīśvarbās'] request, Bhaṭobās initiates [Keśavācārya] as an ascetic.

Then Kavīśvarbās brought him to Bhaṭobās. He told him everything that had happened. He had him prostrate himself to Bhaṭobās.

Then Kavīśvarbās made a request of Bhaṭobās. "Bhaṭ, Keśavācārya says, 'I will take initiation as an ascetic.' So you should give him initiation."

Bhaṭobās said, "I don't want him, Bhaṭ.[198] He is not qualified."

Kavīśvar said, "Bhaṭ, do it for me." So Bhaṭobās gave [Keśavācārya] instruction and initiated him as an ascetic.

118. And [Bhaṭobās] takes the supreme *dharma* away from him.

Then Bhaṭobās gave Keśavācārya some [relics] to reverence.

One day, when [Bhaṭobās] was teaching him "Mahāvākya,"[199] he said, "Bhaṭ, if you think about it, this fits in with our [Brāhmaṇical] tuft and thread."[200]

Bhaṭobās said, "Burn up your topknot and thread! Burn it up! Throw it in water! You go away now. Give me my things." And he took back the [relics] he had given him to reverence. Then he dismissed him.

He left. As he was leaving, Keśavācārya said, "Bhaṭ, you have taken this away. But now how will you take away what is in my heart?"

Bhaṭobās said, "The one who identifies himself with me[201] will take it away."

Then [Keśavācārya] left.

Addendum: Later that is exactly what happened to him.[202]

119. During a discussion with a paṇḍit, [Bhaṭobās] reveals that [Kavīśvarbās] is Bhānu from Borī.

One day when Bhaṭobās was sitting there, a paṇḍit came along. He began to have a discussion with Bhaṭobās. In the course of the discussion the man said to Bhaṭobās, "That is not right. It cannot be."

Meanwhile, Kavīśvarbās was a little way off, sewing his shirt. The man had not even noticed him. From there, Kavīśvarbās said, "How can it not be?"

The paṇḍit looked at him and said, "What do you know about it?"

And Bhaṭobās said, "How can he not know about it? Isn't he Bhānu from Borī? You should talk with him."

So he began to have a discussion with Kavīśvarbās. And Kavīśvarbās silenced him and refuted his arguments.

Addendum: And he was amazed.

120. He tells Kavīśvar not to evoke the emotions of Purāṇic stories (*kathās*) elsewhere, but to expound the *Bhāgavata* in his presence.

One day Kavīśvar was sitting right at the side of the river. (*Addendum:* He was reciting something—to whom is not known. But he was expounding a Sanskrit text.) And one after another, people were drawn to him. He evoked intense emotion. The whole town was attracted.

Someone came and told Bhaṭobās. Bhaṭobās said, "What has happened to this Bhaṭ? Go and call him here," and he sent the man to summon him. He brought him back.

[Kavīśvar] came. Then Bhaṭobās said, "Bhaṭ, if you are addicted to [lecturing], then explain the *Śrī Bhāgavata*[203] or the *Gītā*[204] to me."

Kavīśvar agreed. So from then on, Kavīśvarbās gave Bhaṭobās a lyrical *(rasvṛtī)* exposition of the *Śrī Bhāgavata.* It melted Bhaṭobās' heart, and turned it completely to nectar.[205]

121. And he allows Haribhaṭ to expound the *Gītā.*

Kavīśvarbās finished expounding the *Śrī Bhāgavata.* Then he said to Bhaṭobās, "Bhaṭ, now may I expound the *Gītā?*"

Bhaṭobās replied, "Bhaṭ, don't you expound it now. When you speak, my heart turns completely to nectar."

Kavīśvarbās said, "So may I have this Hari expound it?"

Bhaṭobās agreed. Then Kavīśvarbās said to Vāṅkle Haribhaṭ, "Hari, now you expound the *Gītā.*"

So Vāṅkle Haribās expounded the *Gītā.* He too was learned, but his speech was a bit rough, and he was less lyrical. Fewer of the disciples came to listen to him.

122. When he sees how handsome Kavīśvar is, he tells him what kind of clothes to wear.

Kavīśvarbās was handsome. When he wore a sewn inner shirt and a shawl over it, he would look all the more handsome. Seeing that, one day Bhaṭobās said, "Bhaṭ, wrap yourself in a garment with unhemmed ends. You look too good."

So Kavīśvarbās got rid of his sewn shirt and wore a patched cloth wrapped around his shoulders. He wholeheartedly agreed with this. He was happy.

123. When he hears Māhādāï sing *ovīs*, he says that Rūpai's speech is that of a Siddha.

One day—it is not known on what occasion—Māhādāïsẽ sang some *ovīs*. Māhādāïsẽ said,

> 1. King Cakradhar placed his hand on Nāgdev's shoulder,[206]
> and went away.
>
> 2. Wearing a silk garment with golden threads, knotted in the fashion
> of a wrestler,
> Mhāïyā came to meet [Śrī]prabhu.[207]

Bhaṭobās heard her and said, "A Nāth speaks like a Nāth, and Rūpai speaks like a Siddha."[208] Bhaṭobās praised her in this way.

124. He admonishes Keśav and Paṇḍit for having a discussion inappropriate to a time of solitude.

One day Keśav, Paṇḍit, and others were sitting in solitude. Bhaṭobās came to check up on their solitude, to see who was doing what kind of religious exercise. Paṇḍit and Kesobās were sitting in solitude having a lively discussion, with much give and take, in the early morning. They did not even see that Bhaṭobās had arrived, so engrossed were they in their conversation.

Seeing that, Bhaṭobās did not approve. Bhaṭobās said, "How can you argue with each other all the time? If you just have discussions all the time, when will you think of God?" He admonished them this way.

Addendum: Then he instructed them; he told them to do religious practices appropriate to the time of day.

125. He explains that offering a grain of food in a mendicant's bowl is the same as offering a mountain of food.

One day—it is not known on what occasion—Bhaṭobās said, "Can anything done for this order *(mārg)* be a waste? For some it will lead to devotion *(bhakti);* for some it will lead to knowledge; for others it will lead to dispassion *(vairāgya).* How is that? By offering a single grain of food in these mendicants' bowls, one gets the benefit of giving a mountain of food.[209] How so? Because the Gosāvī said to Dāïmbā: 'Bhojā, I cannot express the greatness of someone who contemptuously tosses a few grains of food into your begging bowl.' "[210]

In this way he explained the greatness of the order *(margmāhātmya)* and the greatness of food offerings *(bhajanmāhātmya)*.[211]

126. When a Brāhmaṇ hears him called Bhaṭ, he does away with his ignorance.

One day Bhaṭobās was sitting there. A Brāhmaṇ was sitting nearby. [The disciples] were saying to Bhaṭobās, "Bhaṭ, how is this? Bhaṭ, how is that? Bhaṭ, may we do this? May we not do that?" In this way they would ask Bhaṭobās about whatever they wanted to do.

Hearing that, the Brāhmaṇ said, "Your disciples call you Bhaṭ. Why don't they say, 'Bhaṭ, Lord'?"

Bhaṭobās replied, "I myself tell them to address me that way."

"Why is that?"

" 'Lord, Lord' should be used only for God (Īśvar). It cannot be used for a *jīva.*"

And the man remained silent.

127. After forbidding a lay disciple to drink the water from washing his feet, [Bhaṭobās] accepts his retort.

One day a certain lay disciple washed Bhaṭobās' feet and drank the water. Seeing that, Bhaṭobās said, "You should drink the water from washing only God's feet. And you should eat only God's leftovers as *prasād.*"[212]

The man said, "Yes, Bhaṭ. It is as God's that I am taking it."

Bhaṭobās remained silent.

128. He disparages himself when he is paid special homage.

Bhaṭobās did not allow people to make prostrations to him or to place their heads on his feet. Disciples would do this, but he would disapprove and say, "You should prostrate yourself this way to the Gosāvī's holy feet. You should not do this to me."

He would disparage himself this way.

129. When a stranger asks him, he says that he is essentially a devotee.

One day when Bhaṭobās was sitting there, a stranger came to have his *darśan.* He asked Bhaṭobās, "Bhaṭ, are you God (Īśvar)?"

Bhaṭobās said, "No. I am a devotee of God."

With that, the man kept silent.

130. When Paṇḍit questions him after he has scorned Ākāī's homage, he accepts her objection to his rule.

One day when Bhaṭobās was sitting there, Ākāïsē arrived. She bowed to him repeatedly, and then, absentmindedly, she placed her head on Bhaṭobās' feet and prostrated herself lovingly to him.

Bhaṭobās said, "Ākāï, don't prostrate yourself to me this way. I have told you over and over again not to do this, but you keep on doing it." And he got angry. He threw her out.

The next day she returned. She bowed to him, and went and sat down near Paṇḍitbās. Softly she said to Paṇḍitbās, "Paṇḍit, religion *(dharma)* means going toward God, but Bhaṭ gets upset when we do homage to him. Though I [try to] do what is right, I end up doing wrong, and that makes me sinful. So ask Bhaṭ, 'May we or may we not do homage to Lord Cakradhar's connection *(sambandh)* [with him]?' "[213]

So Paṇḍitbās said to Bhaṭobās, "Ākāïsẽ says, 'Religion means going toward God, but Bhaṭ gets upset when we do homage to him. . . . So may we do homage to Lord Cakradhar's connection [with you]?' This is what she asks."

Then Bhaṭobās said, "You may."

So she came and prostrated herself to Bhaṭobās.

131. Kesobās disciplines Vaṅki when Kaṭak Demāïsẽ arranges their meeting.

Once Kesobās went to meet Kaṭak Demāïsẽ. He met her. Kaṭak Demāïsẽ invited Kesobās for a meal, and, without letting Kesobās know, she also invited Vaṅki. He was a fellow disciple of Demāïsẽ's: both of them had previously received instruction from Nāthobā; and then, when Bhaṭobās came, the two of them had prostrated themselves to Bhaṭobās.[214]

But Vaṅki had many vices. He behaved in a wayward manner. The disciples would not greet him. But Demāïsẽ still had affection for him. So she secretly invited him as well.

Then, when it was time for the meal, Demāïsẽ asked Kesobās, "Keśobā, may I invite Vaṅki to eat in the same row with you?"

Kesobās said, "No. He has many vices."

Demāïsẽ kept quiet. Then she prepared a plate for Kesobās inside her house. Kesobās sat down to eat. And she invited Vaṅki to eat too, and served him on a leaf plate in the cattle shed.

Inside, Demāïsẽ prostrated herself to Kesobās, and then she came outside and asked Vaṅki too to start eating. Then she rushed inside.

As he took his first bite, Vaṅki said, "Śrī Cakradhar!"

Kesobās heard this and said, "Who said the Gosāvī's name here?"

Demāïsẽ said, "If you promise not to get angry, I'll tell you."

"All right. Tell me."

"Bhaṭobās said, 'In this world, is God (Īśvar) hard to find, or is someone who remembers God hard to find?'[215] That's why I invited Vaṅki without telling you."

Then Kesobās said, "You did right, Demāïsẽ. Now go and invite him in."

She went. She invited him in. Vaṅki smeared his body with cow dung and mud, and prostrated himself to Kesobās, [saying], "Forgive me for everything."

Kesobās said, "You are forgiven. Now from now on restrict your future behavior and repent for the past. Don't associate with adulterers or with those who practice the seven vices. Do not stand near them."

Saying, "All right," Vaṅki agreed. He prostrated himself again. Then Kesobās allowed him to eat in the same row with him. Demāïsẽ was pleased.

Then from then on Vaṅki gave up all his vices.

Addendum: Then Kesobās came and told Bhaṭobās everything that had happened. Then one day Vaṅki came too. He took initiation as an ascetic from Bhaṭobās, and became a disciple.

132. When he tells Demāïsẽ that she should not go to Ujjain, and explains how to be a follower, he tells her about the renewed meeting [with God].

Once bards came from Ujjain to Kaṭak Devgiri. They met Demāïsẽ. They spoke to Demāïsẽ; they pronounced the Gosāvī's name and said, "The Gosāvī is in Ujjain."[216]

Then Demāïsẽ said to herself, "Now I will go and tell this to Bhaṭobās. I will take initiation as an ascetic, and I will go to Ujjain." So she arranged all her affairs and came to Bhaṭobās. She met him. As soon as she arrived, she told him what had happened, and said, "So, Bhaṭ, I will go there."

Bhaṭobās replied, "What will you do when you get there?"

She said, "Why, Bhaṭ?"

Bhaṭobās said, "No, you won't meet him. When the Gosāvī was [here], Rūpai[217] asked the Gosāvī, 'If you are leaving, Lord Gosāvī, after how long will you let us meet you again, Lord?'

"The Gosāvī replied, 'My woman, now you will not meet me in this [form]. Now you will meet me in a new [form].'[218]

"Rūpai said, 'How is that, Lord?'

"The Gosāvī said, 'If you do what I have said, you will be born as a man in the home of happy, rich people. Then after twelve years I will meet you anew.'[219] This is what the Gosāvī explained to her. So what he said to her is the same thing he says now to those who do not have his presence. Whether he said it with his own holy mouth or said it through a deputy *(adhikārdvārẽ),* they should accept it. Then he will meet them anew."

And with that, Demāïsẽ accepted it. She prostrated herself to him.

133. And she becomes a follower.

Then Demāïsẽ asked Bhaṭ, "Bhaṭ, now give me initiation as an ascetic." Bhaṭobās agreed. So Demāïsẽ became a follower. She took initiation as an ascetic. She became an ascetic.

Addendum: She became a follower—it is not known whether on that same occasion when she came [to see Bhaṭobās] or at some other time.

Then the group of disciples [began] to call her Demāïsē from Kaṭak.

134. And he sends her to Kaṭak to disarm criticism.

After Demāïsē had taken initiation, she was criticized a great deal in her hometown. Hearing that, one day Bhaṭobās said, "Demāyā, you go and show yourself in your hometown. Go on. Your relatives are criticizing you."

She agreed. Then she went to Kaṭak and showed herself to everyone. Then, seeing her firmness in religious practice *(ācār)*, they came to have a high opinion, a good opinion of her.

Addendum: She stayed there this way until their doubts were removed.

Then she came to Bhaṭobās. Bhaṭobās was pleased.

135. And he forbids [her] to force tasty food onto an immature [ascetic] at mealtime.

Addendum: One day Demāïsē invited the mendicants for a meal. She served everything, and then poured sumptuous amounts of ghee over it. She forced it on those who refused it. This is what she always did.

Then one day Bhaṭobās said, "Demāï, you [should not] force ghee this way on anyone at all. Some who are immature [in asceticism] may not want to eat or drink it. When such a one turns against you, then who will protect you?"

And she was frightened.

Addendum: In this way Bhaṭobās stated the distinction between mature and immature ascetics (*puruṣas*) with respect to serving them food.

After that she no longer did what she had been doing.

136. When he looks at the food she has gotten while begging, he talks about the hot and the cold.

One day Demāïsē returned from begging. She had her begging bag purified by Bhaṭobās' glance.[220] Bhaṭobās looked into the begging bag. Half of the food she had received as alms was warm, and half of it was cold.

Seeing that, Bhaṭobās said, "Demāï, use the hot food, and save the cold. The cold is cold today, and it will be just as cold tomorrow."

Addendum: That is what she did. She was a bit fastidious [about food]. He said this because he knew she could not swallow [stale food].

137. When Remāïsē becomes a disciple, he gives her the name "Princess."

Remāïsē was Bhaṭobās' disciple. Her blood relatives were in Rāmpurī, and her in-laws were from Kheḍ.

One day her husband beat her. Her husband was a devotee of Nṛsiṃha. That same night [Nṛsiṃha] appeared to him in a dream. He said, "Hey, why did you beat her? She is a princess! Now you will live [only] one more year, and then she will become a Mahātmī.

Then the next morning he got up and told his parents. After that he lived only one more year. Then Remāïsē came to Rāmpurī; from there she came to Bhaṭobās. She took initiation as an ascetic, and then she told him everything that had happened, including the dream.

Hearing that, Bhaṭobās said to everyone, "Call her 'Princess Remāïsē.' " So from then on they called her "Princess Remāïsē."

138. And when she has prepared Vāṅkuḍe Dāïmbhaṭ by arguing with him, Bhaṭobās gives him initiation as an ascetic.

One day Princess Remāïsē went to Taḍasmukh to go begging. In the course of her begging, she went to Paṇḍit Vāṅkuḍe Dāïmbhaṭ's house. Boys were studying there. They said to Remāïsē, "O Mahātmā, spread out this bundle of grass for the calves. Then we will give you alms. Otherwise we can't give you anything."

She said, "Why can't you give me anything?"

The boys said, "You have not received the initiation *(upadeśu)* that we have."

Remāïsē said, "Have the sparrows to whom you give water received the initiation that you have?"

They replied, "If that is how you feel about it, why do you come to our door?"

Remāïsē said, "The god whose order *(mārg)* this is said, 'If you want food, go to a Brāhmaṇ's house; if you want shoes, go to a leatherworker's house.' "

And with that they kept silent.

Vāṅkuḍe Dāïmbās was sitting there. He heard everything.

Then Remāïsē did her begging and came to the river. She completed the whole ritual [of eating]. At that point, Vāṅkuḍe Dāïmbhaṭ came along. He sat down and asked Remāïsē, "Mother, what god's order *(mārg)* is this?"

Remāïsē said, "It is that of the God who is the supreme one *(parameś-varu)* above all."

Then Vāṅkuḍe said, "Can he not be reached by performing regular and occasional works *(nitya naimityaka karma)*?"

Remāïsē said, "There are four kinds of works: regular *(nitya),* occasional *(naimityaka),* optional *(kāmya)* and forbidden *(niṣedhē).* Of these, the regular and occasional are used up in getting rid of daily sins. The optional are used up when they have borne fruit. The forbidden are used up in going to hell. So tell me, what works are there to offer to God (Īśvar)?"

And [Vāṅkuḍe Dāïmbhaṭ] was silent. Then he said, "It is true. I have realized that I do not see any works to offer to God." Then he said to Remāïsẽ, "So, mother, tell me this. How does one reach Him?"

Remāïsẽ replied, "That I do not know. Bhaṭobās knows that."

He said, "Where is he?"

"He is in Nimbā."

"In that case, now *you* please tell me." And he prostrated himself and took her to his house.

Then after four days, seeing his determination, Remāïsẽ told him about the religion *(dharma).* Then she brought him to Bhaṭobās. They met. She told [Bhaṭobās] everything that had happened. Then [Vāṅkuḍe Dāïmbhaṭ] took initiation as an ascetic.

139. Mhāībhaṭ is distressed when he realizes that it is Gadonāyak whom he has seen in the course of his wanderings.

One day Mhāībhaṭ had gone out to wander. He was sitting in solitude somewhere. Gadonāyak[221] was passing along the road, and saw him from a distance. And he got down from his horse. He prostrated himself completely to Mhāībhaṭ, and asked, "Who are you, Mahātmā?"

But Mhāībhaṭ did not break his silence. And Gadonāyak prostrated himself and left. Mhāībhaṭ did not recognize Gadonāyak.

Then [Mhāībhaṭ] saw his attendant coming along behind him. And he went up to him and asked, "Who is that?"

He said, "That is Gado the treasurer."

At that, Mhāībhaṭ felt distressed. And he began to say, "Oh, dear! What a sinner I am! If I had spoken with him, I could have asked him about the Gosāvī's *līḷā*s."[222]

Then Mhāībhaṭ spoke an aphorism:

> "You should do nothing without looking into it.
> You should act after a full investigation.
> Afterwards comes remorse—
> as in the case of the Brahmaṇ woman and the mongoose."[223]

He said this, then kept quiet.

140. And, after hearing God's (Īśvar's) *līḷā*s, [Mhāībhaṭ] accepts relic water and then a meal from Kheibhaṭ.

Similarly, in the course of his wanderings, Mhāībhaṭ went to Kheibhaṭ's village. He met him there. Mhāībhaṭ's purpose was to discover *līḷā*s of the Gosāvī.

Kheibhaṭ would go to work in his fields. Mhāībhaṭ would go along with him. Kheibhaṭ would do his farming, and Mhāībhaṭ would follow along with him, asking him about the Gosāvī's *līḷās*. Kheibhaṭ would tell them to him, and Mhāībhaṭ would accept them with reverence. Then he would go begging and eat his meal. He would take no food from [Kheibhaṭ].

One day Mhāībhaṭ said, "Kheibhaṭ, wash the bread relic *(prasādācī roṭī)* that you have, and give me the water to drink."

[Kheibhaṭ] replied, "If you will accept some food from me, I will give you the water to drink."

Then Mhāībhaṭ said, "I will accept it."

Then he washed the bread relic and gave the water to Mhāībhaṭ to drink. Then Mhāībhaṭ accepted some food from him. Then he set out and came to Bhaṭobās.

141. When he hears the *līḷās* from Mhāībhaṭ, Bhaṭ tells him to verify the *līḷās*.

Then Mhāībhaṭ told Bhaṭobās everything that had happened. They discussed the *līḷās* of the Gosāvī that Mhāībhaṭ had collected. Bhaṭobās approved the ones that were correct; of those that were wrong, he said, "These are not the words of his holy mouth. These are."

Then he said to Mhāībhaṭ, "Ask Upādhye about the ones that Upādhye experienced; ask Nātho about the ones that Nātho experienced; ask Sādhē about the ones that Sādhē experienced." In this way, Bhaṭobās commanded Mhāībhaṭ to ask only the person who had experienced each *līḷā* about it.

So Mhāībhaṭbās did this, and then he discussed them with Bhaṭobās in the same way as before. Then he divided them into two parts, "Uttarārdha" and "Pūrvārdha."[224]

142. And [Bhaṭobās] says that [Mhāībhaṭ] did wrong in rejecting Sāraṅgpaṇḍit's meal of rice pudding.

Once Mhāībhaṭ went to Pratiṣṭhān[225] in search of *līḷās*. He met Sāraṅgpaṇḍit.[226] [Sāraṅgpaṇḍit] invited him for a meal.

Mhāībhaṭ replied, "First tell me the Gosāvī's *līḷās*; then I will eat."

While [Sāraṅgpaṇḍit] first told him *līḷās* of the Gosāvī, Umāïsē prepared all the food, with rice pudding as the main dish.

She prepared a plate for Mhāībhaṭ. When [Sāraṅgpaṇḍit] invited him to start eating, Mhāībhaṭ said, "If you will serve me the Gosāvī's sweet-ball relic *(prasādācā lāḍu),* I will eat the meal."

So Umāïsē crumbled the Gosāvī's sweet-ball relic, and sprinkled it over the rice pudding. Then Mhāībhaṭ picked out the bits of sweet ball and ate them. He ate two bites of the top of the rice pudding.

And then, pretending that he had to vomit, he got up from his place. He went begging and then ate at the river.

Then he came to see Bhaṭobās. He told him everything that had happened. And Bhaṭobās said, "You did wrong, Mhāībhaṭ."

143. When Mhāībhaṭ asks about the validity of nondualism,[227] [Bhaṭobās] says that activity begins with God.[228]

144. And Bhaṭ says that he forgot to ask the Gosāvī about inappropriate religious exercises.

Both of these chapters (*smṛtis*) are in the version of Kavībās.

145. Kāmāïsẽ from Bhadra meets him and receives instruction.

Kāmāïsẽ from Bhadra was King Rāmdev's[229] queen. Her dealings were with Ānobās. She was always listening to Purāṇa recitals. Ānobās would argue with the Purāṇa reciter.

At that time [Ānobās] was a lay disciple; his name at that time was Gopāḷpaṇḍit.

The Purāṇa reciter would not be able to answer Gopāḷpaṇḍit's arguments, and that would amaze him. Then he would ask him, "How [can] this [be refuted], Paṇḍit?"

Then Ānobās would answer [his own] argument.

Kāmāïsẽ would notice this, and say, "Paṇḍit, how do you know this?"

He would say, "I have a *guru* to instruct me."

Then one day she asked, "Where is your *guru*?"

He said, "He is in Nimbā, near Mudgal."

Then one day Kāmāïsẽ asked the king, "[Pilgrimage to] Mudgal gives sons to barren women. So may I go there?"

The king said, "Go ahead."

So Kāmāïsẽ made her preparations and said to Gopāḷpaṇḍit, "Paṇḍit, give me a note introducing me to Bhaṭobās."

So Gopāḷpaṇḍit gave her an enthusiastic letter.

Then she came to Nimbā. She handed the note to Bhaṭobās. Bhaṭobās looked at it. Then he gave Kāmāïsẽ instruction.

She was there for a couple of days; then she left.

As she was leaving, she said, "Bhaṭ, I will come again."

Bhaṭobās said, "Do not come without asking [your husband]. Come if the king allows you to come. Otherwise we will keep in touch through letters."

And with that, she left.

146. And when she arrives, he reveals where her toe ring is.

King Rāmdev became a member *(upadeśīya)* of a certain sect *(mārg)*.[230] Afterwards Kāmāïsẽ asked the king, "Then may I make the charismatic *(vedhavantī)* Nāgdevbhaṭ my *guru*?"

The king said, "Go ahead."

Then she came back to Nimbā. Bhaṭobās was not in the temple [where he was staying]. He had gone off to be in solitude. She came straight [to where he was]. She greeted Bhaṭobās. She sat down.

A golden toe ring had fallen off her foot along the way. When she sat down in front of him, she did not see the ring on her toe. And she held that toe in her hand.

Bhaṭobās saw that, and said, "What, have you lost your toe ring?"

She said, "Yes. Let it go."

Bhaṭobās said, "Why let it go? Go on. It has fallen in a wheelcart rut near the Gaṇeś temple. Send your trusted servant. He will bring it."

She sent her trusted servant. It was there, just where [Bhaṭobās] had said.

Kāmāïsẽ said, "Bhaṭ, how did you know?"

Bhaṭobās said, "I knew by the grace of Śrī Cakradhar."

Kāmāïsẽ was very surprised. Then Bhaṭobās went with her to the place where he was staying.

147. And when he is asked about recollection *(smaraṇ)*, he explains that the name Pratiṣṭhān is to be remembered.

This title [is found in the version of] Kavibās. The chapter about this is not available.

148. And he refuses her initiation as an ascetic.

One day Kāmāïsẽ asked Bhaṭobās, "Bhaṭ, may I take initiation as an ascetic?"

Bhaṭobās said, "You may not take initiation."

"Why is that?"

"The land that the Gosāvī told us to stay in[231] belongs to [your husband,] the king.[232] And we cannot go to lands that have been forbidden to us.[233] So I cannot let you take initiation."

Kāmāïsẽ kept silent.

149. And he tells her not to enter fire of her own accord.

After that Kāmāïsẽ spoke again: "Bhaṭ, the king will die, and they will throw me into the cremation fire."

Bhaṭobās said, "But you must avoid [entering it] of your own accord."

"Then they will throw me in by force."

"Still you won't go to the hell reserved for those who commit suicide."

With that, she kept silent.

Then she gave Bhaṭobās a certain kind of food that she had brought. Then she took his leave and went home.

Then, some time later, the king died. And they did just what she had said they would. In many ways she tried to avoid her previous duty. But they forced her into it.[234]

150. And, when he hears that she has entered fire, he explains about God's gifts.

Then Bhaṭobās heard all about it. *Addendum:* The group of disciples of the five *gurus*[235] was very sad. Some of them asked Bhaṭobās, "Bhaṭ, since Kāmāïsē died this way, in agony, what happened to her?"

Then Bhaṭobās had a discussion about religion *(dharmavārtā).* Bhaṭobās said, "If one has attraction *(vedhu)* and enlightenment *(bodhu),* and a strong desire to become a disciple, then one will get the knowledge of the body."[236]

Addendum: "If one's discipleship is obstructed by some problem, one will still get God (Īśvar).

"If one has attraction and enlightenment, but not the strong desire to become a disciple, the world will become empty (for one)."

Addendum: "But one will get the reward of enlightenment, and one will still have the joy of having maintained the enlightenment.

"If one has no enlightenment, but does have a strong desire for discipleship, one will be born as a son. . . .[237] Then God (Īśvar) will give one knowledge *(jñān).*"

Addendum: "He will come greatly to one's help and liberate one."

Bhaṭobās taught this way on the subject of Kāmāïsē.

151. When Pāṭhak's son comes, [Bhaṭobās] tells him where Pāṭhak is.

Once Pāṭhak from Seigāv took initiation as an ascetic from Bhaṭ. Then he went to another area to wander. He went toward the region of Meghaṅkar.

The official of Seigāv heard that Pāṭhak had taken initiation as an ascetic. Still, he would not transfer [Pāṭhak's] hereditary income *(vṛti)* to his son. He said to him, "Go and bring him here. Then I will transfer it."

[Pāṭhak's son] said, "All right," and came to Nimbā. He told Bhaṭobās the whole situation, [and said], "So, Bhaṭ, you should send him."

Bhaṭobās said, "Go to Loṇār. He is doing his religious exercises there."

[The son] came directly to Loṇār. He met [his father] and told him everything, [and said], "So, Pāṭhak, come there."

Pāṭhak replied, "Whether he transfers it to you or not, I cannot go [back to my earlier] connections. Go away."

So he went to the village. He told the headman everything, and said, "He refuses to come."

Then the headman said, "He is firm in his resolve. If he had come, I would not have transferred the hereditary income to you. Now I will definitely transfer it."

And he transferred his hereditary income.

152. He admonishes Dīṇḍorī Gondobā for improperly accepting money.

Then, some time later, Dīṇḍorī Gondobā took initiation as an ascetic from Bhaṭobās. Then one day Gondobā heard that his mother and father had died, and he went directly from where he was to his home village. There he took his share of the inheritance from his brother. And he came to see Bhaṭobās.

Addendum: Bhaṭobās would not embrace him. Bhaṭobās said, "Oh, why have you put out your hand to accept vomit?"

Addendum: "You have picked up again the same thing you had given up as feces."[238]

Bhaṭobās admonished him this way. The whole group of disciples also admonished him.

Addendum: Then he went back and gave up [the money], and [his brother] accepted it.

153. When a Brāhmaṇ asks, [Bhaṭobās] says [that he gives his relic ring] food and water.

One day in the cold season Bhaṭobās had eaten his meal in the early morning. He was sitting down. In front of Bhaṭobās was a pan of hot coals. He was warming his hands over it. On Bhaṭobās' hand he was wearing a ring made of metal[239] that had come into contact [with the Gosāvī]. A grain of rice had stuck to the ring.

A certain Brāhmaṇ came to have *darśan* [of Bhaṭobās]. He bowed to Bhaṭobās and sat down. He saw the grain of rice and said, "Bhaṭ, what is that, a grain of rice?"

Bhaṭobās said, "Yes. When it needs a grain of rice, I give it a grain of rice. When it needs water, I give it water." And he poured water over his hand.

The man kept silent.

154. When he explains about the world, he talks about [why one should] study the scripture.

Someone who was ignorant asked Bhaṭobās a question: "Bhaṭ, is this world eternal or not?"

Bhaṭobās said, "It is not eternal."

With that, the man kept silent.

Then Bhaṭobās said, "If one does not study this scripture *(śāstra)* for the good of one's Self *(ātmahītākāraṇē),* one should study it at least to learn how this world is constructed."

Addendum: "But [you are] not [interested in] that either."

155. Bhānubhaṭ from Kaṭak becomes a disciple.

Bhānubhaṭ was from Kaṭak Devgiri. He received instruction from Bhaṭobās. He was very young. One day he came to Bhaṭobās. He took initiation as an ascetic. He stayed with Bhaṭobās and served him. Bhaṭobās was very friendly to him; he called him "Bhānu."

156. When [Bhānubhaṭ] makes a relic into beads, [Bhaṭobās] explains that its identity has been destroyed.

One day Bhānubhaṭ made two necklaces out of the old cot.[240] *Addendum:* One was made of [beads] shaped like *pīpaḷ* fruit, the other of round beads. And he made two fine earrings and fitted them with golden hooks. Then he brought them and handed them to Bhaṭobās. Bhaṭobās did reverence to them, and said, "Bhānu, the necklaces have come out nicely, but I don't know what will come of destroying [the cot's] identity."

Then Bhaṭobās explained the greatness of relics (*prasāds*). Bhaṭobās said, "A relic should be reverenced just as it was given by the one who gave it.[241] If the relic is dismantled, then the fact of its being a gift *(prasannatā),*[242] the fact of its being a relic *(prasādatva)* is lost; then [only] the contact *(sambandh)* [with God] remains."

In this way Bhaṭobās explained the flaw in destroying [a relic's] identity.[243] Bhānubhaṭ accepted [the teaching] with reverence.

Then Bhānubhaṭ put the necklace of *pīpaḷ*-fruit-shaped beads around Bhaṭobās' neck. He put the earrings in Bhaṭobās' ears. He put the other necklace around Sādhẽ's neck, and prostrated himself.

157. And [Bhaṭobās] has [Bhānubhaṭ] crack a betel nut.

Once Bhaṭobās had gone from Nimbā to some village—it is not known which one. As he was going along the road, he ate at a certain place. Bhānubhaṭ was with him. Bhaṭobās said, "Bhānu, crack this betel nut."

He took it. When he looked, he could not find a stone. Bhānubhaṭ said, "Bhaṭ, there's no stone. How can I crack it?"

Bhaṭobās said, "Crack it with your teeth."

"Bhaṭ, how can I crack it with my teeth? It will get polluted by my saliva *(usītẽ hoil).*"

Bhaṭobās said *(addendum):* "In service, there is no sense of saliva pollution."

So Bhānubhaṭ cracked it. Bhaṭobās took [some] as a mouth-freshener.

158. And, in making peace with [Bhānubhaṭ], he calls him his betel nut cracker.

Once Bhaṭobās got angry with Bhānubhaṭ. He said to him, "Bhānu, you go away."

He replied, "Give me my golden earrings, and then I will leave."

Bhaṭobās said, "Take them," and he turned his ear toward him.

[Bhānubhaṭ] took them off him and kept them. Then he went home to Kaṭak Devgiri. He stayed there.

One day Bhaṭobās went there. Bhaṭobās embraced Bhānubhaṭ and said, "Bhānu, you are my betel nut cracker." In this way he made peace with him and brought him back.

But he did not stay. He left again.

159. Kesobās admonishes a Mahātmā when he sees him eating out of his begging bag.

A Mahātmā was eating his meal out of his begging bag at the river. Kesobās had come there. He saw this. And Kesobās came to their quarters. [The Mahātmā] followed him. Then, in Bhaṭobās' sight, Kesobās said, "Hey, why did you eat your meal out of your begging bag?"

The man replied, "What, did someone see me?"

And Kesobās said, "Just as I saw you, others will see you too, and they will denigrate the order *(mārg)*.[244] From today on, may Bhaṭobās' curse be on anyone who eats from his begging bag." Kesobās [spoke] angrily this way. At that, Bhaṭobās said, "You should put all your food onto a plate and then eat it. But do not [eat directly from] your begging bag."

Afterwards no one ate [that way].

160. And he uses the threat of Bhaṭobās' curse in forbidding onions as a vegetable.

One day Gaurāïsẽ cooked some nice onions. Then she served them to everyone in Bhaṭobās' row. Keśav, Paṇḍit, and all the others sat down to eat. Kesobās looked at the food and said, "What is this you have cooked?"

Gaurāïsẽ said, "It is onions."

Kesobās said, "You should not cook them. From today on, if you cook them, may Bhaṭobās' curse be on you." Kesobās forbade her this way in the sight of Bhaṭobās.

So from then on they did not cook [onions].[245]

161. He sends Rambhā away when he hears her talking about other things.[246]

One day when Bhaṭobās was sitting there, Rambhāïsẽ was arguing with someone—what they were arguing about is not known. Bhaṭobās heard this and said, "Hey Rambhāï, you are constantly arguing. You must leave," and he sent her away. He abused her. He [spoke] angrily this way.

So she went off to practice solitude. She completed her solitude. In the evening she returned. She prostrated herself to Bhaṭobās.

162. And when he gives instructions [to put aside] his leavings [for Rambhāïsẽ], he says, "I am her duty."

Then Bhaṭobās sat down to eat his meal. He and the others sat in a row to eat. He ate his meal. He rinsed his mouth.

About the leavings from his meal he said to Gaurāïsẽ, "Gaurāï, keep these. Save these leavings for Rambhāï."

Gaurāïsẽ said, "But you sent her away, Bhaṭ!"

Bhaṭobās said, "Still, a pebble placed in a sloping channel will roll down the channel. If I am her duty *(dharma)*, she who is mine will come to me."

At that point she returned from her solitude. She prostrated herself to Bhaṭobās. Bhaṭobās said, "Go on, Rambhā, take the leavings I have saved for you."

"All right."

Then she went and took them, and ate her meal.

163. When Nāïkbāï insists, Māhādāïsē gives her instruction.

One day Māhādāïsē went to Naugāv. The village head there was Nāïkbāï. One day she had the sight *(darśan)* of Māhādāïsē. She said to Māhādāïsē, "Mother, when the Gosāvī Śrī Cāṅgdev Rāüḷ[247] was living in Pīpaḷgāv,[248] I caught a glimpse of his brilliance. So tell me, in what way is he God (Īśvar)?" She insisted on [being told] this.

So Māhādāïsē gave her instruction. She received enlightenment.

164. And she gives her initiation as an ascetic.

Then, some time later, she took initiation as an ascetic. She was initiated as a follower by Māhādāïsē.

165. And Māhādāïsē listens to her songs of separation.

One day Nāïkbāï composed verses about separation [from God], and recited them to Māhādāïsē. Māhādāïsē was delighted.

The verses are as follows:

1. One [of the *gopīs*] says to another:
    "Hear about Kṛṣṇa's power of attraction:
   I caught a glimpse of his lustrous personality;
    it sent my mind into a whirl.
   This is a miracle to my heart:
    how can one who has experienced Kṛṣṇa survive?
   Would not one's life leave one immediately?

Refrain: "My mind has been attracted in a strange way, my friend.
    I saw him in a dream.
   From then on I've spent my life
    counting the days.

2. "You may say that I love the sight of him,
    and that what I love more is [my own feelings of] desire.
   But don't go on thinking this—
    it's not the way to reach the lord of the soul.
   You'll say I love the state of Nirvāṇa,
    but I swear by you, I don't aspire to that.
   But when your heart has been pierced,
    who but you knows it?

3. "The many kinds of austerities, vows, and almsgiving;
the disciplines *(yama),* restraints *(niyama),* and the means to merit;
the Vedic scriptures and the Purāṇas:
through none of these can that Kṛṣṇa be reached.
To whom shall I go for help in getting him?
Whose feet shall I hold in supplication?
Who will save my anguished life-breaths
by uniting me with that King Kṛṣṇa?

4. "How strange is this possession by love!
How was my mind unwittingly attracted to him?
How can I want to see him
who is hard for even perfected *yogīs* to obtain, however hard they try?
I have neither service nor faith, neither love nor devotion,
neither intense desire nor mental inclination.
Now how can I attain
that lord of my life?

5. "I see in myself no special merit
that would allow me to see his feet.
If he himself has mercy on me,
then I will get to see him.
When will these desires be fulfilled?
Even if my longing is great,
how will I who am without love
reach that unmanifest infinite form?

6. "This sinful mind is attached to [its] nature.
When I say I will think of Him in solitude,
it shows me everything else.
That makes my mind wander.
But an extremely knowledgeable one has told me
that the sign I see is that
of the king of the Yādavs.[249]

7. "Now enough of all this talk.
In the end, my real friend is she[250]
who has told me about Śrī Cakrapāṇī.[251]
I see no other than her.
Now I pay homage to the best of the Yādavs.
Of all those who are unfortunate, I am the worst.
But include me among those you remember;
and protect me."

She sang these verses. (According to some, she composed them after she had received instruction, and then she became a follower.)

166. Māhādāïsē checks on the mendicants' behavior and admonishes a woman.

The mendicants would go off to solitude. They would sit in solitude, and Māhādāïsē would go and check on their practice of solitude. She would point out the men's and the women's mistakes at the place where they were sitting. She would awaken them [to the proper way to act]. She would check who was in whose company. She always used to do this.

One day, after a woman had completed her solitude and returned to their quarters, Māhādāïsē went to the place [where the woman had been sitting]. There were some *kuhīrī* seeds and some scraps of cloth on the ground there. When Māhādāïsē saw that, she did not approve. She returned to their quarters and admonished the woman in front of Bhaṭobās.

The woman prostrated herself in acknowledgment.

167. And she snubs a woman because she has sung *Rukmiṇī Svayaṃvar.*

Māhādāïsē had gone out to wander. Another woman was preceding her in wandering. At night that woman sang *Rukmiṇī Svayaṃvar*[252] on the veranda [of the house where she stayed]. In the morning she left, and the next day Māhādāïsē came to that place to sleep. The woman of the house said, "Mother, will you sing a song?"

Māhādāïsē replied, "Mother, I don't know any songs."

And the woman said, "What a fine song the woman who came yesterday sang!"

Māhādāïsē heard that, and she did not approve.[253]

Then later the woman met Māhādāïsē, but Māhādāïsē would not talk with her. She parted from her.

168. Bhaṭ admonishes the woman, and says, "The old woman is the protection of the religion."

Bhaṭobās heard that Māhādāïsē would not have anything to do with that woman. And he was pleased, and said, "The old woman is the protection of my religion *(dharma)*."

Then, after some time, that woman came [to where Bhaṭobās was]. Bhaṭobās admonished her.

Addendum: Then from that time on no one sang anything anywhere.

169. Māhādāïsē admonishes Mhāībhaṭ about his choice of a place for solitude while wandering.

Māhādāïsē had gone wandering,[254] and Mhāībhaṭ had also gone. In a certain village, Māhādāïsē heard that Mhāībhaṭ was there, and she went to meet him.

When she looked in the appropriate places for solitude, Mhāībhaṭ was not there. He was in an orchard. They met there. They did the whole ritual [of meeting].[255]

When it was time for conversation about religion *(dharmavārtā)*, Māhādāïsē said, "Such places are not appropriate for solitude for a man *(puruṣ)* suffering from separation from God (Īśvar). They are for the solitude of men who have attachments."

Māhādāïsẽ pointed this out through *dharma*. Mhāībhaṭ agreed. He was very happy.

170. He explains the reward for one who falls away.

Once, on some occasion, Bhaṭobās said, "If someone who has been instructed *(upadeśiyā)* in absolute knowledge *(brahmavidyā)* completes his religious exercises, he will attain God (Īśvar). If he falls away, he gets the reward of the chief *devatā*."[256]

This is what Bhaṭobās taught.

171. He has them teach women the meaning of the words.

One day Bhaṭobās said, "Women cannot retain a [whole] sermon. Teach them the words and their meanings together."[257]

172. Mhāībhaṭ makes a retort to a Brāhmaṇ.

Mhāībhaṭ was reading a *pothī*[258] somewhere when a paṇḍit came along. He stood and listened to a word or two, and said three times, "Wrong, wrong, wrong!"

Mhāībhaṭ looked at him and said, "If the mouth is wrong, [the text] can still be read; if the *pothī* is wrong, it can be torn up."[259]

And the man got angry.

173. And he makes a retort to a Brāhmaṇ whom he hears say, "There is nothing auspicious about a Śūdra."

In a certain village, Mhāībhaṭ went begging and then went to the river for water. He was taking water from a hole dug in the sand.

There was a paṇḍit there. He said, "There's nothing auspicious about a Śūdra."

Mhāībhaṭ looked at him and said, "And so much the less about a Brāhmaṇ."

With that, the man got angry.

174. Mhāībhaṭ [helps] compose *Rukmiṇī Svayaṃvar*.

One day Mhāībhaṭ and Lakṣmīdharbhaṭ said to Māhādāïsẽ, "Why don't you go on with *Rukmiṇī Svayaṃvar?*"

Māhādāïsẽ said, "How can I do it? At that time[260] the Gosāvī gave me a boon, and that is why I was inspired."

Mhāībhaṭ and Lakṣmīdharbhaṭ said, "Then we will make up the words, and you sing them."

Māhādāïsẽ agreed. So they made up the words and composed the verses, and Māhādāïsẽ sang them.

In this way the second part was composed.

175. When Māhādāïsē asks, [Bhaṭobās] says that those who do not have [God's] presence will end up just like Bāïsē.

One day, seeing the [new disciples'] firmness in detachment, Māhādāïsē said to Bhaṭobās, "Nāgdev, we followed the Gosāvī because he caressed us and fondled us. And these have followed for the sake of a God they have never seen, [because] they were suffering and afflicted. So what will happen to them?"

Bhaṭobās said, "Rūpai, they will end up just like Bāïsē,[261] who had [God's] presence."[262]

Bhaṭobās praised them this way.

176. And, when he is asked, he says that they should do twice as many religious exercises on a festival day.

Once, on a festival day, Māhādāïsē asked Bhaṭobās, "Nāgdev, what should one do on a festival day?"

Bhaṭobās said, "On a festival day, one should do twice the regular amount of repetition of the names of God *(jāpya)*. One should do twice as much worship of relics *(prasādsevā)*. For one who is intent on God (Īśvar), it is always the right time for recollection *(smaraṇ)* of God (Parameśvar). This is the rule for Mahātmās.

"The rule for lay disciples is to give time, hospitality, and clothes to those who yearn [for God]."

Addendum: "[A lay disciple] should do all this with whatever means he has."

Bhaṭobās said this. Māhādāïsē bowed in acceptance.

177. He meets Māhādāïsē at Naugāv. He decides with respect to Kothaḷā the rule about the number of days [to stay together].

Māhādāïsē was in Naugāv. One day Bhaṭobās came from Nimbā to meet Māhādāïsē. They greeted one another. When they had done the rites of meeting[263] for twelve days, Kothaḷobās came as a guest. They greeted him. They eased his weariness.[264] Then, while they were eating their meal, Bhaṭobās said, "Rūpai, the days of my meeting with you are over. Now you do the rites with Kothaḷā."

Kothaḷobās said, "Bhaṭ, how many days may we stay together?"

Bhaṭobās said, "The text *(pāṭh)* says twelve days;[265] but the meaning *(artha)*[266] is eighteen days." *Addendum:* "The final answer *(si[d]dhānta)* is that you may stay together as long as you do not become [aware of one another's] faults, and as long as nothing but new attainments comes of it."

Then Māhādāïsē and Kothaḷobās ate and drank together and exchanged clothes.[267] Then Bhaṭobās came to Nimbā.

178. When mendicants go to Varāḍ, he tells them to be sure [to meet] Śrīprabhu's daughter and Āü.

Bhaṭobās would say to mendicants who were going to Varāḍ,[268] "First you should meet the Gosāvī's daughter,[269] and then you should go to Ṛddhipur. In Ṛddhipur, first you should meet Āü,[270] and then you should pay homage to the [Rāj]maḍh.[271] Then you should wander around in the region."

He would instruct in this way those who were going there, and the mendicants would do just what he said.

179. He tells where his sandals are.

The disciples would brush Bhaṭobās' sandals and put them carefully away. Sometimes, when someone would forget, Paṇḍitbās would brush them and put them away.

One day nobody put them away. A dog carried off one of the sandals. When it was time to use them, [the disciples] looked for them, but one was missing. Seeing this, Bhaṭobās said, "Paṇḍit puts my sandals away, so they are kept safe. Go on now. A dog has left [my sandal] in that ditch over there. Bring it here."

Someone went and found it in the ditch. He brought it back. Everyone was amazed.

180. He says that Gaurāï's initiation will be fruitful.

One day Indrabhaṭ's [wife] Gaurāï took initiation as an ascetic. Bhaṭobās said, "Gaurāï, your initiation will be fruitful. The Gosāvī has described your qualities of mind."[272]

Gaurāïsẽ was happy.

181. He says that Lakhudevobā is married to his begging bag.

One day Bhaṭobās said to Lakhudevobās, "Lakhudev, you have gotten married to your begging bag."[273]

182. He tells Upādhye to stay in Rāvasgāv.

Upādhye took initiation as an ascetic from Bhaṭobās.

[Later, Upādhye] became very weak. Then Bhaṭobās said, "Upādhye, you (*Addendum:* "Dādo, you . . .") stay in Rāvasgāv. No one will criticize you. The Gosāvī has given you a boon."[274]

So he stayed in Rāvasgāv.

183. And Kamaḷāïsẽ becomes a disciple.

Kamaḷāïsẽ was Upādhyabās' niece. Hearing that she had been widowed, Upādhyabās went and got her. On the way he gave her instruction. Then he brought her to Bhaṭobās, and entrusted her to him. He had Bhaṭobās instruct her again and give her a begging bag.

Before giving her instruction, Bhaṭobās said, "What, Dādo, did you tell her about one God, while I will tell her about another?"

"No, Bhaṭ. The Gosāvī made *you* his deputy *(adhikaraṇ).* You will tell her about the God that God told you about."

So Bhaṭobās instructed her again, and gave her initiation as an ascetic.

She was with Bhaṭobās for some time. But the group of disciples used to call her Upādhyabās' disciple.

Later she went to Rāvasgāv. There she nursed Upādhyabās.[275]

184. He predicts that guests will come and that there will be a discussion about religion.

Early one morning, Bhaṭobās said to everyone, "Today no one should go out to solitude. Today guests will come. There will be a great discussion about religion *(dharmavārtā).*" He made this prediction.

So no one went out to solitude.

Then Kesobās and Gopāḷpaṇḍit arrived together. Everyone greeted them. It was a festive occasion. Then there was a fine, unprecedented discussion of religion *(dharmavārtā).* It was an auspicious time for everyone. They were amazed.[276]

185. He says that the water jar is empty, and accepts water brought by Ānobā.

Bhaṭobās got thirsty one night. He looked for water in his drinking vessel, but it had no water. So he went to fill it at the water storage jar. But there was none there either. So he said, "There is no water in the water jar."

Ānobās heard this, and he took a pitcher and went to get water. He went and fetched water from the river. He filled Bhaṭobās' drinking vessel.

Addendum: He prostrated himself and said to Bhaṭobās, "Drink this water, Bhaṭ." Bhaṭobās drank it.

Then [Ānobās] poured the rest into the water storage jar. He brought another pitcherful. He poured it too into the water jar, and then looked at Bhaṭobās. But Bhaṭobās did not say, "That's enough."

So he brought another [pitcherful]. He emptied it too into the water jar. Again he looked at Bhaṭobās, but Bhaṭobās still remained silent. So Gopāḷpaṇḍit[277] filled the whole water jar.

Addendum: [This took place] while he was still a lay disciple.

186. And when Gopāḷpaṇḍit comes again, [Bhaṭobās] removes his grief over his wife.

Gopāḷpaṇḍit went to his village. His wife died. He felt great grief. Then he came to meet Bhaṭobās, and [Bhaṭobās] took away his grief.

Addendum: He told Bhaṭobās [about his wife's death].

187. He talks about the discipleship of the servant Anantkocā.

One day Bhaṭobās said, "This servant Anantkocā has followed me completely, from his ears to his hooves." This is what Bhaṭobās said.

Anantkocā was Ānobās' grandfather, and Sāraṅgpāṇī was his father. All of them had had *darśan* of the Gosāvī.

188. He gives a retort to a Brāhmaṇ and initiates him as an ascetic.

One day when Bhaṭobās was sitting there, a certain Brāhmaṇ came to have *darśan* of Bhaṭobās. [The Brāhmaṇ] sat silently without bowing to him.

Someone said, "Bhaṭ,[278] aren't you going to bow?"

The man said, "He has no [Brāhmaṇical] tuft or thread. I won't prostrate myself to him."

At that, Bhaṭobās said, "You prostrate yourself to your mother and sisters. Do they have tufts and threads?"

And the man came and prostrated himself. He took initiation as an ascetic, and became a disciple.

189. He says that Mahātmās should conduct themselves like Gaurāï.

One day Bhaṭobās said in connection with someone: "You should behave the way this Umbarī Gaurāïsẽ behaves."

Addendum: What he meant was that if one does not know on one's own how to act, if one does not understand, one should act the way someone senior to you does.

190. He sets out for Ṛddhipur.

Once Bhaṭobās set out to go to Ṛddhipur. *Addendum:* along with everyone. Stopping at the regular places along the way, he came to Sāvaḷāpur.

It is not known whether the Gosāvī's daughter[279] was there or not at the time. Those who say that she was there say that he met her and then came to Ṛddhipur.

191. He meets Āü. He bows to the [Rāj]maḍh.

Āüsẽ was there then. First he met her, and then he bowed to the [Rāj]maḍh[280] and its compound wall. Then he stayed there for some days.

192. When a man who looks like God (Īśvar) comes, [Bhaṭobās] has Mhāībhaṭ ask him the same question that [Cakradhar] had asked earlier.

Once Bhaṭobās had gone wandering, visiting certain holy places (*tīrthas*). He was nearby, at Taḷegāv.

Mhāībhaṭ and everyone else was in the [Rāj]maḍh, when a man who looked like the Gosāvī arrived. The man came and sat quietly on Ābāïsẽ's platform *(oṭā)*. Mhāībhaṭ and everyone else was delighted. They were attracted to him. They felt that he was the Gosāvī.

So Mhāībhaṭ sent someone to get Bhaṭobās. Bhaṭobās was right there, at Taḷegāv.

[The messenger] told Bhaṭobās what had happened. Bhaṭobās listened, and said, "Go and say to Mhāībhaṭ, 'Ask him the question the Gosāvī asked you when you first met him. If he gives the same answer [as you gave], then send for me again.' "[281]

So [the messenger] left. He gave Mhāībhaṭ the message. Mhāībhaṭ said, "All right," and asked the man the question. Mhāībhaṭ said, "[Do you have] an experience that cuts away worldly existence *(saṃsṛtī)?*"

The man replied, "Nāth[282] knows that," and he placed his hands on his ears.[283]

So Mhāībhaṭ intentionally led him outside, and then sent word to Bhaṭobās. Bhaṭobās returned. [Mhāībhaṭ] told him everything that had happened. Hearing about it, Bhaṭobās said, "This [Rāj]maḍh would have been ruined."

193. Mhāībhaṭ admonishes Umāï when she gets angry with Kothaḷobā for drinking her water.

One day when Kothaḷobā was thirsty, he drank some water from Umāïsẽ's cup without asking her permission. And Umāïsẽ got angry. "You are a Śūdra. Why did you drink water from my cup?"

Mhāībhaṭ heard that, and said, "What is this, Umāïsẽ? You have had contact with both Gods,[284] and you have a mother like Ābāïsẽ and a brother like Bhaṭobās. But still you have not lost your ignorance? What has happened to you? If someone as worthy as Kothaḷā drinks water from your cup, is that not your good fortune?" He admonished her this way.

Then she felt remorse. Mhāībhaṭ said, "Prostrate yourself to Kothaḷā."

"All right." And Umāïsẽ prostrated herself to Kothaḷobās. "I am ignorant. I did wrong. I am a sinner."

Addendum: Then Kothaḷobā lifted her to her feet.

194. And at Mhāībhaṭ's suggestion, [Bhaṭobās] teaches her "Mahāvākya."

On that same occasion, Mhāībhaṭ prostrated himself to Bhaṭobās and said, "Bhaṭ, teach 'Mahāvākya'[285] to Umāïsẽ."

Bhaṭobās said, "Why don't you teach it to her?"

[Mhāībhaṭ] said, "The Gosāvī made *you* his deputy *(adhikaraṇ).*"

Bhaṭobās replied, "Mhāībhaṭ, how will she learn from me what she did not learn from the Gosāvī? The Gosāvī once said to me, 'Will she get my benefit by having you as a brother?' "[286]

Mhāībhaṭ replied, "In Belopur the Gosāvī said that five or six[287] people would be [enlightened] by you."[288]

Addendum: So Bhaṭobās taught the religion *(dharma)* to Umāïsẽ. Then from then on Umāïsẽ had great respect for the order *(mārg).*

195. When Kothaḷobā sets out after hearing about independence *(nirālambanatā)*, [Bhaṭobās] praises lonely places.

One day Bhaṭobās was having a discussion about religion *(dharmavārtā)*, and in particular about "Asatīparī."[289] Bhaṭobās said, "Some are dependent *(koṇhāṃsi ālamban)* on relics *(prasād)*; some are dependent on scripture *(śāstra)*; some are dependent on Yelho;[290] some are dependent on me. But there is no one born of a mother who draws his sword and goes to another land."[291]

As [Bhaṭobās] taught this way, Kothaḷobā said, "How is there no such one? Here am I, Kothaḷā!" and he patted himself on the arms.[292] And he prostrated himself to Bhaṭobās and set out.

Bhaṭobās said, "Kothaḷā will go to a place where if he is hit on the leg his head will not feel it."[293]

Addendum: In this way he praised lonely places.

196. He admonishes Mhāībhaṭ for refusing Āü's hospitality.

Once Āüsē asked Mhāībhaṭ, "Please accept some food from me." Mhāībhaṭ refused.[294]

Addendum: Bhaṭobās had gone out wandering. There he heard that Mhāībhaṭ would not accept Āü's food.

Later, in the course of his wandering, Mhāībhaṭ met Bhaṭobās. And Bhaṭobās got angry. Bhaṭobās said, "If you don't accept food from the Āü who would run ahead while the Gosāvī would run after her to pacify her,[295] the Āü without taking whose food [the Gosāvī] would not eat a meal,[296] whom he indulged this way—if you don't accept that Āü's food, it is the same as not accepting God's."

In this way he praised Āü to Mhāībhaṭ.

197. And, remorseful, Mhāībhaṭ asks Āüsē for a meal.

Addendum: With that, Mhāībhaṭ felt remorse. So Mhāībhaṭ took leave of Bhaṭobās and returned. He prostrated himself fully to Āüsē, and said, "Āü, feed me a meal. It was wrong of me not to accept it when you offered. Now serve it to me."

Āüsē said, "All right. Get up! Get up!" and she lifted him to his feet. "You are my Cakrasvāmī's hero."

And Āüsē prepared food, and she served it to Mhāībhaṭ in a dish that was a relic *(prasād)*. And Mhāībhaṭ ate his fill.

Addendum: Bhaṭobās heard about this, and he was happy.

198. Mhāībhaṭ dies.

Once when Mhāībhaṭ had gone out to wander, he became ill in the course of his wandering.

Addendum: Umāïsē had come to that same area. She met Mhāībhaṭ. Mhāībhaṭ said to her, "Umāï, take me to Ṛddhipur."

She said, "All right, Mhāībhaṭ. I will take you."

So Umāïsē pawned the bracelet and chained ring that she had with her. Then she hired a palanquin and brought him to Ṛddhipur.

The palanquin was set down at the main gate [of the Rājmaḍh]. Hearing that Mhāībhaṭ had arrived, Bhaṭobās came to receive him. They met near the main gate.

Mhāībhaṭ said to Bhaṭobās, "Bhaṭ, put your foot on my forehead," and he held Bhaṭobās' foot in his hands.

Bhaṭobās said, "It is the Gosāvī's holy foot that should go on one's forehead. I should put my *hand* on your forehead," and he placed his hand there.

Addendum: Then they brought him into the compound. They made a place for him in a nice spot.

Then one day Mhāībhaṭ said to Bhaṭobās, "Bhaṭ, will I attain God?"

And Bhaṭobās, wondering, Why has he said this? remained silent for a moment.

That made [Mhāībhaṭ] feel even worse. "I am a sinner," said Mhāībhaṭ. "How can I attain God?" he lamented.

Then Bhaṭobās said, "Mhāībhaṭ, you have had the presence *(sannidhān)* of both Gods[297] and the opportunity to serve them *(sannidhāndāsya)*. So why are you talking this way?"

Mhāībhaṭ said, "Bhaṭ, nothing untrue comes from your mouth."[298]

Bhaṭobās said, "When the Gosāvī was living in Nivāse, you came along with the headmen, and you left without having *darśan* of the Gosāvī. At that time, I pointed out to the Gosāvī, 'Lord Gosāvī, your Mhāyā came here, but he would not come for *darśan.*'

"At that, the Gosāvī said, 'It is all right if he does not come. When he comes, he is the one who will know when to come.'[299]

"That is how the Gosāvī described you. If you do not attain God, no one will attain God. Therefore, you will attain God." Bhaṭobās explained this to him.

Then Mhāībhaṭ said, "Forgive whatever wrongs I have done," and he folded his hands and placed them on his forehead. "And bury me near Caṇākhya."[300]

With that, Mhāībhaṭ died. Then Bhaṭobās buried him there.

Addendum: Bhaṭobās and all the others were very sad. Then Bhaṭobās immediately set out for the Gaṅgā Valley.[301]

199. When he sets out for the Gaṅgā Valley, he says to Āü, "Come on."

Bhaṭobās set out for the Gaṅgā Valley. As he was leaving, he said to Āüsē: "Come on, Āü. Let's go to the Gaṅgā Valley."

Āüsē replied, "I won't come, Nāganā. Without Cakrasvāmī, that Gaṅgā Valley is burning with red flames!"[302] This is what she said, and she would not come along.

So Bhaṭobās bowed to the [Rāj]maḍh and set out.

200. On the road, he drinks water from the coconut shell given him by Gaurāï from Paraṇḍ.

Gaurāïsẽ from Paraṇḍ (according to Kavībās, Pomāïsẽ[303]) was Bhaṭobās' disciple. For six months she carried a coconut shell filled with water and sealed with wax in the roll of sari folds at her waist. Every day she would throw one away and fill another. But no one knew about it.

One day as Bhaṭobās was traveling along the road, he felt thirsty. He asked everyone, "Does anyone have any water?" They looked in their water pots, but there was no water. Then he asked Gaurāïsẽ, "Gaurāï, do you have some water?"

"Yes, Bhaṭ, I do." And she took out the coconut shell from her sari fold. She gave the water to Bhaṭobās. Bhaṭobās drank the water. And, holding the coconut shell in his hands, he said, "She has been carrying around this coconut shell full of water for six months. The whole six months have been put to use."

Everyone was amazed. Then they arrived at the village where they were going to spend the night.

201. He arrives at Pratiṣṭhān.

So then Bhaṭobās traveled stop by stop to Pratiṣṭhān. *Addendum:* He bowed to Pratiṣṭhān and immediately set out to leave.

At that, Kesobās said, "Bhaṭ, let's stay here."

Bhaṭobās said, "I cannot stand [even] to cook rice in Paiṭhaṇ or Ṛddhipur.[304] I cannot stand to accept homage here. So I cannot stay here for too many days."

Addendum: Then he stayed there for a day or two.

202. In accordance with Bhaṭ's command, Bhāskarbhaṭ defeats the *sannyāsīs* in Pratiṣṭhān.

Kavībās: One day Kavīśvar said, "Bhaṭ, may I have a discussion with [the] *sannyāsīs* [here]?"

Bhaṭobās said, "Bhānubhaṭ,[305] do not do so at your own initiative. Do so if they create the occasion."

Then one day—it is not known where—the occasion arose. Kavīśvar silenced them. The *sannyāsīs* were humiliated.

203. And he tells him not to go to the Pīṃpaḷeśvar temple.

Then one day—it is not known whether at that time or at another time—Bhaṭobās said to Kavīśvarbās, "Bhaṭ, don't you go to the Pīṃpaḷeśvar temple."

But in his heart, Kavīśvar wanted to go.

204. Kavīśvar has a discussion in the Pīṃpaḷeśvar temple.

A certain paṇḍit came to Pratiṣṭhān. He used to claim that he had reduced all other paṇḍits to straw. No one was a match for him. He began to expound a Purāṇa in the Pīṃpaḷeśvar temple.

Bhaṭobās had forbidden Kavīśvar [to go to the Pīṃpaḷeśvar temple]. But, while that man was showing off his learning there, Kavīśvarbās went there without anyone realizing it. The temple hall was crowded. Kavīśvarbās leaned against the door frame and began to listen.

At one point, Kavīśvar noticed a mistake, and he said, "That's wrong, that's wrong, that's wrong."

The man said, "Come forward. How is it wrong?"

So he went up to him and sat down. Then he had [the man] recite the verse he had been expounding. Then he said, "You have the text wrong." Then he recited it himself. It made sense [to the paṇḍit].

Addendum: Then [Kavīśvarbās] said, "Now explain it." So he explained it. Kavīśvarbās refuted [the explanation].

The man said to Kavīśvarbās, "Now you explain it." So Kavīśvarbās explained the verse. He said to the man, "Well, is this the right meaning?"

The man said, "Yes, it is."

Kavīśvarbās said, "It is not the right meaning." Then he refuted that interpretation too. Then he said, "This is the meaning," and he explained it another way. "Now, is this the right meaning?"

"Yes, it is right."

Again he said, "It is not right."

In this way he gave ten different explanations. *Addendum:* This melted the man's heart. The audience was astonished.

Then the paṇḍit said, "Who are you?"

Kavīśvarbās improvised this verse as an answer:[306]

> Some inspired ones have punished the broken pride
> of heroic leaders of the world;
> some very stupid ones are mounted on the mountain
> of false pride in much logic;
> some, expert in the play of bunches of poetic sounds,
> are surrounded by the moods of love and heroism;
> Some have alert minds that are [set] on the stories of Kṛṣṇa—
> [such a one] am I, the poet Bhāskar.

"I am that poet Bhāskar," he said.

Then the paṇḍit said: "You are not human. You are the deity of this place, embodied to do away with my pride."

Kavīśvarbās replied, "I am not a god. I belong to the charismatic *(vedhavantī)* Nāgdevbhaṭ."

In this way, he destroyed [the man's] pride. Then he returned to their lodgings.

Addendum: Then it is not known whether or not he told Bhaṭobās, but the people of the town were astonished.

205. He goes to Nimbā and stays there again.

Addendum: Then Bhaṭobās went to Nimbā. He stayed in Nimbā again. This was his third visit. And besides, he came and went there many times in the course of his wandering.

206. He calls Gaurāïsẽ of Vihīṭā back from her relatives.

Addendum: Gaurāïsẽ of Vihīṭā took initiation as an ascetic from Bhaṭobās. One day she took leave of Bhaṭobās and went out to wander. In the course of her wanderings, she went to Vihīṭā. She stayed there, in her relatives' village.

Some time later, her companions in wandering came to meet Bhaṭobās. Bhaṭobās said to them, "Where is Gaurāï?"

They said, "She is in her relatives' village."

Bhaṭobās said, "If you can get *dharma* from the Mahārvāḍā,[307] then the Mahārvāḍā is [where] your relatives [are]. And I, her *dharma,* am here. Why did she go there? Go on. Call her back."

So they went. They brought her back. Then Bhaṭobās instructed her, primarily about relatives.

Then she said, "Bhaṭ, how far away is the end [of the land]?"[308]

Bhaṭobās said, "If you go seven provinces (*maṇḍaḷ*s) away from your own village, that is called the end." *Addendum: maṇḍaḷ* means "region" *(pradeśu).*

This is how Bhaṭobās instructed her.

207. He denies that attraction or enlightenment can come from the written word.

Once during a discussion about religion *(dharmavārtā),* Bhaṭobās said, "One should not study this scripture *(śāstra)* on one's own. Written words cannot bring about attraction *(vedhu)* or enlightenment *(bodhu).* When the scripture is heard from the mouth of one's *guru,* it comes alive. Why is this? God (Parameśvar) himself gives absolute knowledge *(brahmavidyā),* or he depends on a deputy *(adhikaraṇ)* to give it.[309] Therefore the written word cannot produce attraction or enlightenment."

Addendum: "So one should not study the scripture on one's own. One should study and discuss it at the mouth of the scripture."[310] This is what he said.

208. He says that religion is destroyed by resorting to the passionate or the turbid.

One day during a discussion about religion *(dharmavārtā),* Bhaṭobās said,

"Do not keep company with people who are passionate *(rājasē)* or turbid *(tāmasē)*. The moment that you resort to people who are sensualists or to objects that give sense pleasure, religion *(dharma)* will be destroyed."

Another version:[311] "Through discipline, restraint, and scripture *(yema-nemaśāstrē)*, take away the passion *(rajas)* and turbidity *(tamas)* of passionate and turbid people, and then keep company with them."

209. When Nāgāïsē reports on a discussion of scripture, [Bhaṭobās] says that both [she and those who took part in the discussion] have profited.

Nāgāïsē was Bhaṭobās' granddaughter and Maheśvarpaṇḍit's daughter. She had received instruction from Bhaṭobās and had been initiated by him as an ascetic.

Bhaṭobās used to go out to solitude with his followers. And he would leave Nāgāïsē behind to take care of their lodgings. Because of the [precept about sitting under a] thorn bush,[312] he would usually sit in solitude under a *rui* tree. Sometimes he would sit on a rocky stretch of ground, and then they would have a discussion about religion *(dharmavārtā)* there.

After one and a half watches,[313] they would return to their lodgings. And Nāgāïsē would ask Paṇḍit, Kesobās, and Kavīśvarbās, "What religious discussion *(dharmavārtā)* took place today?"

Then they would tell her what had taken place.

Nāgāïsē would go and report it to Bhaṭobās.

One day as she was reporting it to Bhaṭobās, Nāgāïsē said, "Today Paṇḍit said so-and-so, and Keśav said such-and-such, and Kavīśvar said so-and-so."

At that, Bhaṭobās said, "I taught them that, and now this marvelous thing has happened, that both [you and they] have profited."

210. He tells about an animal incarnation.[314]

One day Bhaṭobās said to Kesobās and Paṇḍitbās, "There is a parrot in a prostitute's house in Devgiri who is an incarnation of God (Īśvar)."

Kesobās and Paṇḍitbās replied, "Bhaṭ, should we go and see?"

Bhaṭobās said, "Don't go. Our Gosāvī commanded us to serve Śrī-prabhu,[315] so we did so. The [parrot] is an incarnation of God, but not one we have been commanded [to serve]."

Bhaṭobās instructed them this way, telling them not to go.

211. He forbids speaking untruth.

Once during a discussion about religion *(dharmavārtā)*, Bhaṭobās said, "Do not tell lies to your friends, to your relatives, to dependents of the order *(mārgīcāṃ parīvārīyāṃ)*, or to others—except when the person would die otherwise—or to people who are lustful[316] or turbid *(tāmas)*."

This is what he taught.

212. When a woman asks about wandering, he says that she will be directed from village to village.

Once when a woman was setting out to wander, she asked Bhaṭobās, "Bhaṭ, how should wandering be done?"

Addendum: Bhaṭobās said, "Go from one village to another.[317] In one village they will tell you about another village. As you beg, at one house they will tell you about another house."

Then she set out to wander.

213. He picks up vegetables that the women had discarded, and says, "Half in the winnowing fan and half in the well."

The women were cleaning vegetables. They were throwing away the leaves; they were throwing away the tender stalks.

Bhaṭobās saw this, and he sat down and picked them up. He brought them and handed them to the women and said, "Why are you throwing half into the well and keeping half in the winnowing fan?[318] If my Mahātmās eat this they will get good at practicing recollection *(smaraṇ).*"

Addendum: So, from then on, they would not throw anything away. They would work carefully.

214. He tells a Mahātmā how many days to stay in a place in the course of constant wandering.

One day someone asked Bhaṭobās *(addendum):* "Bhaṭ, when we are wandering, how long should we stay in what village?"

Bhaṭobās said, " 'One night in a village; five nights in a town.'[319] And the Gosāvī [also] said, 'Stay as long as no one realizes your good and bad qualities.' "[320]

The man bowed in acceptance.

215. He criticizes a Brāhmaṇ's song and initiates him as an ascetic.

One day Bhaṭobās was sitting in solitude near a sacrificial altar when a certain Brāhmaṇ came along. He recited to Bhaṭobās a song that he had composed himself. Then he asked, "Bhaṭ, how was the song?"

Bhaṭobās said, "It was such that the one who composed it will go to hell."[321]

Then he instructed the man, and the man immediately took initiation as an ascetic.

216. When Sāraṅgpaṇḍit dies, [Bhaṭobās] meets Umāïsē̃, and she becomes a disciple.

Sāraṅgpaṇḍit died in Pratiṣṭhān. Then Umāïsē̃[322] made all the necessary arrangements.

Addendum: Sāraṅgpaṇḍit was ill. Umāïsē̃ had gone outside. When she came back home, he was dead. And immediately she closed the door to the courtyard.

Then she took her relic *(prasād)* stool and Dhānāïsē,[323] and came to Bhaṭobās. She told him what had happened when she set out.

Then both [Umāïsē and Dhānāïsē] took initiation as ascetics from Bhaṭobās.

Kavibās: As Dhānāïsē took initiation, Bhaṭobās said, "Dhānāï, you have fulfilled the promise [you made] when [the Gosāvī] tucked in your sari."[324]

Bhaṭobās rejoiced this way.

217. He explains how to act in accordance with scripture *(śāstra)*.

One day during a discussion about religion *(dharmavārtā)*, Bhaṭobās said, "The deputy *(adhikaraṇ)* has[325] explained the number of years [to perform religious activities]. Then when a man is in another land, he should adjust them for himself. If there is something he does not understand, he should come and ask the deputy, or he should ask those who are senior to him. He should distribute his time among different religious activities *(kriyā)*. Then he will not be lax in conduct *(ācār)* or thought *(vicār)*."

This is what he taught.

218. When Keśavdev gives up his sandals because he has heard someone criticize him, [Bhaṭobās] says, "You are my only Mahātmā."

Once Kesobās, Paṇḍitbās, Kavīśvarbās, and a few others were going along the road. Kesobās had on sandals, while all the rest of them were barefoot.

A passerby saw them and said, "These are all Mahātmās of the Bhaṭmārg — all except for this one. He has on sandals."

Kesobās heard this. "So because of these sandals I am not a Mahātmā of the Bhaṭmārg!" he said, and he ripped them up and threw them away on the spot.

Then he came and told Bhaṭobās what had happened. Then Bhaṭobās said, "Keśavdev, you are the only true Mahātmā of my order *(mārg)*," and rejoiced.

219. People are attracted by Bhaṭ's cry for alms.

Bhaṭobās used to go begging. Bhaṭobās' sonorous call for alms would fill the air. When a baby who was crying heard the sound, it would give up its demands; it would take its mouth from its mother's breast and start looking at Bhaṭobās. Someone who was suffering would forget his misery. Others would be made happy by the sight *(darśan)* of him. People who were quarreling would lose their anger.

So on both banks of the Gaṅgā[326] they called Bhaṭobās "the charismatic *(vedhavantī)* Nāgdev Bhaṭ." He was known by this name.

220. When Sādhẽ has learned about hells, [Bhaṭobās] tells her [to study] a holy man.

The Gosāvī had had Sādhẽ look at the hells [portrayed in] the Kaḷaṅki Nārāyaṇ temple.[327] [Doing so] had filled her with misery. Then she came to the Gaṅgā Valley, and told Bhaṭobās about it.

At that, Bhaṭobās said, "You should look at and listen to a most faithful holy man *(puruṣ)* in the same way that God (Īśvar) had you look at the eighty-four kinds of hells in Kaḷaṅki Nārāyaṇ. That will give you peace, and you will come to love [God]."

This is how he instructed Sādhẽ.

221. As Dādos is dying, Upādhye and Nāthobā take care of him.

Dādos was in Pīpaḷgāv. One day he became very ill. Hearing this, Upādhyabās and Nāthobās came to take care of him. Upādhye said, "Dādo, who am I?"

Dādos said, "You are Jāno."[328]

Upādhyabās said, "Dādo, do you remember the Gosāvī's name?"

Rāmdev[329] replied, "The name and the bearer of the name are you and your Nāgdev."[330]

Upādhyabās replied, "All right, so be it." And immediately they stood up and left.

Later he died.

Addendum: Tradition *(mārgrūḍhi)*[331] holds that he was buried [near] a stream to the east of the Somnāth temple.

222. Upādhye dies.[332]

Once Upādhye became ill. He died from the illness. Kamaḷāïsẽ[333] gave him a proper burial. Then she left there and went to Vālsā.

She stayed in Vālsā. That is where she died. *Addendum:* This was after Bhaṭ's death.

223. Nāthobā defecates when he sees a treasure chest.

It is not known in what village Nāthobā was staying, but once when he went out to an open area [to defecate], he found an iron treasure chest lying there.

Nāthobā saw it, and said, "Why are you appearing now? If I had found you earlier, I would have put you to use for the Gosāvī. Instead, I spread out a cloth [to sit on and beg].[334] Am I not that same Nātho?" And he defecated on it and left.

Addendum: Bhaṭobās heard about this. He was pleased.

224. Nāthobā dies; [Bhaṭobās] sleeps at [Rākṣas]bhuvan.

Bhaṭobās came to Rākṣasbhuvan, and he heard that Nāthobā had died there. So Bhaṭobās said, "Spread my bedding at the very place where Nātho died. That is holy *(satvastha)* ground. The Gosāvī was there.[335] God will come into my heart."

They spread it there.

225. He says that Keśavdev's work will be of use to the order *(mārg)*.

From here on, everything is from the Kavibās version.

One day Bhaṭobās said, "Keśavdyā, there is no doubt about what I myself say, but you have arranged that the scripture *(śāstra)* will not be lost after I am gone. This scripture will settle arguments within the order *(mārg)* in the future."

In this way Bhaṭobās praised Kesobās' editing of the scripture.[336]

226. He says that seniority is connected with authority.

One day Bhaṭobās said, "To avoid sins having to do with respect and disrespect, you should take as senior to you anyone who is one Cāturmās[337] senior to you [in the order]. You should be subject to him. Otherwise, whomever the one in authority[338] appoints as senior is senior to you. And one who is advanced in knowledge of the scripture *(jñānvṛddhavacanē)* is senior to all."

This is what [Bhaṭobās] said.

227. He prostrates himself when he sees a mendicant in solitude.

One day when Bhaṭobās was going along the road, he saw a certain mendicant sitting in solitude. And [Bhaṭobās] said, "I have seen God . . ." *(Addendum:)* "and that got me started." "[But] it is for the sake of a God he has never seen . . ." *(Addendum:)* "that this man is sitting here."

"How great you are!" [Bhaṭobās] said, and prostrated himself from afar. He was pleased.

Addendum: Then they met.

228. A Brāhmaṇ is affected by hearing a discussion about religion; [Bhaṭobās] gives him initiation as an ascetic.

One day Bhaṭobās was sitting in a temple having a discussion about religion *(dharmavārtā)* with his disciples. There was much give and take. A certain paṇḍit was standing outside the temple listening. He would listen, and immediately say, "Bhaṭ has said this, so now what will Bhaṭ's disciples say?" Then when they had given their answer he would nod to himself.

He was engrossed in their conversation this way for several hours,[339] nodding his head. Then the discussion was over.

So he came inside. He prostrated himself completely to Bhaṭobās. He became his disciple *(siṣya)* and said, "Bhaṭ, for you it was a search for knowledge, but for me it was instruction."

Then immediately he took initiation as an ascetic.

229. He says, "You should at least become a disciple to amaze people."

One day during a discussion about religion *(dharmavārtā)*, [Bhaṭobās] proved a doctrine in an original way. And at the end he said, "If God's desire to arrange for the salvation of your soul *(jīvoddharaṇ)* does not enable you to become a disciple, then at least become a disciple to show yourself off *(ātmadarśanārtha)*, so that everyone will be amazed."

This is what he said.

230. He says that no action goes to waste.

One day Bhaṭobās said, "In this order *(mārg)*, not even the smallest action goes to waste. For some, unworthiness is the cause of renunciation; for some, worthiness[340] is the cause; for others, yearning is the cause; and for still others, [God's] presence is the cause."

231. He forbids them to wear new clothes, and praises food and clothes obtained by begging.

One day Bhaṭobās said, "Do not put on new clothes. You never get tired of patched clothes or of food obtained by begging. They save you from much [harm]."

232. When he hears that [the Gosāvī] is living in Ujjain, he obeys the Gosāvī's explicit orders.[341]

Once someone came from Ujjain. He said that the Gosāvī was living there.

Someone said, "So may we go there, Bhaṭ?"

Bhaṭobās said, "Is Pīpaḷgāv far away for a possessed man?[342] But the Gosāvī has given a command.[343] If we obey that command, we will be happy."

Then the man kept quiet.

233. When Lakṣmīdharbā says that when one has given up what is wrong one attains God by even a little positive action *(ācār)*, [Bhaṭobās] agrees.

One day Bhaṭobās was sitting there. All the Mahānubhāvs, from Lakṣmīdhar on down, were sitting in front of him in a tightly packed group. During the discussion about religion *(dharmavārtā)*, Lakṣmīdharbās said, "Avoiding these three forbidden things . . ." (According to some: "One who avoids these four forbidden things . . .") ". . . one attains God (Īśvar) by even a little religious practice *(dharmānuṣṭhān)*."

Lakṣmīdharbā said this, and Bhaṭobās agreed.

Addendum: The fourth forbidden thing is the displeasure of a deity.[344]

234. He talks about faith in keeping one another company.

Once during a discussion about religion *(dharmavārtā),* Bhaṭobās said, "One who is senior should give his company to his juniors; one who is junior should seek the company of his seniors. They are protection for each other. So you should give and seek [one another's] company."

Ānobās heard this teaching *(smṛti)*[345] and held it in his heart. Later Ānobās showed its application.

When he heard it, he was a lay disciple. Then, after Bhaṭobās had died, he took initiation as an ascetic; and one day, when it was time to go to sleep in some village, he said to his own disciples, "You sleep around me. You will protect me; I will protect you. Let us bring our religion *(dharma)* to perfection by keeping one another company."

So they slept [around him].

235. He teaches about refreshment and tarnishment.

One day during a discussion about religion *(dharmavārtā),* Bhaṭobās said, "A man who gets tired and tarnished doing practice *(ācār)* alone gets refreshed in the presence of the deputy *(adhikaraṇ).* He also gets refreshed by a discussion in a large group. And one who is tarnished by laxness gets refreshed by doing practice alone.

"And when these activities are allotted to different times, one gets refreshed in all ten ways."[346]

236. He says that interpretation should be confined to the scriptural works themselves.

On the subject of context *(prakaraṇ),*[347] Bhaṭobās said, "The meaning *(arthu)* of revelation *(śruti)*[348] should be explained through revelation. The meaning of a biographical episode *(līḷā)* should be explained through the episode; the meaning of parables (*dṛṣṭānta*s) should be explained through the parables. The meaning of the *Gītā*[349] should be explained through the *Gītā.* The meaning of the *Bhāgavata*[350] should be explained through the *Bhāgavata.* There is one Meaning[351] that should be explained through all of them." *Addendum:* "Thus works should be explained through the works themselves, according to their context."

This is what he said.

237. Keśavdev gets angry with Kavīśvar over a discussion about religion.

Once Bhaṭobās was holding a discussion about religion *(dharmavārtā).* During the discussion, Bhaṭobās and Kavīśvarbās did most of the talking. They had a huge debate, with objections and answers.

Kesobās spoke to Kavīśvarbās about it: "Bhaṭ, it is wrong to argue that much with the deputy *(adhikaraṇ).* The deputy *(adhiṣṭhān)* gets displeased. Can any understanding emerge from this? What Bhaṭobās says is the word of God *(īśvarvāṇi)*. You should bow your head and accept it as you have heard it. If you cannot accept it, then think it over to yourself. Then in time, when your unworthiness has gone away, you will come to understand."

Kesobās spoke angrily to Kavīśvar this way.

238. Gati Gondobā receives instruction.

Gati Gondobā was Kavīśvarbās' [niece] Nāgāïsē's grandfather. He lived in Rāmpurī. One day he received instruction from Bhaṭobās. (Some say he took initiation as an ascetic.)

239. He argues with a paṇḍit who has heard him called the "charismatic teacher," and he gives him initiation as an ascetic.

There was a certain paṇḍit who said, "What is this 'charismatic *(vedhavantī)* Nāgdevbhaṭ' like?" and came to have *darśan* of him.

He had a huge debate with Bhaṭobās. Bhaṭobās silenced him. He said, "He *is* the charismatic Nāgdevbhaṭ."

Immediately he renounced all attachments and took initiation as an ascetic.

240. [Kesobās] justifies the word *"mātrā."*

Keśavdev justified the word *"mātrā"* in "Asatīparī"[352] to the paṇḍits by denying that it is any of the three [kinds of] utterance *(yuktitrayē)* rejected by the grammarians and explaining that it is the fourth [kind of] utterance, the word of God *(īśvarokti)* instead.[353]

Sic.[354]

241. He calls Hīrāï the touchstone of the dispassionate.

Hīrāïsē was Paṇḍitbās' [wife]. She would point out anyone's mistakes anywhere. She would tell people how to behave. She would make a big fuss over any little thing.

Hearing this, Bhaṭobās said, "Hīrāï is the touchstone of the dispassionate. One who can pass her test is truly dispassionate."

242. He says, "Bhaṭ, you are a poet of love."

One day—it is not known in what context—Bhaṭobās said to Kavīśvarbās, "Bhaṭ, you are a poet of love."[355] He praised him this way.

243. He says that an external act will have an internal effect.

A Mahātmā had given up all the duties of mendicants. He had taken off his [mendicant's] garb.

Someone said, "He has gone away from the religion *(dharma)*."

Bhaṭobās said, "As long as he was not doing forbidden things and was wearing the garb, he had not gone away. An external act will have an internal effect."

244. Nāmdev the devotee of Viṣṇu is attracted through Paṇḍit's words.[356]

One day Nāmdev the tailor[357] met Paṇḍitbās. They had a debate. Paṇḍitbās defeated him, and then he began to ask for initiation *(upadesu).* But [Paṇḍitbās] would not give it to him. Then [Paṇḍitbās] brought [Nāmdev's] thoughts to the Kṛṣṇa incarnation. Then [Nāmdev] composed the poem "My days have passed to no purpose."[358]

According to some, it was Kavīśvarbas who defeated him, and Kemdyā[359] as well.

245. He says not to allow a man who is respected and pedantic to participate in a discussion of the scripture.

One day—it is not known on what occasion—Bhaṭobās said to Keśo, Paṇḍit, and the others, "Do not allow someone who is respected and pedantic to participate in a discussion of the scripture *(śāstra).*"

Everyone agreed with this.

246. Using the metaphor of daughter and daughter-in-law, he calls the Gaṅgā Valley an in-laws' house from the point of view of the practice of religion.

Addendum: This is according to some. According to Kesobās' version, Bhaṭobās said, "Varāḍ is our maternal home, and the Gaṅgā Valley our in-laws' house."

Addendum: "Therefore, *dharma* does not get accomplished there as it does here."

This is what he said.[360]

247. He says "I challenge" with respect to Mhāībhaṭ's service.

One day Bhaṭobās said, "I will expound 'Mahāvākya'[361] to anyone who shows me Mhāībhaṭ doing anything but serving Śrīprabhu." *Sic.*[362]

This teaching *(smṛti)*[363] is from Ṛddhipur, while Śrīprabhu Gosāvī was alive. It could not be included in the biography *(caritra),*[364] so it was put in [here], in [the account of what happened at] Nimbā.[365]

248. He says that a man who is doing practice gets direct experience just through verbal testimony.

One day—it is not known on what occasion—Bhaṭobās said, "A man who is doing practice *(ācār)* gets direct experience *(aparokṣa)* just through verbal testimony *(śābda).*"[366]

249. He says that when a person has achieved particular [knowledge], he belongs to a divine incarnation.

One day Bhaṭobās said, "When a person *(jīva)* has achieved particular [knowledge] (*viśeṣ[jñān]*),[367] then he belongs to a divine incarnation *(avatār)* and the divine incarnation belongs to him."

250. He says that to interpret [God's] words wrongly is to be a sinner against the words.

One day, in a certain context, Bhaṭobās said, "God (Parameśvar) takes form in his words *(vacan).* When one expounds the words wrongly, one is called a sinner against the God (Parameśvar) who has the form of words. One has distanced oneself from that God (Īśvar)."

251. He says that a half hour of seeking knowledge will accomplish what wandering would.

One day Bhaṭobās said to a Mahātmā who was setting out to wander, "Stay here. Don't go out to wander today. Today there will be a discussion about religion *(dharmavārtā).*"

So the man stayed, and an unprecedented discussion took place. Then Bhaṭobās said to him, "A half hour of seeking knowledge *(jijñāsā)* will accomplish all that your wandering would."

252. He explains that one attains God by making the decision to become a disciple.

One day during a discussion about religion *(dharmavārtā),* Bhaṭobās said, "If a sensualist dies the moment that, pan in his mouth and flowers on his head, he sets out to become a follower, he attains God (Īśvar), even though he has not done any practice *(nācāratāṃci).*

Addendum: He explained this through the parable of the prostitute.[368]

253. He challenges anyone to [show him] Keśav and others idle.

One day Kesobās, Paṇḍitbās, and Rāghobhaṭ were discussing the scripture *(śāstra).* Seeing this, Bhaṭobās said, "I challenge anyone to show me Keśav, Paṇḍit, or Rām standing or sitting idle, not engaged in a discussion of scripture."

He praised them this way.

And when he saw the three of them standing, sitting, and doing everything exactly the same, he would say, "Rām, Paṇḍit, and Keśavdyā are three parts of a single image *(mūrti).*"

(Up to here is [from the] Kavibās [version].)[369]

254. Māhādāïsē dies in Naugāv.

Māhādāïsē was in Naugāv. One day she became ill with a boil. Hearing that, Bhaṭobās came from Nimbā to take care of her.

She met Bhaṭobās. Bhaṭobās tried some remedies. But Māhādāïsē said, "No, Nāgdev. I am not going to live." So Bhaṭobās did not try anything further.

Then one day she was much worse. Bhaṭobās asked, "Rūpai, do you remember God?"

"Yes, Nāgdev. I do remember him."

Bhaṭobās said, "How do you remember him, mother?"

Māhādāïsē said, "With a turban on his head, fashioning a pumice stone that [he called] a floating horse." And she told him of the way [the Gosāvī] had played in Belopur.[370]

At this, Bhaṭobās said, "Rūpai, as long as you have lived you have not failed to perform proper recollection *(smaraṇ)*. You alone have remembered God from the first day to the last day." And Bhaṭobās felt grief.

With that, Māhādāïsē died. She was buried in Naugāv.

Bhaṭobās said, "The old woman was a protector of the religion *(dharma)*, a protector of love. She was my friend, and so I feel bad." He mourned her with these words.

Then he returned to Nimbā.

255. When Gaurāïsē admonishes Hīrāïsē, [Bhaṭobās] says that [Gaurāïsē] keeps up the standards in the order.

It is not known which Hīrāïsē it was, but she was a lay disciple. One day in the course of wandering, Umbarī Gaurāïsē went to meet her. She saw that hard chick-peas[371] had been set out in her courtyard to dry. So Gaurāïsē admonished her, saying, "What is this, Hīrāï?"

Bhaṭobās heard about this, and said, "Since Māhādāïsē died, Gaurāïsē keeps up the standards in the order *(mārg)*."

256. When Bhaṭobās gets a fever, he accepts a bed from Paṇḍit.

Once Bhaṭobās had a fever. Paṇḍitbās bought a cot made of cloth tapes. He spread a fine sheet on it. He said to Bhaṭobās, "Please lie on this, Bhaṭ."

Silently, Bhaṭobās lay down.

257. He stops his fever by making a review of the order *(mārg)*.

Then on the third day, Bhaṭobās said, "How long have I had this fever?"

Paṇḍitbās said, "This is the third day."

Bhaṭobās said, "Since the Gosāvī made me his deputy *(adhikaraṇ)*, I have finally told the old woman[372] the same thing that I told Paṇḍit and Keśavdev. I don't know why I have gotten a fever." And he reviewed [the order].

Kesobās said, "Bhaṭ, there is nothing to worry about, is there?"

Bhaṭobās said, "No, Paṇḍit, there isn't."

This made everyone happy.

Then Bhaṭobās said, "Don't anyone speak. Be quiet. I will remember the Gosāvī's play *(līḷā)*."

So Paṇḍitbās made everyone be quiet. Then [Bhaṭobās] practiced recollection—it is not known how. He was very quiet for a while, and then he said, "Here am I, Cakradhar's Vānarā."[373] And he stretched, with a loud voice said "Śrī Cakradhar!" and sat up. With that, his fever stopped completely.

Addendum: Kesobās, Paṇḍit, and the others were very happy.

258. Paṇḍit is told something in a dream.

One day Paṇḍitbās had a dream. Outside the temple *(maḍh)* there was a woman in a freshly starched sari, with her hair hanging loose. She was outside the temple, in the corner of the compound wall. She began crying, saying over and over again, "What will I do now?"

Paṇḍitbās heard those words. "What is this I have seen?" he said, and he awoke, frightened. He sat up. Those words kept sounding in his ears.

Then he went to that spot and looked. He saw light, but no one was there. So he came back and sat down.

The first thing in the morning he told Bhaṭobās what had happened. "So, Bhaṭ, what is this that I have seen?"

And Bhaṭobās said, "Now the Gosāvī will send for me. She was the deity of this place. She showed you an omen."

Addendum: Everyone felt sorrowful.

259. When Bhaṭ gets a fever, he asks his fellow disciples' forgiveness.

One day Bhaṭobās said, "Today the Gosāvī will send for me." Paṇḍit and all the others got frightened. Someone asked him something about his will.

Bhaṭobās said, "Don't ask me this kind of thing. Ask me something about "Nirvacan," "Mahāvākya," or "Uddharaṇ."[374]

So Paṇḍit asked him questions and Bhaṭobās taught.

Then, after some time, he said, "Paṇḍit, don't ask any more now. The time is getting very close now. Now I will fold my hands and say to you, the disciples of the five *gurus*,[375] "If I have offended anyone in carrying out the Gosāvī's work, you must all forgive me." Having said this, he gave a shout of victory.

260. Bhaṭobās sees God.

Then Bhaṭobās said, "Now no one must talk; no one must cry. Do not touch me for a watch or so after I have died. Now I will remember Bāïsẽ's God, Śrī Cakradhar." Having said this, he lay down and departed.

Then the lay disciples decorated a bier. On the bier they set a plate and copper water pots. They waved [coins before him] and placed them [on the bier]. They hired musicians.

In this way they brought him to the bank of the river. They did the rites for a *yogī.* In Śaka 1224, in the Saṃvatsar year named Śubhakṛt, on the twelfth day of the dark half of the month of Bhādrapad,[376] Bhaṭobās had *darśan* of God (Īśvar).

He became a disciple in his thirty-second year. He was in the Gosāvī's presence for four years, during six months of which period he was in Śrīprabhu's presence. Then, after the Gosāvī died, he was in Śrīprabhu's presence for fourteen years. After that he lived for sixteen more years. Thus he lived sixty-six years. He lived thirty-four years within God's grace.

261. Paṇḍit composes a poem in his distress at being separated from Bhaṭ.

Then—it is not known whether right there on the river bank or after he had come back to the temple—Paṇḍitbās composed a poem *(dhuvā)* in his distress at his bereavement:

1. He served Śrīprabhu's feet; that purified his body and mind
   and sanctified all three worlds.
   Listen: no one knows how many have been enlightened
   in his company.
   They go into trance through natural bliss:
   that Avadhūt plays on earth.

Refrain: Leaving behind the net of delusion,
   holding to the pure form of the Self,
   that servant *(margaḷā)* of the king of gods
   became separated from worldly life.

2. He learned to distinguish the essential from the non-essential,
   so he disregarded censure.
   He held firmly the one savior;
   his mind merged into him.
   Becoming detached from the senses' objects,
   in the company of absolute knowledge
   (brahmavidyā)
   his essential nature reached the Lord of the Absolute *(kaivalyapati)*.

3. He left all *karma* behind.
   The Supreme One *(parampuruṣ)* favored him,
   So he was not affected by the sufferings of existence.
   He was filled with supreme joy.
   He was appointed by the primordial Lord,
   the supreme *yogī* whom Ṛddhis obey,
   whose Siddhis[377] are hidden,
   who cools [suffering] people.

4. The supreme object of meditation,
   the limitless, unqualified Brahman,
   the formless one took form
   to save people.
   Listen: By his natural luster
   the state of the Self was illumined.
   Then, remaining motionless, they come;
   they have reached the supreme reward.

5. He described the supreme path
   to tell of the secret of a *guru*,

he became a *jīvanmukta*[378]
  and showed the supreme way.
He obeyed King Śrī Cakradhar,
  who confirmed him as a leader.
He called Nāgārjun
  and placed him near his lotus feet.

[Epilogue.]

Bhaṭobās' fellow disciples *(gurubhāü),* and, from one point of view, his own disciples *(siṣya),* were (1) Vīrahe Lakṣmīndharbhaṭ, (2) Kothaḷobā, (3) Pomāïsẽ, and (4) Vairāgyadev.

Next, those who were only his fellow disciples *(gurubhāvaṇḍẽ)* were (1) Bāïsẽ, (2) Sāntibāïsẽ, (3) Māhādāïsẽ, (4) Mhāībhaṭ, (5) Sādhẽ, (6) Āüsẽ, (7) Nāthobā, (8) his mother, Ābāïsẽ, (9) Khei, and (10) Goi.

These are his fellow disciples who were initiated in [the Gosāvī's] presence *(sannidhānīṃ anusarauni gurubhāvaṇḍe).*

Next, his fellow disciples who were not initiated *(nanusarauni gurubhāvaṇḍe)*: (1) Dāïmbā, (2) Demāïsẽ, and (3) Upādhye. Two of these[379] lost their enlightenment *(bodhu).* Upādhye was initiated by Bhaṭobās *(bhaṭobāsāṃjavaḷī anusaralẽ)* after the Gosāvī was gone.

Dādos was different: he had *darśan* [of the Gosāvī, but was never initiated]. Of all the others who had *darśan* [of the Gosāvī], some received instruction from Bhaṭobās and became disciples.

All of these, and others as well, who had not been told of before, have been told about [in this book].

Notes to *Smṛtisthaḷ*

1. "The supreme Lord," also called Parameśvar, Īśvar, or *dev*. All of these terms are translated here as "God."

2. Cakradhar's.

3. The edition of V. N. Deshpande (Puṇē: Venus Prakāśan, 1939; 2d ed., 1960; 3d ed., 1968) and the 1990 edition by S. G. Tulpule (Puṇe: Anamol Prakāśan) include at this point a list of each type of follower. See the Appendix, below. For a discussion of this typology of disciples, see the Introduction, above, chapter 4. *Darśan* is the sight of a holy person or object.

4. Bhaṭobās or Nāgdev, the central character of this text.

5. Their *guru*. Also called Rāmdev.

6. Bhaṭobās' cousin, his father's brother's daughter.

7. Sinnar.

8. Cakradhar and Śrīprabhu (= Guṇḍam Rāüḷ) are both considered incarnations (*avatārs*) of the one God, Parameśvar or Īśvar, and hence both are referred to as "the Gosāvī." Bhaṭobās' six months in the presence of Śrīprabhu and three and a half years in the presence of Cakradhar add up to a total of four years in the divine presence.

9. Cakradhar's. Cakradhar is sometimes called "our Gosāvī" to distinguish him from Śrīprabhu.

10. Mahānubhāv tradition holds that Cakradhar did not die, but left for the North.

11. That is, in January–February of A.D. 1273.

12. Some of the symptoms are mentioned toward the end of this chapter: he fell unconscious, mushrooms grew on him, and so on.

13. The valley of the Godāvarī River. At the time of Cakradhar's final departure, he and his followers were in Belopur, on the Pravarā, a tributary of the Godāvarī.

14. Ṛddhipur, in Vidarbha, Śrīprabhu's town.

15. *melī,* a variation on Śrīprabhu's more usual form of address, "Drop dead!" See *The Deeds of God in Ṛddhipur,* translated by Anne Feldhaus (New York: Oxford University Press, 1984), passim.

16. *karavanda,* corinda?

17. *Līḷācaritra,* "Uttarārdha," chaps. 625 and 649 (*Mhāībhaṭ Saṅkalit Śrīcakradhar Līḷā Caritra,* 2d ed., ed. V. B. Kolte [Mumbaī: Mahārāṣṭra Rājya Sāhitya-Saṃskṛti Maṇḍaḷ, 1982]); *Sūtrapāṭh* 12.208 (Anne Feldhaus, *The Religious System of the Mahānubhāva Sect: The Mahānubhāva Sūtrapāṭha* [New Delhi: Manohar, 1983], 85–169). Cf. Feldhaus, *The Deeds of God in Ṛddhipur,* chap. 322.

18. Chapter 1, above.

19. Cf. Feldhaus, *The Deeds of God in Ṛddhipur,* chap. 85. Here, Cāṅgdev Rāüḷ is a name of Cakradhar.

20. That is, in January–February of 1286 (counting the thirteen years from the Śrīmukh to the Vyaya Saṃvatsar, the seventh and twentieth years, respectively, in the sixty-year Jupiter cycle) or 1287 (accepting the text's statement that it was fourteen years from the death of Cakradhar to that of Śrīprabhu). Feldhaus, *The Deeds of God in Ṛddhipur,* chap. 322 gives the date of Śrīprabhu's death as "the fourth day of the dark half of Bhādrapad [August–September] in the Vyaya year."

21. Literally, "changed his inclination *(pravṛtti),*" the choice of words serving to emphasize the voluntary character of Śrīprabhu's death. The same expression is used in chapter 1, above, with respect to Cakradhar's departure, as well as in the title of the present chapter.

22. The valley of the Godāvarī River, the principal region in which Cakradhar lived and traveled. The places named are all places where Cakradhar had stayed.

23. The spittle is, of course, dried up and washed away by the time Nāgdev and the others come, but perhaps a betel-colored red stain remains.

24. A Nṛsiṃha temple in which Cakradhar had stayed.

25. The feet of a divine incarnation. In this case, Cakradhar's feet, although the term is also used for Śrīprabhu's feet.

26. See Feldhaus, *The Deeds of God in Ṛddhipur,* chap. 258.

27. See ibid., chap. 259.

28. *kāṃbi.* See ibid., chap. 310.

29. Possibly the one in Feldhaus, *The Deeds of God in Ṛddhipur,* chap. 293.

30. Bhaṭobās' grandson.

31. Commentaries on the "Ācār" (chap. 12) and "Vicār" (chap. 10) chapters, respectively, of the *Sūtrapāṭh.*

32. A commentary on the first nine chapters of the *Sūtrapāṭh.*

33. He was trying to claim an inheritance for his daughter, who had been "married" to Śrīprabhu (Guṇḍam Rāüḷ) in an episode narrated in Feldhaus, *The Deeds of God in Ṛddhipur,* chap. 224. For Śrīprabhu, the wedding was temporary fun, and he soon "lost interest," but, as the next sentence of this passage reveals, the girl considered it a valid marriage.

34. Appendix 1 of Deshpande's edition includes the following additional chapter, explaining the decision against Īśvarnāyak. The chapter is from a manuscript of *Ajñāt Smṛti.*

20. When Īśvarnāyak asks for a share, Mhāībhaṭ silences him [before] Nyāyabhārati and the 500 *sannyāsīs.*

Then, after Bhaṭobās had left for Mātāpur, Īśvarnāyak began to ask Mhāībhaṭ for a share [of Śrīprabhu's estate]. And Mhāībhaṭ said, "Come on, let's go before the four *mahājans* and before the *sannyāsīs.* Let's plead our cases; then if they decide we should give it to you, we will. What more could you ask?"

So Mhāībhaṭ and Īśvarnāyak both set out for Deuḷvāḍā. The *mahājans* and the 500 *sannyāsīs* held an assembly there. Both parties presented their arguments. The *sannyāsīs* and *mahājans* held a discussion about whether or not Īśvarnāyak had a right to get something. Then the *sannyāsīs* and *mahājans* said to Īśvarnāyak: "One who is active *(pravṛt)* in the world cannot claim a share of the property of one who has withdrawn from the world *(nivṛt)*. Only those who follow the Rāüḷ after giving up all attachments are entitled to [a share]; others are not."

They gave Mhāībhaṭ a letter of judgment to this effect.

35. A verse text in Sanskrit on the life of Cakradhar.

36. Śuka is a figure who appears in Sanskrit epic and Purāṇic literature as a son of Vyāsa and a model of ascetic control.

37. Place names.

38. "Uddharaṇ" is the title of chapter 8 of the *Sūtrapāṭh*. It describes the process by which liberation or salvation (*uddharaṇ* [Sanskrit, *uddharaṇa*], literally "uplifting") is attained.

39. *mājhiyā mhāṃtārīyā*. Not just the old ladies, but all those without Sanskrit learning would be unable to understand the work if it were written in Sanskrit verse.

40. *prakaraṇānvayo*. This probably refers only to the first nine chapters ("Navprakaraṇ") of the *Sūtrapāṭh*. "Ācār" (chap. 12) and "Vicār" (chap. 10) are mentioned separately, in chapter 17, below. "Ācār Mālikā" (chap. 13) and "Vicār Mālikā" (chap. 11) are not mentioned, nor are the three short chapters—"Pūrvī," "Pañcakṛṣṇa," and "Pañcanām"—that are found at the beginning of some manuscripts and most printed editions of the text. See Feldhaus, *The Religious System of the Mahānubhāva Sect*, 9–22.

41. The text whose composition is described here is the *Dṛṣṭāntapāṭh*, a collection of 114 parables illustrating aphorisms of the *Sūtrapāṭh*. Each chapter of the *Dṛṣṭāntapāṭh* consists of an aphorism, a parable, and a conclusion *(dṛṣṭāntik)*. H. N. Nene and N. B. Bhavalkar (Nāgpur, 1937), Bhagavant Deshmukh and S. R. Gadgil (Aurangabad: Jośī Brothers, 1965), and S. G. Tulpule and Kumudini Gharpure (Puṇe, 1964; 2d ed., Venus Prakāśan, 1989) have edited the text.

42. A chapter entitled "Lāpikā" is found in most *Sūtrapāṭh* manuscripts after the first nine (or twelve) short chapters and before the longer chapters on "Ācār" and "Vicār."

43. This is probably the commentary listed as "*Ācārādi naū prakaraṇē*" in I. M. P. Raeside, "A Bibliographical Index of Mahānubhāva Works in Marathi," *Bulletin of the School of Oriental and African Studies, University of London* 23 (1960): 469.

44. Different from the Lakṣmīdharbā of Rājaur who is mentioned in the preceding chapter.

45. A work in Sanskrit verse.

46. A *stotra* is a eulogistic work in verse.

47. A *yogabhraṣṭa* is someone who has been reborn after failing to complete his *yoga* in a previous life.

48. Sanskrit words meaning "Either a fever or a weapon," two ways to die. Cf. the proverb *śāpādapi śarādapi,* "through a curse or an arrow," the two ways a Brāhmaṇ can destroy his foes.

49. Cf. chapter 30, below.

50. A senior disciple.

51. "Ease [one another's] weariness." *Sūtrapāṭh* 12.130.

52. A *prasād* garment is a relic, a garment that had been used by the Gosāvī and is his gift to his disciples.

53. That is, Bhaṭobās too is like a *prasād* relic, because he too has been touched by the Gosāvī and is the Gosāvī's gift to the other disciples.

54. *Līḷācaritra,* "Uttarārdha," chap. 12.

55. That is, the chapter belongs to the second half of the *Līḷācaritra,* "Uttarārdha," rather than to *Smṛtisthaḷ.*

56. That is, to renounce the world and become an ascetic.

57. "Mahādevobā who had contact with God."

58. Feldhaus, *The Deeds of God in Ṛddhipur,* chap. 204.

59. Ibid., chap. 205.

60. That is, even though he had been fed as a guest at lay disciples' houses, Cāṅgdev still followed the *Sūtrapāṭh* injunctions to beg for his food and then to eat it on the bank of a river. *Sūtrapāṭh* 13.59 and passim.

61. Although the disciples have mixed together and are sharing the food they have severally obtained by begging, each of them is eating only from his own bowl. The extra food the generous disciple gives to Bhaṭobās is polluted *(usītē, uṣṭa)* by having been on the plate from which the disciple was eating.

62. *Līḷācaritra,* "Pūrvārdha," chap. 118.

63. *Sūtrapāṭh* 12.115: "A puddle and the Gaṅgā should be the same to you."

64. Cāturmās is a four-month period, roughly corresponding to the monsoon season, when asetics generally suspend their normal peregrination and stay in some one place.

65. This is a modification of the *Sūtrapāṭh*'s command, "Practice constant peregrination" (13.132), but it is closer to the usual practice of Indian ascetics, including Buddhists and Jains.

66. That is, they began to wear distinctive clothing, something they had apparently not done during the lifetime of Cakradhar and Guṇḍam Rāüḷ (Śrīprabhu).

67. The three categories *sattva* ("goodness"), *rajas* ("passion"), and *tamas* ("darkness") are widely used in Indian thought to classify—and to hierarchize (*sattva* being the best, *tamas* the worst, and *rajas* in between)—various aspects of nature: here, personality types.

68. The five names are those of the "five Kṛṣṇas," five principal divine incarnations in the Mahānubhāv system: Kṛṣṇa, Dattātreya, Cāṅgdev Rāüḷ, Guṇḍam Rāüḷ, and Cakradhar.

69. That is, spending one's life this way is *not* a waste. The phrase "spends his life at the foot of a tree" echoes the language of *Sūtrapāṭh* 12.26, 12.72, and 13.219.

70. Govind = Kṛṣṇa.

71. The twelfth day of the fortnight is the day on which the eleventh-day *(ekādaśī)* fast is broken; sweets are prepared on the twelfth day. The eleventh-day fast is associated with devotion to Viṣṇu. If, as exclusive devotees of Parameśvar, and hence *not* of Viṣṇu, Mahānubhāv lay disciples did not practice the eleventh-day fast—or the

twelfth-day feast—the twelfth day of the fortnight would be a good day to beg at the homes of lay Mahānubhāvs. Even if they were one's acquaintances, they would not have as rich alms to give as would devotees of Viṣṇu who had practiced the eleventh-day fast and were feasting on the twelfth. One manuscript used for Deshpande's edition has a variant reading that could be translated: "they may *not* go to beg. . . ." If this reading were to be accepted, the assumption would be that lay Mahānubhāvs also, like Vaiṣṇavas, observed the eleventh-day fast and the twelfth-day feast.

72. Cf. *Sūtrapāṭh* 12.82–83: "Beg without picking and choosing the houses [at which to beg]. Do not go to the houses of your acquaintances."

73. *Sūtrapāṭh* 12.14.

74. *Sūtrapāṭh* 12.278: "Self service for ascetics."

75. A ritual gesture of worship or respect, consisting of waving a tray of small lighted lamps, burning camphor, or, as in this case, incense in front of the person or object to be honored.

76. *Sūtrapāṭh* 9: "To one who, free from passion and error, with his nature restrained, independent, spends his life in recollection of God, Parameśvar again gives union with himself."

77. That is, for someone other than me.

78. A Sanskrit verse *(śloka)* whose source we have not been able to locate.

79. See *Sūtrapāṭh* 12.136ff.

80. *Sūtrapāṭh* 13.26.

81. For *rājas, tāmas,* and *satvastha,* see note 67, above.

82. That is, the regular rules are more comfortable and familiar, as a girl's parents' home is to her, but the occasional rules must nevertheless also be followed, as, after marriage, a girl must live and work in her in-laws' house. The regular rules *(nityavidhi)* are *aṭan,* peregrination; *vijan,* solitude; *prasādsevā,* worship of relics; and *īśacintan,* thinking about God; while the occasional rules *(naimittikvidhi)* include *prasaṅgopātta gurubandhūṃcī sevāśuśrūṣā,* serving one's fellow disciples as occasion demands.

83. That is, just as a ladle is dipped into every dish on the stove, one should be of service to everyone.

84. While Bhāndārekār was practicing only the regular rules.

85. Feldhaus, *The Deeds of God in Ṛddhipur,* chap. 196.

86. This is the term that Bhaṭobās uses to refer to himself. The term is recorded as having been used by Cakradhar: see, for instance, *Sūtrapāṭh* 10.113 and 13.35. In *Līḷācaritra,* "Uttarārdha," chap. 623, Cakradhar uses the term in connection with Bhaṭobās.

87. Divine musicians.

88. *pāṭhīceyā vāṃsācī upapati.* Possibly the reverberations of *karma.*

89. Both cowrie shells and betel nuts were used as currency.

90. By contact with money.

91. This is a commentary on *Sūtrapāṭh* 12.35, *gaḍīṃ sīḍīṃ asāvē,* "Stay in *gaḍīs* and *sīḍīs.*"

92. This is a commentary on *Sūtrapāṭh* 12.36, *hāḷiyāṃ pāḷiyāṃ asāvē,* "Stay in *hāḷīs* and *pāḷīs.*"

93. This is a commentary on *Sūtrapāṭh* 13.20, *tumhīṃ pūrīṃ pāṭanīṃ na vasāvē,* "Do not live in *purs* or *pāṭans.*"

94. Chardobā (Deshpande has "Chardobās") was a disciple of Cakradhar who was

a model of dispassion: he would even eat vomited *(chardit)* food. But he gradually allowed himself to fall prey to attachments, and eventually gave up the ascetic life. See *Līḷācaritra,* "Uttarārdha," chap. 481 and *Sūtrapāṭh* 12.202.

95. Paṇḍitbās was Dāmodarpaṇḍit, the author of *Vacchaharaṇ* (ed. V. B. Kolte. Malkāpūr: Aruṇ Prakāśan, 1953; 2d ed., 1965).

96. For the sequel to this episode, see chapter 58, below.

97. = Bhāskarbhaṭ Borīkar, the author of *Śiśupāḷvadh* (ed. V. B. Kolte. Malkāpūr: Aruṇ Prakāśan, 1958) and *Uddhavgītā* (ed. V. B. Kolte. Amrāvatī, 1935; 2d ed., Malkāpūr: Aruṇ Prakāśan, 1962).

98. To get her son to eat fine food that she had prepared.

99. A reference to *Sūtrapāṭh* 10.158, "You are not that sort of fraudulent preceptor; you are a preceptor who leads people away from evil and places them in the good."

100. That is, why have you become a disciple?

101. Caitanya is the highest of the *devatās*, deities of the relative sort utterly inferior to Īśvar. See Anne Feldhaus, "The *devatācakra* of the Mahānubhāvas," *Bulletin of the School of Oriental and African Studies, University of London* 43 (1980): 101–109.

102. See chapter 54, above.

103. That is, do you want to suffer maltreatment from your daughter-in-law in the same house where you were once well cared for by your wife?

104. That is, we are the ones who will be inconvenienced if you die. *Jogīs* and *jaṅgams* are wandering holy men. The term *jogī* is derived from *yogī,* the term for a practitioner of *yoga.* A *jaṅgam* is an itinerant Liṅgāyat priest.

105. *Sūtrapāṭh* 13.132: "Practice constant peregrination."

106. Various types of Marāṭhī verses. *dhuvā* = *dhāvā,* a cry to God to come to the help of his devotee.

107. Instead of cold leftovers.

108. = Kesobās.

109. Deshpande's edition has Mayaṅka.

110. "*Rūṃ-rūṃ*" is the sound of Paṇḍit singing, and "*ṭhak-ṭhak*" the sound of Kesobās lecturing. See the previous chapter.

111. Chapter 6 of the *Sūtrapāṭh.* It consists of the text, and a word-by-word gloss, of the following "great statement" *(mahāvākya):* "There is a single Parameśvar, distinct from the *jīva* and the world, and composed of being, consciousness, and joy. He possesses all powers."

112. Imitating the cry Māhādāïsẽ and the other mendicants made in begging? Cf. chapter 4, above.

113. Cf. *Sūtrapāṭh* 13.99 ("One who meditates on me is hard to find") and 13.241 ("One who loves God is better than one whom God loves"). Cf. chapter 131, below.

114. This word indicates that the sentence, chapter, or paragraph that follows occurred only in Kavībās' version of the *smṛtis*, and not in other versions. "Kavībās" could be Kavīśvarbās, but Deshpande, the editor of the text, thinks Kavībās is Kavi Mālobās, "the poet Mālobās." See the Introduction, above, chapter 5.

115. A place where Cakradhar had once stayed.

116. Literally, "Why have you held the preliminary sip of water in your hands?"

117. Apar Rāmdev may be a name, or it may mean "the other Rāmdev"—that is, a different Rāmdev from the one in chapters 56, 57, 59, 60, and 61.

118. "*Asmāt*" and "*kasmāt*" are Sanskrit for "therefore" and "wherefore," words that often come up in learned arguments.

119. Chapter 8 of the *Sūtrapāṭh.*

120. *Sūtrapāṭh* 8.46. Part of the chapter "Uddharaṇ." The whole *sūtra* is as follows: " '*Karma*' is so named because of the definition, 'What is done *(krīyate)* is *karma.*' *Karma* is expressed by the word '*karma*'; the stain, too, is expressed by the word '*karma.*' " The part of this *sūtra* quoted in the present chapter is in Sanskrit, but the rest of the *sūtra* is in Marāṭhī.

121. The highest of the four levels of speech: *parā, paśyantī, madhyamā,* and *vaikharī.* See *Sūtrapāṭh* 8.21, 10.15–18, and 11.23.

122. *Sūtrapāṭh* 10.164.

123. *Līḷācaritra,* "Uttarārdha," chap. 17.

124. Nine hours.

125. During the late afternoon. *Sūtrapāṭh* 13.53.

126. *Sūtrapāṭh* 13.59: "Having completed your begging, take your meal on the bank of a river."

127. *Sūtrapāṭh* 13.66: "Sleep outside a village in an abandoned temple or under a tree."

128. Cf. *Sūtrapāṭh* 13.74: "Take off the stench of dirt; put on the stench of water."

129. Literally, he could not arrive at *satva* (= *sattva*), purity or goodness of mind.

130. A divine or holy person. Here, a *yogabhraṣṭa,* someone who has failed to complete his yogic regime in one lifetime, and must be reborn to complete it in the next.

131. A commentary on chapter 12 of the *Sūtrapāṭh,* "Ācār."

132. The word we have translated "medium" is *jhāḍ,* a term whose most common meaning is "tree," but which is also used for a person who becomes possessed by a ghost (or sometimes a deity) and through whom the ghost (or deity) speaks.

133. Chapter 9 of the *Sūtrapāṭh.* See note 76, above.

134. *Sūtrapāṭh* 13.253: "Even a lump of salt is an object of sense pleasure."

135. This is generally taken to refer to the invasion of the Deccan by Malik Kāphur, in A.D. 1310. It thus renders problematic the statement in chapter 260, below, that Nāgdev died in Śaka 1224, or A.D. 1302. See the Introduction, above, chapter 1. On the other hand, perhaps the invasion referred to here is that of Ala-ud-Din Khilji, the nephew of the Sultan of Delhi, in A.D. 1294.

136. Ābāïsẽ was Bhaṭobās' mother, and Vaijobā his brother. See chapter 1, above.

137. *Sūtrapāṭh* 12.1: "Renounce your attachment to your own land; renounce your attachment to your own village; renounce especially your attachment to your relatives."

138. Cakradhar and Guṇḍam Rāüḷ, the two divine incarnations whom the early Mahānubhāvs had a chance to meet.

139. See chapter 85, below. The sign to flee is the appearance of the Sultan's army's banners.

140. Perhaps the Bāleghāṭ mountain range. (See the map.)

141. *Sūtrapāṭh* 12.104: "Do not be afraid, Sādhẽ. I will hold the roaring wind above you." Cf. *Līḷācaritra,* "Uttarārdha," chap. 185.

142. Bhaṭobās' son.

143. An ironical echo of *Sūtrapāṭh* 13.81: "Rise at daybreak and set off on the road. Look for company. Those behind you [will] say you are with the ones in front of you; those in front of you [will] say you are with the ones behind you."

144. The Yādav king who is also called Rāmcandra or Rāmcandradev, ruled 1271 to 1311.

145. The verse is in Sanskrit.

146. For Bhaṭobās, the most notable example of this was certainly Cakradhar, whose treatment at the hands of the Yādav king and his minister Hemāḍpaṇḍit is described in *Līḷācaritra,* "Uttarārdha," chaps. 547, 649–651. See Günther-Dietz Sontheimer, "God, Dharma and Society in the Yādava Kingdom of Devagirī According to the *Līḷācaritra* of Cakradhar," in *Indology and Law: Studies in Honour of Professor J. Duncan M. Derrett,* ed. Günther-Dietz Sontheimer and Parameswara K. Aithal (Wiesbaden: F. Steiner Verlag, 1982), 329–358.

147. Songs in various meters with various themes.

148. *Sūtrapāṭh* 13.171.

149. *Līḷācaritra,* "Uttarārdha," chap. 345.

150. The capital of the Yādav kingdom, present-day Daulātabād.

151. Probably the Dematī of *Līḷācaritra,* "Uttarārdha," chap. 520, who is identified there as the wife of Hemāḍi Paṇḍit (Hemāḍpaṇḍit or Hemādri), the minister of the Yādav king. Here she is called Kaṭak Demāïsẽ or Demāïsẽ from Kaṭak to distinguish her from Cakradhar's disciple Demāïsẽ.

152. Māhādāïsẽ. See chapter 111, below.

153. Literally, "my people with patchwork quilts," *kanthaḍīkār.*

154. Parameśvarpur is Ṛddhipur.

155. A *coḷī* is a woman's blouse. This may be a reference to the rite of *ghaṭakañcuki,* which is described as follows in M. Monier-Williams' *Sanskṛit-English Dictionary* (Oxford: 1899; reprint New Delhi: Munshinam Manoharlal, 1976): "an immoral rite practised by Tāntrikas and Śāktas (in which the bodices of different women are placed in a receptacle and the men present at the ceremony are allowed to take them out one by one and then cohabit with the woman to whom each bodice belongs)."

156. Cf. *Sūtrapāṭh* 10.257: "One who is very old is not qualified for *dharma.*"

157. Just as an insect might by chance carve out the holy syllable, so someone who is too old to be qualified in the normal course of things could by chance be qualified anyway. This exemplifies what is called the *ghuṇākṣaranyāya,* the rule of the woodworm's writing.

158. *Molesworth's Marathi-English Dictionary,* corrected reprint (Poona: Shubhada-Saraswat, 1975): "A leguminous plant and its pod, Cowhage or Cowitch, Carpopogon pruriens."

159. S. S. Hanamante, *Saṅket Koś* (Sholapur: Kamalābāī Bendre, 1963) identifies the eighteen kinds of foods *(pakvānna)* as a variety of sweet and/or rich dishes: *mānḍe, vaḍe, ghṛtapuryā, lāḍū, tiḷave, guḷvaryā, teḷvaryā, pheṇyā, kuravaṇḍīyā, ghāryā, ghārge, vaḍorīyā, corve, veṭhnīge, khānḍvī, śikharaṇī, sāñjoryā* and *khirī.*

160. Deshpande's edition gives the word *puruṣ* in parentheses after *tridaṇḍī.* "*Tridaṇḍī*" is the name of a type of renouncer. Here the name is implicitly interpreted to mean "one who punishes or restrains *(daṇḍī)* the three *(tri),* body, senses, and

mind." Cf. *Mānavadharmaśāstra* 12.10–11. On the question of the meaning of *tridaṇḍī,* see Patrick Olivelle, *Renunciation in Hinduism: A Medieval Debate,* vol. 1 (Vienna: Publications of the De Nobili Research Library, 1986), 35–54, 138–139; and Patrick Olivelle, "Renouncer and Renunciation in the Dharmaśāstras," in *Studies in Dharmaśāstra,* edited by Richard Lariviere (Calcutta: Firma KLM Private Limited, 1984), 121–126.

161. On the term *vastu,* see S. G. Tulpule, "The Vastu, or the Reality, of Medieval Indian Saints," in *Bhakti in Current Research, 1979-1982,* ed. Monika Thiel-Horstmann (Berlin: Dietrich Reimer Verlag, 1983), 403–411.

162. Ānobās is another name for Gopāḷpaṇḍit.

163. The notes to Deshpande's edition identify the fourteen as the five organs of action (*karmendriyas*), the five organs of knowledge (*jñānendriyas*), the *manas (sensis communis),* the *buddhi* (intellect), the *ahaṃkāra* (ego), and *cetanā* (=? Caitanya, the highest of the deities in the *devatācakra*).

164. See Feldhaus, "The *devatācakra* of the Mahānubhāvas."

165. A temple of the god Śiva.

166. From gossip.

167. A gesture of self-congratulation, similar to patting oneself on the back in some other cultures.

168. According to Deshpande's introduction to his third edition (1968), 7, Malekoyābā was a fifth-generation disciple of Bhaṭobās.

169. A *jogiṇī* is a female *yogī.*

170. This is a ritual that Cakradhar also performed.

171. That is, not as a funeral meal for your father.

172. *Sūtrapāṭh* 13.188: "In going out to solitude [you should feel] as if you are being led to sit on a raised seat."

173. Rich, festive foods.

174. Literally, by "the five-faced line of *gurus,*" *pācāsyā* (later *pāṃcāsyā*) *gurukuḷ.* The five are Cakradhar, Guṇḍam Rāüḷ (= Śrīprabhu), Cāṅgdev Rāüḷ, Dattātreya, and Kṛṣṇa.

175. This conversation is found in *Līḷācaritra,* "Uttarārdha," chap. 623.

176. "Seven or five," in the Marāṭhī idiom.

177. Of the *mantra. Sūtrapāṭh* 13.121: "A *jīva* gives the syllables; Parameśvar gives enlightenment." In Mahānubhāv thought, a *jīva* is to be distinguished not only from Parameśvar and from material things, but also from the many gods (*devatās*) different from and inferior to Parameśvar.

178. Not of *jīvas.* Acyut, "the steadfast one" or "the unfallen one," is a name for the god Kṛṣṇa. Cf. *Sūtrapāṭh* 12.136: "You are the lineage of Acyut! You should have the highest affection for one another."

179. See above, chapters 2–4.

180. See *Līḷācaritra,* "Uttarārdha," chap. 625; Feldhaus, *The Deeds of God in Ṛddhipur,* chap. 322; and chapters 1 and 3, above. Not just Māhādāïsẽ but all the other disciples are entrusted to Bhaṭobās.

181. The ending *-kavi* means "poet."

182. Presumably Marāṭhī renditions of the famous Sanskrit works with these names. Neither of these two Marāṭhī works is now extant.

183. The Yādav king mentioned in chapters 86, 113, 145, 146, 148, and 149.

184. That is, Kṛṣṇa's.

185. On the marriage of Kṛṣṇa and Rukmiṇī, a subject quite popular with Mahānubhāv authors. Narendrakavi's version has been edited by V. B. Kolte as *Mahākavī Narendra-Viracit Rukmiṇī-Svayaṃvar* (Malkāpūr: Aruṇ Prakāśan, 1966), and by G. M. Dolke and S. M. Dolke as *Narīndra Viracit Rukmiṇīsvayaṃvar* (Nāgpur: Vidarbha Saṃśodhan Maṇḍaḷ, 1971).

186. This is verse 312 in V. B. Kolte's edition.

187. Two types of gold coins.

188. = Hayagrīva.

189. *Gadyarāj* or *Gadyarāj Stotra,* a work in verse based on the tenth chapter of the *Bhāgavata Purāṇa.* This work has been edited and translated by I. M. P. Raeside, *Gadyarāja: A Fourteenth Century Marathi Version of The Kṛṣṇa Legend* (Bombay/London: Popular Prakashan/School of Oriental and African Studies, University of London, 1989).

190. Govind, Murārī, and Gopāl are all names of Kṛṣṇa.

191. Both sandalwood paste and the moon are supposed to cool the longing of one who suffers the pangs of separation *(viraha),* but the *gopīs* find these remedies of no help at all.

192. Vṛndāvan is the grove where Kṛṣṇa's love play with the *gopīs* took place.

193. The *rās* is the circle dance that Kṛṣṇa danced with the *gopīs.*

194. Kṛṣṇa.

195. To call Kṛṣṇa Nāgdev's patron is to emphasize the identity with Kṛṣṇa of Cakradhar, who can more properly be called Nāgdev's patron.

196. That is, have you acquired exceptional knowledge and skill?

197. The verse is in extremely corrupt Sanskrit. This translation is at best a guess at its meaning.

198. Here, Kavīśvar.

199. *Sūtrapāṭh* 6. See note 111, above.

200. That is, the topknot of hair, and the thread worn looped over the left shoulder and hanging below the waist on the right side of the body. The tuft and thread are the marks of an orthodox Brāhmaṇ man.

201. That is, God. Cf. *Sūtrapāṭh* 10.247: "My woman, I identify myself with him. This is not said to him; it is said to me."

202. That is, he forgot what Bhaṭobās had taught him.

203. The *Bhāgavata Purāṇa.*

204. The *Bhagavadgītā.*

205. Literally, "made it completely into the moon"—but the moon is filled with nectar.

206. That is, appointed him his deputy.

207. Cf. Feldhaus, *The Deeds of God in Ṛddhipur,* chap. 97, where Mhāībhaṭ offers Śrīprabhu a gold-worked shawl and a basket of jaggery. Mhāībhaṭ's own clothes are not mentioned, except that on his way he trades his shawl for a coarse blanket, and sells half of another shawl for the money to buy the jaggery and the basket.

208. A Siddha is a perfected *yogī.* "Nāth," here, may refer to a mendicant Nāthpanthī or to a Kānphaṭā Nāth.

209. Literally, of offering [Mount] Meru, the highest mountain in the world, at

the center of the world. In the title of this chapter as well, we have translated "*meru*" as "mountain."

210. *Līḷācaritra,* "Ajñāt Līḷā," chap. 14.

211. In the language of the Mahānubhāv texts, the term *bhajan,* which ordinarily means worship or devotion, is equivalent to *bhojan,* which ordinarily means eating.

212. *Prasād,* here, is food that has been offered to, and presumably tasted by, a deity or holy person.

213. Cf. *Sūtrapāṭh* 12.185: "Parameśvar is to be worshipped; connection *(sambandh)* with him is to be revered."

214. See chapters 92–93, above.

215. See chapter 62, above, where it is Māhādāïsẽ, not Bhaṭobās, who says this. Cf. *Sūtrapāṭh* 13.99 and 13.241.

216. Ujjain is where Cakradhar goes in the last chapter of the *Līḷācaritra: Līḷācaritra,* "Uttarārdha," chap. 655. Here too there are reports that he has been sighted in Ujjain, and Bhaṭobās discourages the disciples from going there to find him. See chapter 232, below.

217. Māhādāïsẽ.

218. Cf. *Līḷācaritra,* "Uttarārdha," chap. 646 and *Sūtrapāṭh* 11.139: "Now there will be contact anew *(naveyāṃ sambandhu).*"

219. Cf. *Sūtrapāṭh* 12.262: "She will be born as a man in the home of happy, rich people; after twelve years, [God] cannot fail to give her union [with himself]." See *Līḷācaritra,* "Uttarārdha," chap. 646.

220. Cf. chapter 107, above.

221. The Yādav king's treasurer.

222. Mhāībhaṭ was the author of the *Līḷācaritra,* the biography of Cakradhar. For a general description of Mhāībhaṭ's methods of research, see chapter 141, below. The episodes in Cakradhar's life, and the chapters in the biography, are called *līḷās*. Gadonāyak's testimony would have been particularly valuable to Mhāībhaṭ because Cakradhar stayed in Gadonāyak's house for a month (*Līḷācaritra,* "Uttarārdha," chaps. 299–301). For an additional example of Mhāībhaṭ's diligence in researching the *līḷās*, see Feldhaus, *The Deeds of God in Ṛddhipur,* chap. 252.

223. A reference to a *Pañcatantra* story about a Brāhmaṇ woman who killed a mongoose. The mongoose had protected the woman's son by killing a snake as it was about to bite the child. The woman saw the mongoose's blood-smeared face and jumped to the conclusion that the mongoose had killed her son. Later she felt remorse. *Pañcopākhyān,* ed. V. B. Kolte (Bombay: Mahārāṣṭra Rājya Sāhitya-Saṃskṛti Maṇḍaḷ, 1979), chap. 5.1, 148.

224. The former ("Pūrva-") and latter ("Uttara-") halves of the *Līḷācaritra,* corresponding to the parts of Cakradhar's life before and after Bhaṭobās became his follower.

225. Pratiṣṭhān, present-day Paiṭhaṇ, is the town that had been Cakradhar's headquarters.

226. Sāraṅgpaṇḍit was a learned Brāhmaṇ from Paiṭhaṇ who was a professional narrator of Purāṇic stories. His first meeting with Cakradhar is narrated in *Līḷācaritra,* "Pūrvārdha," chap. 115. Sāraṅgpaṇḍit became one of Cakradhar's close associates, but never took ascetic initation from him. In the end, Sāraṅgpaṇḍit left Cakradhar. The Umāïsẽ who appears in this chapter was Sāraṅgpaṇḍit's wife.

227. Nondualism is *advaita,* a philosophical system in which a theism like that of the Mahānubhāvs is ultimately meaningless.

228. For this chapter and the next, only the titles are given in the text. The next chapter explains only that the two chapters belong to a variant version, that of Kavībās. See Introduction, chapter 5.

229. The Yādav king mentioned in chapter 86, above.

230. According to *Ajñāt Smṛti,* chap. 140 and *Smṛtisamuccaya,* chap. 169, the Yādav king Rāmdev was a member of the "*kāmbaḷī mārg*" (Deshpande, *Smṛtisthaḷ,* 123). We do not know what group this was. However, the Paṇḍharpur stone inscription (A.D. 1273–1277), column 1, line 31, refers to king Rāmdev as "*pāṇḍarīphaḍamuṣya,*" chief of the *phaḍ*s (groups) in Pāṇḍarī (Paṇḍharpur); this seems to indicate that the king was a Vārkarī. See *Prācīn Marāṭhī Korīv Lekh,* ed. S. G. Tulpule (Poona: Poona University Press, 1963), 179.

231. Probably this is a reference to *Sūtrapāṭh* 12.24: "Stay in Maharashtra." If so, the implication is that Bhaṭobās understood "Maharashtra" to be coterminous with the Yādav kingdom.

232. And one cannot live as a celibate renouncer in land that belongs to one's husband. According to *Sūtrapāṭh* 12.1, "One should renounce one's attachment to one's own land. . . ."

233 *Sūtrapāṭh* 12.23: "Do not go to the Kannaḍ land or the Telaṅga land. . . ."

234. *Ajñāt Smṛti,* chap. 141 (cf. *Smṛtisamuccaya,* chap. 173) (Deshpande, *Smṛtisthaḷ,* 123) adds the following, more detailed account of Kāmāïsē's being forced to commit *satī:*

> Then, a considerable time after Kāmāïsē had gone home, the king died. Then the king's son Sīṅgaṇ said to Kāmāïsē, "Hurry up. Get ready to enter the fire."
>
> Kāmāïsē replied, "I do not have the courage *(satva).* I will live on, eating sorghum mash from your kitchen."
>
> Sīṅgaṇ replied, "If you do not have the courage, you will have to be tied up and thrown in."
>
> Then Kāmāïsē's father, the provincial governor *(māndaḷīyā)* Māhādaraṇā, came. He held her hand, and said, "What is this, Kāmāī? Will you eat the sweet and reject the bitter? Get up! Why are you making them tie up Māhādaraṇā's daughter and throw her in?"
>
> Then she set out without bathing. She stood on the rock *(sīḷā)* [the *satī* stone], and said, "Please don't, Sīṅgaṇ! I am a member of the Bhaṭmārg *(maja bhaṭmārgīṃcā upadesu ase).* Spare me, and I will take initiation as an ascetic. That will assure your lifelong future. Otherwise, if you throw me in, you will have no offspring."
>
> He said, "Throw her in! Throw her in!" and they threw her in.

235. *pāṃcāṃsyā gurukuḷ.* The five *guru*s are Cakradhar, Śrīprabhu (Guṇḍam Rāüḷ), Cāṅgdev Rāüḷ, Dattātreya, and Kṛṣṇa. Cf. chapter 111, above.

236. The "knowledge of the body," *dehavidyā,* is the knowledge of how to prolong one's life. See *Sūtrapāṭh* 10.38–40 and 11.70–75.

237. Cf. *Sūtrapāṭh* 12.262: "She will be born as a man in the home of happy, prosperous people; after twelve years, [God] cannot fail to give her union [with himself]."

238. See *Sūtrapāṭh* 12.249, which describes the different kinds of renunciation, and 13.109, which praises the type of renunciation in which one gives up worldly possessions and pleasures as if they were feces *(maḷavat tyāg).*

239. The phrase "made of metal" translates a variant reading in Deshpande's edition.

240. Presumably the one on which Guṇḍam Rāüḷ used to sit. See Feldhaus, *The Deeds of God in Ṛddhipur,* passim.

241. "The one who gave it" is an incarnation of God.

242. This is a play on the meaning of *prasād,* which we have been translating "relic": it is a gift that a divine incarnation gives out of graciousness *(prasannatā),* because he is pleased *(prasanna).*

243. Contrast chapter 8, above, where Bhaṭobās has a wooden threshold made into bowls.

244. That is, they will say that we are poor beggars rather than ascetic mendicants.

245. Ascetics are forbidden to eat onions because of their reputed aphrodisiac qualities.

246. *anyavārtā,* things other than religion. Cf. *Sūtrapāṭh* 12.151: "It is better to sleep than to talk about irrelevant matters *(anyavārtā).* Sleep, rather, but do not talk about irrelevant matters."

247. That is, Cakradhar, who is a reincarnation of Cāṅgdev Rāüḷ. See *Līḷācaritra,* "Pūrvārdha," chaps. 16–17.

248. The *Līḷācaritra* refers to five different Pīpaḷgāvs where Cakradhar lived. This is most likely the one in modern-day Paiṭhaṇ Tālukā, Auraṅgābād District, near Naugāv. It is mentioned in *Līḷācaritra,* "Pūrvārdha," chap. 127, and "Uttarārdha," chap. 33.

249. The king of the Yādavs is Kṛṣṇa.

250. Māhādāïsẽ. See above, chapter 163.

251. The name Śrī Cakrapāṇī can refer to either Cakradhar or Kṛṣṇa—both of whom are ultimately identical, anyway, in the Mahānubhāv system.

252. A poem about the ceremony *(svayaṃvar)* in which Rukmiṇī chose Kṛṣṇa as her husband. This subject is very popular with Mahānubhāv poets. Perhaps the woman sang one of the Mahānubhāv versions, possibly the one composed by Māhādāïsẽ herself (see chapter 174, below).

253. *Sūtrapāṭh* 13.171: "Song is an object of sense pleasure." Hence it is forbidden to Mahānubhāv ascetics. But cf. chapters 89 and 90, above.

254. The word for "wandering," *aṭan,* is not found in Deshpande's edition. It is supplied in parentheses in Tulpule's.

255. See *Sūtrapāṭh* 12.128–135, quoted in the Introduction, above, chapter 3. The ritual includes conversation on religious matters: "Talk about what I have said and done" (*Sūtrapāṭh* 12.133).

256. A *devatā* is one of the numerous deities inferior to Īśvar or Parameśvar ("God"). The highest of the *devatā*s is Caitanya. See Feldhaus, "The *devatācakra* of the Mahānubhāvas."

257. That is, do not make the women memorize a whole text before explaining it to them.

258. A *pothī* is a manuscript of a holy book, one of the sort that is read aloud and explicated by a learned man.

259. If the *pothī* Mhāībhaṭ was reading was an exclusively Mahānubhāv scripture,

its contents may have seemed wrong to the Brāhmaṇ; if it was a scripture (such as the *Bhagavadgītā)* accepted by both Mahānubhāvs and non-Mahānubhāvs, the Brāhmaṇ was objecting to Mhāībhaṭ's interpretation. In the latter case, Mhāībhaṭ's retort and the anger it evoked in the Brāhmaṇ make more sense.

260. That is, during the lifetime of Śrīprabhu, when Māhādāïsẽ composed and sang to him what the present chapter reveals to have been only the first part of *Rukmiṇī Svayaṃvar.* See Feldhaus, *The Deeds of God in Ṛddhipur,* chap. 224.

261. Bāïsẽ was the first of Cakradhar's followers, and in some ways a model for subsequent ones. See *Līḷācaritra,* "Pūrvārdha," chaps. 105–107.

262. The word *sannidhāniceyā,* which we have translated as "who had [God's] presence," is given in parentheses in Deshpande's edition.

263. See chapter 169, above, and *Sūtrapāṭh* 12.128–135.

264. *Sūtrapāṭh* 12.130: "Ease [one another's] weariness."

265. Taking *Sūtrapāṭh* 12.134 *(sāt pāṃc dīs ekatra asīje. . . .)* to mean, "Stay together for seven *plus* five days [rather than five *or* seven]; then you must go your own ways."

266. On the contrast between text and meaning, see *Sūtrapāṭh* 12.147: "These are the words *(vacan)* and this is the meaning of the words *(vacanārthu).* Do not let go of the words."

267. In obedience to *Sūtrapāṭh* 12.131, "Eat and drink together," and 132, "Exchange your ragged clothes."

268. Varāḍ is Varhāḍ or Vidarbha, the region that includes Śrīprabhu's town of Ṛddhipur.

269. This was a young woman who considered herself Śrīprabhu's daughter, and whom he treated as his daughter. The story of her relationship with Śrīprabhu is told in Feldhaus, *The Deeds of God in Ṛddhipur,* chaps. 156 and 323. She is also mentioned in chapter 190, below. She lived in Sāvaḷāpur, near Ṛddhipur.

270. Āü is Āüsẽ, a devotee of Cakradhar and Śrīprabhu who was sent by Cakradhar to stay with Śrīprabhu in Ṛddhipur (*Līḷācaritra,* "Uttarārdha," chap. 649; *Sūtrapāṭh* 12.208). Chapter 11, above, indicates that she stayed on in Ṛddhipur after Bhaṭobās left for the Godāvarī Valley.

271. The Rājmaḍh was the Nṛsiṃha temple in Ṛddhipur that served as a dwelling place for Śrīprabhu. See Feldhaus, *The Deeds of God in Ṛddhipur,* chap. 120. In chapters 190 and 191, below, Bhaṭobās is shown following his own instructions for a visit to Ṛddhipur.

272. See *Līḷācaritra,* "Pūrvārdha," chap. 397.

273. See S. G. Tulpule, *Mahānubhāv Panth āṇi tyāce Vāṅmay* (Puṇe: Venus Prakāśan, 1976), 278.

274. In *Līḷācaritra,* "Pūrvārdha," chap. 118, Cakradhar promises Upādhye that no one will criticize him for the kind of pollution involved in ingesting pan that has previously been chewed by Cakradhar.

275. Three of the manuscripts used for Deshpande's edition add: "Upādhye died there. Then she went to Vāle. She was at Vāle. Later she died in Khaḷadī." Cf. chapter 222.

276. What amazed them, apparently, was Bhaṭobās' foreknowledge.

277. Gopāḷpaṇḍit is another name for Ānobās.

278. "Bhaṭ" is used as a form of address for *any* Brāhmaṇ, not just for Nāgdev (Bhaṭobās).

279. See note 269, above. Notice that in this chapter and the next, Bhaṭobās is shown obeying his own instructions in chapter 178.

280. See note 271, above.

281. The episode referred to is narrated in *Līḷācaritra,* "Uttarārdha," chap. 133. Mhāībhaṭ repeats the question below.

282. The name Nāth means "Lord" and is generally used to refer to Śiva. This could also be a reference to the group of Śaiva *yogīs* called Nāths.

283. Placing one's hands on one's ears is a gesture of ignorance.

284. "Both Gods," here, refers to Cakradhar and Guṇḍam Rāüḷ (Śrīprabhu), the two divine incarnations whom some of the Mahānubhāv disciples had had the opportunity to meet.

285. *Sūtrapāṭh,* chapter 6. See note 111, above.

286. *Līḷācaritra,* "Uttarārdha," chap. 566.

287. "Seven or five," in the Marāṭhī idiom.

288. *Līḷācaritra,* "Uttarārdha," chap. 623. Cf. chapter 111, above.

289. *Sūtrapāṭh,* chapter 9. The text of this chapter, which is extremely brief, is as follows: "To one who, free from passion and error, with his nature restrained, independent *(nirālambī),* spends his life in recollection of God, Parameśvar again gives union with himself."

290. Sādhẽ.

291. That is, there is no one who renounces completely. The wording here is almost identical with that of *Sūtrapāṭh* 13.215, except that the *sūtra* uses a rhetorical question rather than a negative statement: "Who born of a mother will be such as to draw his sword and go to another land?"

292. Patting oneself on the arms is a gesture of self-congratulation, similar to patting oneself on the back in some other cultures. Cf. chapter 106, above.

293. That is, he will be detached from his body.

294. Again, as in chapter 193, above, the problem seems to have been one of caste distinctions. From her speech as recorded in the *Līḷācaritra,* Āüsẽ seems to have been a tribal.

295. Cf. *Līḷācaritra,* "Uttarārdha," chap. 549.

296. This time "the Gosāvī" is Śrīprabhu. See Feldhaus, *The Deeds of God in Ṛddhipur,* chaps. 189–190.

297. Cakradhar and Śrīprabhu.

298. Cf. *Sūtrapāṭh* 10.159: "Nothing contrary to the scripture leaves your mouth."

299. *Līḷācaritra,* "Uttarārdha," chap. 228; *Sūtrapāṭh* 10.238.

300. Caṇākhya or Caṇākṣī was a temple near the cremation ground in Ṛddhipur. It is mentioned in the *Sthānpothī,* an early Mahānubhāv text listing and identifying holy places, edited by V. B. Kolte (Malkāpūr: Aruṇ Prakāśan, 2d ed., 1976), 77.

301. The valley of the Godāvarī River.

302. Āüsẽ says much the same thing in Feldhaus, *The Deeds of God in Ṛddhipur,* chap. 186. She cannot bear to see the Godāvarī Valley, since Cakradhar is no longer there.

303. Pomāïsẽ was the disciple who served as water carrier for Guṇḍam Rāüḷ. See Feldhaus, *The Deeds of God in Ṛddhipur,* chap. 167.

304. Paiṭhaṇ (= Pratiṣṭhān), on the Godāvarī River, was the town that Cakradhar made his headquarters, and Ṛddhipur was Guṇḍam Rāüḷ's town. Bhaṭobās is saying

that it makes him sad to stay in either of these places, since Cakradhar is gone and Guṇḍam Rāüḷ dead.

305. Bhānubhaṭ is Bhāskarbhaṭ, also called Kavīśvar and Kavīśvarbās.

306. The verse is in Sanskrit.

307. *Sūtrapāṭh* 12.149: "Draw out *dharma* from the Mahārvāḍā." The Mahārvāḍā is the part of a village where the Untouchable Mahārs live.

308. A reference to *Sūtrapāṭh* 12.26: "Throw away your life at the foot of a tree at the end of the land," and other similar injunctions to be at "the end of the land," rather than in one's own village or in other familiar places. Gaurāïsẽ has violated the command of *Sūtrapāṭh* 12.1: "Renounce your attachment to your own land; renounce your attachment to your own village; renounce especially your attachment to your relatives."

309. Cf. *Sūtrapāṭh* 11.a6: "He gives directly, or he gives through an agent."

310. *jeth śāstrācẽ mukh teth.* The mouth of the scripture is one's *guru*'s mouth.

311. This variant *(pāṭhāntar),* like those introduced with the words "According to some" *(ekī vāsanā),* "Kavībās," and so on, is included in the text as part of the manuscript tradition. See Introduction, above, chapter 5.

312. *Sūtrapāṭh* 12.73: "There are also some who make themselves dry up and fall at the foot of a thorn bush."

313. Four and a half hours.

314. Cf. *Sūtrapāṭh* 10.106: "God becomes a tortoise, he becomes a fish; he descends among the gods, he descends among men, he descends among animals. When he has descended among men, God becomes a madman, he becomes a possessed man, he becomes a mute; but a walking, talking God is rare."

315. Śrīprabhu was a divine incarnation who was mad. He exemplified the phrase, "When he has descended among men, God becomes a madman," in *Sūtrapāṭh* 10.106. See Anne Feldhaus, "God and Madman: Guṇḍam Rāüḷ," *Bulletin of the School of Oriental and African Studies, University of London* 45 (1982): 74–83. Cakradhar's command is found in *Līḷācaritra,* "Uttarārdha," chap. 649, and *Sūtrapāṭh* 12.208, and it is referred to in Feldhaus, *The Deeds of God in Ṛddhipur,* chap. 322.

316. An example of a lie told to a lustful person is found in chapter 105, above.

317. *Sūtrapāṭh* 13.41.

318. This is a proverb. Bhaṭobās apparently finds such fastidiousness and waste inappropriate for ascetics.

319. *Sūtrapāṭh* 13.133; *Mitākṣarā* 3.58 (Benares: Chowkhamba Sanskrit Series, 1928) (quoting Kaṇva); cf. *Bṛhatkathāślokasaṃgraha* 22.220 (ed. Félix Lacôte [Paris: Mouton and Company, 1964]).

320. *Sūtrapāṭh* 13.9.

321. Cf. *Sūtrapāṭh* 13.171: "Song is an object of sense pleasure." Cf. chapters 89–90 and 167, above.

322. Sāraṅgpaṇḍit's wife, not Bhaṭobās' sister.

323. Her daughter.

324. In *Līḷācaritra,* "Pūrvārdha," chap. 126 the Gosāvī (Cakradhar) tucks in Dhānāïsẽ's (Dhāï's) sari folds for the first time after she has come of age. When he asks her for whom she has put on a sari and for whom she has adorned herself, she answers, "For Śrī Cāṅgdev Rāüḷ"—that is, for Cakradhar himself.

325. That is, "I myself have. . . ."

326. That is, in the valley of the Godāvarī River.

327. This temple was in Aḷajpur. See *Līḷācaritra, Ajñāt Līḷā,* chap. 39.

328. This is the correct answer. The name Upādhye is short for Jānopādhye.

329. Rāmdev is another name for Dādos.

330. Dādos (or Rāmdev) was Bhaṭobās' former guru. He is listed separately in the epilogue (after chapter 261, below) and first in the prologue to Deshpande's edition (Appendix, below), as one who had *darśan* of Cakradhar but did not take initiation as an ascetic. Here, on his deathbed, he appears unrepentant.

331. The term *mārgrūḍhi* is used in the Mahānubhāv tradition to refer to the teachings of disciples of Bhaṭobās' disciples. Thus it has a degree of authority twice removed from the *smṛti* teachings of Bhaṭobās. See V. B. Kolte, "Mahānubhāv Panthāce Avaidikatva," in *Mahānubhāv Saṃśodhan: 1* (Malkāpūr: Aruṇ Prakāśan, 1962), 59–76; and Anne Feldhaus, "The Mahānubhāvas and Scripture," *Journal of Dharma* 3 (1978): 295–308. See the Introduction, above, chapter 5.

332. This chapter is found in the base manuscript used by Deshpande for his edition, but not in the other three manuscripts he used. The other three manuscripts give the kind of information found in this chapter, in similar but not identical wording, at the end of chapter 183. See note 275, above.

333. His niece. See chapter 183, above.

334. In *Līḷācaritra,* "Uttarārdha," chap. 249, Nāthobā sits on a cloth on the ground and begs for food to give to Cakradhar and the disciples.

335. *Līḷācaritra, Ajñāt Līḷā,* chap. 3 reports that Cakradhar told Nāthobā not to live in Sāḍegāv or Pratiṣṭhān, and that after Cakradhar's departure, Nāthobā went to Rākṣasbhuvan and died there. We have not been able to locate an account of Cakradhar's own visit to Rākṣasbhuvan.

336. Kesobās was the editor of the *Sūtrapāṭh,* the aphorisms of Cakradhar. See above, chapters 16–17.

337. See note 64, above.

338. *adhiṣṭhān,* one of the terms translated "deputy" elsewhere in the text. This term, usually reserved for Nāgdev, is here perhaps intended to have a wider application.

339. Literally, for one watch, a *praharu*—that is, three hours.

340. We have read the word *adhikārā* in Deshpande's edition as *adhikār(a).*

341. *Līḷācaritra,* "Uttarārdha," chap. 655 is almost identical to this chapter. Cf. chapter 132, above.

342. Probably the text should read "*pīpaḷ* tree" for "Pīpaḷgāv"—as do all but three manuscripts used for Kolte's edition of the *Līḷācaritra* version of this episode. The sight of a *pīpaḷ* tree, a favorite resting place of ghosts, is understood to intensify a possessed man's symptoms. Bhaṭobās is thus using a proverb to express the fact that he would like very much to see the Gosāvī, and that the sight of the Gosāvī would serve to inflame his devotion further. The text of Bhaṭobās' speech in *Līḷācaritra,* "Uttarārdha," chap. 655 makes this clearer: "Bhaṭ said, 'Yes, you say, "Let's go." Then can I not go? Is a *pīpaḷ* far away for a possessed man? Can I not go to Ujjain? But the Gosāvī has forbidden me. The omniscient one said, "Vānareyā, we will meet anew." So if I went to Ujjain now would I meet the Gosāvī? That is the word of the Absolute *(brahmavācā).* So what is the good of my going to Ujjain now?' "

343. To meet him only in his next incarnation. *Sūtrapāṭh* 11.139: "Now we will have contact anew."

344. *devatecā kṣedu* (variant: *khedu*). The notes to Deshpande's edition, quoting *Smṛtisamuccaya,* chap. 301, identify the other three as sense pleasure *(vikho),* other religions *(anya dharma),* and violence *(hīṃsā).*

345. The term *smṛti* is reserved in Mahānubhāv usage for the teachings of Nāgdev (Bhaṭobās). See V. B. Kolte, "Mahānubhāv Panthāce Avaidikatva"; and Feldhaus, "The Mahānubhāvas and Scripture." See the Introduction, above, chapter 5.

346. Deshpande's edition lists the ten as follows: (1) wandering *(aṭan),* (2) solitude *(vijan),* (3) begging *(bhikṣā),* (4) eating meals *(bhojan),* (5) sleep *(nidrā),* (6) recollection *(smaraṇ),* (7) worship of relics *(prasādsevā),* (8) appropriate food *(ucit anna),* (9) appropriate clothes *(ucit vastra),* and (10) not displaying the external marks of an ascetic *(aliṅga vṛtti).*

347. Cf. *Sūtrapāṭh* 11.135: "The meaning *(arthu)* is subject to the context *(prakaraṇ).* The context makes the meaning applicable. . . ."

348. The term *śruti* is reserved in Mahānubhāv usage for the words of Cakradhar and other divine incarnations. See the Introduction, above, chapter 5; Kolte, "Mahānubhāv Panthāce Avaidikatva"; and Feldhaus, "The Mahānubhāvas and Scripture." Since the *Bhagavadgītā,* which records the words of Kṛṣṇa, is mentioned separately below, "*śruti*" is probably used here for the *Sūtrapāṭh* in particular.

349. The *Bhagavadgītā* is classified as *śruti,* a holy scripture of the highest authority, for Mahānubhāvs because it contains the words of Kṛṣṇa, one of the five major incarnations of God.

350. The *Bhāgavata Purāṇa,* the one that is primarily about Kṛṣṇa.

351. *arthu.* Here, *arthu* (or *artha*) stands for *paramartha,* the Absolute.

352. *Sūtrapāṭh* 9. The second verse of this chapter reads *"svabhāvo-mātrē."* This can be translated "with his nature *(svabhāvo)* restrained," or "not going beyond his nature." The word *mātrā* appearing this way as the final member of a compound means "only."

353. We are indebted to Dr. V. B. Kolte for his suggestion (in a letter to Tulpule dated 16 July 1986) that *"yuktitrayē"* refers to the three kinds of *ukti—svokti, śāstrokti,* and *lokokti*—in *Sūtrapāṭh* 12.141: "Putting aside what you yourself say *(svokti),* what the scriptures say *(śāstrokti),* and what the world says *(lokokti),* become learned in my learning."

354. *hē yathāpratī,* words meaning "It is this way in the manuscript" (that is, literally, *sic*), indicating that this chapter was perhaps as obscure to an early scribe or editor as it is to us. See the Introduction, above, chapter 5.

355. *śṛṅghārīyā kavī,* a poet whose works mainly evoke the romantic sentiment *(śṛṅgāra rasa).* This must be Nāgdev's comment on *Śiśupāḷvadh,* not on Kavīśvar's later work, *Uddhavgītā.*

356. This episode has a rather obvious polemical purpose; its historical validity is questionable. See S. G. Tulpule, "Mahānubhāv Panth āṇi Nāmdev," *Navbhārat* (October 1977): 51–53; and S. G. Tulpule, *Marāṭhī Vāṅmayācā Itihās, Khaṇḍ Pahilā* (Puṇe: Mahārāṣṭra Sāhitya Pariṣad, 1984), 229–231.

357. Nāmdev the tailor was a prominent saint in the Vārkarī tradition. Two of the manuscripts used for Deshpande's edition do not have the word we have translated as "the tailor."

358. No. 1384 in the government edition of Nāmdev's works (Mumbaī: Śāsakīya Madhyavartī Mudraṇālay, 1970). The poem begins and ends as follows:

> My days have passed to no purpose
> because, O God, I never took refuge in you.
>
> I spent my childhood in ignorance.
> I never thought [of God].
>
> The breastmilk of your name saves us from rebirth.
> Says Nāma, the servant of Viṣṇu,
> give me love for your name.

359. We have been unable to identify this Kemdyā.

360. For the early Mahānubhāvs, Varāḍ (Vidarbha) has pleasant associations because it is where Guṇḍam Rāüḷ lived; but the Gaṅgā Valley, where Cakradhar lived and finally suffered, is the proper center of their activities. Similarly, while a young girl in the virilocal society of most of India has a deep and lasting affection for her maternal home, it is in her in-laws' house that she lives out her adult life. See Anne Feldhaus, "Maharashtra as a Holy Land: A Sectarian Tradition," *Bulletin of the School of Oriental and African Studies, University of London* 49 (1986): 539.

361. *Sūtrapāṭh* 6. See note 111, above.

362. See note 354, above.

363. See note 345, above.

364. That is, it could not be included in Śrīprabhu's biography, *The Deeds of God in Ṛddhipur*—perhaps because it is not about Śrīprabhu, but about Bhaṭobās.

365. Notice that this text, which is traditionally called *Smṛtisthaḷ*, refers to itself by the name of the place, Nimbā, which its principal character, Nāgdev, made his headquarters. Similarly, Guṇḍam Raüḷ's biography, the Ṛddhipurcaritra or Ṛddhipurlīḷā; Cāṅgdev Rāüḷ's, the *Dvārāvatīlīḷā;* and Dattātreya's, the *Sahyādrīlīḷā,* are named for the places where their subjects lived.

366. In the context of the next chapter, it is possible that here, rather than having their literal meanings of "direct experience" and "verbal testimony," respectively, the terms *aparokṣa* and *śābda* are technical terms referring to two types of knowledge, *aparokṣa jñān* and *śābda jñān.*

367. *Viśeṣjñān* is the highest of the stages of knowledge outlined in chap. 8 of the *Sūtrapāṭh,* "Uddharaṇ." *Viśeṣjñān* is higher than *sāmānyajñān* ("general knowledge"), which in turn is higher than *sattājñān* ("the knowledge of being," also called "direct knowledge," *aparokṣajñān*).

368. *Dṛṣṭāntapāṭh,* chap. 61: "There was a prostitute who ate up the world's money. Finally someone whose money she was eating died. She entered the fire with him, so she reached the heaven of *satīs*." (Translated from *Līḷācaritra,* "Uttarārdha," chap. 631.) Cf. *Sūtrapāṭh* 12.282: "Just an hour (two *ghaṭikās*) of being a disciple are sufficient."

369. Deshpande gives these words in parentheses, indicating that they are taken from a manuscript other than the one used as the base manuscript for his edition. Taken with the sentence at the beginning of chapter 225, this sentence seems to indicate that the chapters from 225 through 253 are all from Kavibās' version of *Smṛtisthaḷ.* After these chapters, which are especially concerned with doctrinal matters, the

text proceeds to narrate the story of the deaths of Māhādāïsẽ and Bhaṭobās. Chapters concerned with the deaths of such important figures are not likely to have been included in only one version of the text.

370. *Līḷācaritra,* "Uttarārdha," chap. 632.

371. A delicacy. Cf. *Sūtrapāṭh* 13.143: "Chick-peas are an object of sense pleasure"—and therefore to be avoided.

372. Māhādāïsẽ.

373. The name "Vānarā," which means "Monkey," was a nickname that Cakradhar used for Bhaṭobās. *Līḷācaritra,* "Pūrvārdha," chap. 445 relates that Cakradhar gave him this name on an occasion when he showed great agility at climbing around in trees.

374. Chapters 7, 6, and 8, respectively, of the *Sūtrapāṭh.* For "Mahāvākya," see note 111, above.

375. *pāṃcāṃsyā gurukuḷ.* The five *gurus* are Cakradhar, Guṇḍam Rāüḷ, Cāṅgdev Rāüḷ, Dattātreya, and Kṛṣṇa.

376. That is, in August–September of A.D. 1302.

377. Ṛddhis and Siddhis are personified powers that become subjected to an accomplished *yogī.*

378. A *jīvanmukta* is a person who is liberated *(mukta)* while still alive *(jīvan).*

379. Dāïmbā and Demāïsẽ. For Dāïmbā's story, see *Līḷācaritra,* "Uttarārdha," chap. 630; for Demāïsẽ's, *Līḷācaritra,* "Uttarārdha," chap. 564.

Appendix

In the edition of V. N. Deshpande (Puṇẽ: Venus Prakāśan, 1939; 2d ed., 1960; 3d ed., 1968), as well as in the reprint of S. G. Tulpule's edition (Puṇe: Anamol Prakāśan, 1990), the prologue to *Smṛtisthaḷ* includes the names of disciples of the various types. To avoid cluttering our translation with lists of names that will not mean much to most readers at the beginning of the text, we have translated the prologue from the first edition by S. G. Tulpule (Puṇẽ, 1969), which omits the names. The lists in the Deshpande edition are as follows.

Who were those who had the sight of [the Gosāvī]? 1. The learned *(vidyāvantu)* Rāmdev; 2. Sāraṅgpaṇḍit; 3. Indrabhaṭ; 4. Santoṣ; 5. Avaḍa(ḷ)bhaṭ;[1] 6. Avadhut; 7. Mārtaṇḍ; 8. Parasnāyak; 9. Prajñāsāgar; 10. Harīmāïtā; 11. Ghuināyak; 12. Reināyak; 13. Gadonāyak; 14. Padmanābhi; 15. Nāgdev Upādhye; 16. Rāṅkẽ Lakṣmīdharbhaṭ; 17. Kākos; 18. Anno; 19. Ravaḷo; 20. Gondo; 21. Japīya Vīsnubhaṭ; 22. Bhrīṅgī; 23. Vaijobā; 24. Kāḷīdāsbhaṭ; 25. Vāman; 26. Matīvīḷās; 27. Nāgnāyak [of] Ḍombegrām; 28. Bhāïdev; 29. Upāsanīye; 30. Kāḷboṭe; 31. Sāīdev; 32. Kānho Upādhye; 33. Kāḷe Vāsnāyak; 34. Gore Jānopādhye; 35. two Ekāïsẽs; 36. Demāïsẽ; 37. Lakhubāïsẽ; 38. Sobhāgẽ; 39. Yalhāïsẽ; 40. Bhūtānanda; 41. Sāmkosẽ; 42. Laḷītāïsẽ; 43. Ekvīrābāïsẽ; 44. Dravīḷāsbāïsẽ; 45. Ratnamāṇīkẽ; 46. Ābayo; 47. the Māḷī; 48. Ḍāṅgaresu; 49. Kamaḷānāyak; 50. Rāṇāïsẽ, the mother of Rāmdev; and 51. the disciple Rāṇāïsẽ; 52. Vāmdev; 53. Bonebāïyā; and 54. Bonebāïyā [of] Meghaṅkar; 55. Ghāṭe Harībhaṭ who forgot the world;[2] 56. Tīvāḍī;[3] and 57. his wife; 58. in [Bhaṭobās'] household, Sāraṅgpāṇi; and 59. their mother; 60. Māhādev Pāṭhak; and 61. [the Māhādev] from Rāvasgāv; 62. Tika(v)nāyak from Hīvaraḷī; 63. Vāenāyak; 64. Rāhīyā; 65. Govindsvāmī; 66. Sārasvatibhaṭ; 67. the Brāhmaṇ from Kāṇasā; 68. the Brāhmaṇ from Sendurjaṇ; 69. the woman who was fasting for a month; 70. Rāghavdev; 71. Kānhardev at the tank;[4] 72. Māhādevo; 73. Pālhā Ḍāṅgīyā;

74. Kāsta Haridevpaṇḍit; 75. Gopālpaṇḍit of the lesson about the hunt;⁵
76. Sāḷīvāhān; 77. two Rāūts; 78. a Mātāṅg; 79. Deibhaṭ of the grabbing of
the betel roll;⁶ 80. Māydhuvā of Bhognārāyaṇ; and 81. [another] Māydhuvā;
82. Dāṅko; 83. Gaṇpati Āpayo; 84. the woman who was in confinement;⁷
85. the woman gathering cow dung;⁸ 86. the Brāhmaṇ from Pañcagaṅgā;
87. Sukīye Jognāyak; 88. Pāṭhak; 89. Yantrākār Vāsunāyak; and 90. his
brother, Tīkavnāyak; 91. the two Gurjars; 92. Nāgārāūḷ; 93. the sister of the
initiated boy; 94. Chāyāgopāḷi's wife; 95. the Brāhmaṇ at Mārtaṇḍa well;
96. Pāṭhak Degāübāï; and 97. Haṃsubāï; and 98. Ghogargāvbāï; and
99. Dhānāï [of] Aḷajpur; 100. Rāmdaraṇā's mother; and 101. Muktābāï;
102. the Brāhmaṇ from Rāyeri; and 103. the Brāhmaṇ from Bhognārāyaṇ;
and 104. the Ṭhākur's wife; and 105. the Māl [= Malla] of the *jogvaṭā;*⁹ and
106. the Brāhmaṇ to whom [the Gosāvī] gave the *jogvaṭā;* 107. his fellow
sectarian; and 108. Nārobā; 109. the Brāhmaṇ of the watching of the
cows;¹⁰ and 110. the horse-seller. These and others were ones who had the
sight of [the Gosāvī].

Next, those who became enlightened: 1. Demāïsē; 2. Dāïmbā.

Next, those who became disciples in [the Gosāvī's] presence and in his
absence: 1. Bhaṭ; 2. Bāïsē; 3. Sāntībāïsē; 4. Mahādāïsē; 5. Mhāïbhaṭ;
6. Sādhē; 7. Āüsē; 8. Ābāïsē; 9. Nāthobā; 10. Śrīprabhu's Lakṣmīndharbā;
and 11. Kothaḷobā; and 12. Pomāïsē; and 13. Vairāgyadev; 14. Kheibāïsē;
15. Goibāïsē. These are the ones [who became disciples] in [the Gosāvī's]
presence.

Now those who became disciples in his absence: 1. Bhaṭ's sister, Umāïsē;
and 2. his brother Mahādevbā; and 3. Rāmdev; 4. Cāṅgdevbhaṭ; 5. Umāïsē
[of] Paiṭhaṇ; and 6. Dhāṇāïsē; 7. Jāno Upādhye; 8. Kānhopādhye;
9. Gaurāïsē. These became followers after the Gosāvī was gone.

Notes to Appendix

1. In *Līḷācaritra,* "Pūrvārdha," chap. 241, Elhambhaṭ is renamed Avaḍaḷbhaṭ. The word *avaḍaḷ* means "hard-hearted."

2. See *Līḷācaritra,* "Uttarārdha," chap. 323; and Feldhaus, *The Deeds of God in Ṛddhipur,* chap. 19.

3. Of Sāṅgavkheḍā. See *Līḷācaritra,* "Uttarārdha," chap. 71.

4. In Loṇār. See *Līḷācaritra,* "Pūrvārdha," chap. 61.

5. See ibid., "Pūrvārdha," chap. 210.

6. See ibid., "Pūrvārdha," chaps. 112 and 115.

7. See ibid., "Uttarārdha," chap. 169; and Feldhaus, *The Deeds of God in Ṛddhipur,* chap. 72.

8. See Feldhaus, *The Deeds of God in Ṛddhipur,* chap. 199.

9. For this person and the next, see *Līḷācaritra,* "Pūrvārdha," chap. 30. A *jogvaṭā* is a scarf used by *jogīs*, ascetic mendicants.

10. See *Līḷācaritra,* "Pūrvārdha," chap. 60.

Indexes

People in *Smṛtisthaḷ*

Numbers refer to chapter numbers in *Smṛtisthaḷ*.

Places in *Smṛtisthaḷ*

Numbers refer to chapter numbers in *Smṛtisthaḷ*.

Sūtrapāṭh Sūtras in *Smṛtisthaḷ*

THIS INDEX lists *sūtras* of the *Sūtrapāṭh* that are quoted, referred to, echoed, or assumed in *Smṛtisthaḷ*. The *sūtras* are numbered according to the Feldhaus edition, Part II of *The Religious System of the Mahānubhāva Sect: The Mahānubhāva Sūtrapāṭha* (New Delhi: Manohar, 1983). The names of the chapters are as follows: 1. Anyavyāvṛtti, 2. Yugdharma, 3. Vidyāmārg, 4. Saṃhār, 5. Saṃsaraṇ, 6. Mahāvākya, 7. Nirvacan, 8. Uddharaṇ, 9. Asatīparī, 10. Vicār, 11. Vicār Mālikā, 12. Ācār, 13. Ācār Mālikā.

Sūtra	*Chapter of Smṛtisthaḷ*	*Sūtra*	*Chapter of Smṛtisthaḷ*
1–9	10, 16	11.23	67
6	61, 118, 194, 247, 259	11.70–75	150
		11.135	236
7	259	11.139	132, 232
7.21	67	11.a6 (= 11.148)	207
8	15, 67, 249, 259	12.	10, 17, 76
8.46	67	12.1	83, 148, 206
9	40, 76, 195, 240	12.14	37
10	10, 17	12.23	148
10.15	67	12.24	148
10.17	67	12.26	32, 206
10.18	67	12.35	51
10.38–40	150	12.36	51
10.106	210	12.72	32
10.113	47	12.73	209
10.158	56	12.82–83	34
10.159	198	12.104	84
10.164	67	12.115	28
10.238	198	12.128–135	169, 177
10.247	118	12.130	21, 177
10.257	100	12.131–132	177

About the Authors

Anne Feldhaus is professor of religious studies at Arizona State University. She received her Ph.D. from the University of Pennsylvania in 1976. Her first visit to Maharashtra was in 1970, and she has returned frequently to live and travel there. Her work on the religious traditions of Maharashtra includes two other books on Mahānubhāv religious literature—*The Religious System of the Mahānubhāva Sect: The Mahānubhāva Sūtrapāṭha* (Manohar, 1983) and *The Deeds of God in Ṛddhipur* (Oxford, 1984)—and a number of articles on medieval *bhakti,* contemporary religious practice, and the religious geography of Maharashtra. In addition, Professor Feldhaus has translated Günther Sontheimer's *Pastoral Deities in Western India* (Oxford, 1989). Her most recent work focuses on the religious significance of rivers in the Deccan plateau of India.

Shankar Gopal Tulpule received his Ph.D. from the University of Bombay in 1940. From 1950 to 1969, he was professor and head of the Department of Marathi at the University of Poona. More recently he has been a visiting professor in the Department of Indology at the University of Mainz, Germany, and in the Department of History of Religion and Philosophy at the South Asia Institute, University of Heidelberg. He has also been a fellow of the Indian Institute of Advanced Study at Simla. Professor Tulpule is the editor of the corpus of Old Marathi inscriptions and the author of the volume *Classical Marāṭhī Literature from the Beginning to A.D. 1818,* volume 9 in the *History of Indian Literature,* edited by Jan Gonda. He has published a number of other books on the literary and religious history of Maharashtra and is currently at work on a dictionary of Old Marathi.

Production Notes

Composition and paging were done on the Quadex Composing System and typesetting on the Compugraphic 8400 by the design and production staff of University of Hawaii Press.

The text typeface is Garamond and the display typeface is Gill Sans.

Offset presswork and binding were done by The Maple-Vail Book Manufacturing Group. Text paper is Writers RR Offset, basis 50.